RITES

OF

RHYTHM

RITES

❧ OF ❧

RHYTHM

·

THE MUSIC OF CUBA

JORY FARR

ReganBooks

An Imprint of HarperCollins Publishers

HarperCollins books may be purchased for educational, business, or sales promotional use. For information please write: Special Markets Department, HarperCollins Publishers Inc., 10 East 53rd Street, New York, NY 10022.

FIRST EDITION

Designed by Diane Hobbing of Snap-Haus Graphics

Printed on acid-free paper

Library of Congress Cataloging-in-Publication Data

Farr, Jory.
  Rites of rhythm: music of Cuba / Jory Farr.
    p. cm.
  Includes bibliographical references (p.) and
  discography (p.).
  ISBN 0-06-009030-8
    1. Music—Cuba—History and criticism. I. Title.

ML207.C8F37 2003
780'.97291—dc21

2003046682

03 04 05 06 07 BVG/RRD 10 9 8 7 6 5 4 3 2 1

I dedicate this book to my parents, who nurtured my imagination

over many years, had faith in my abilities, and helped me when

I was wounded. And without the love of my children, Zachary,

Joshua, and Hannah, who forgave me, I couldn't have finished.

CONTENTS

Prologue   1

1. Journey to Havana   5

2. The *Son* Rises On Santiago   31

3. Matanzas: The Cradle of Afro-Cuban Culture   71

4. Revisiting Havana   91

5. The Tree of Rhythm: Cuba in New York   133

6. Across the Waters   171

7. Carnival in Santiago   207

Epilogue   231

Appendix A: Selected Discography   235
Appendix B: Trips and Festivals   247
An Afro-Cuban Glossary   255
Bibliography   259
Acknowledgments   261

PROLOGUE

The Yoruba people came to Cuba late in the slave trade, and they brought their gods, called *orishas,* with them. *Orishas* lived in the sacred songs and rhythms that the slaves carried in their throats and bodies. They were summoned with specific rhythms played on drums, as well as sacred chants and dances. Only a fraction of the hundreds of *orishas* worshiped in Yorubaland made it across the ocean to Cuba. But those that did were the most important, and they sustained their initiates through the centuries of terror and sorrow that followed.

The first and last *orisha* to be invoked in any ritual is Eleggua, who possesses the power to bestow transcendent vision or leave one afflicted for life. Positioned at the crossroads, Eleggua stands for chance and destiny. But he's also a lonely, wandering spirit. He survives in American black folklore as Papa Legba, a mysterious apparition who inhabits the crossroads and is hinted at in Robert Johnson's spine-chilling song of the same name. As I traveled through Cuba, I was continually reminded of Eleggua's power. Like an explorer who longs to find the source of a river and so follows it up mountains and down into valleys, I came to Cuba seeking the origins of rhythms that had lifted me up and made my spirit soar. But all true journeys begin with fear and wonder, and have to do with incurable conditions of the soul. Though I couldn't have known it, the land I was traveling in and the myths I was exploring would help throw me into the boiling waters of change, break me open, and allow me to confront my own deep origins. Chance encounters—Eleggua's game of dice—led me down roads I couldn't have imagined. Obstacles were thrown in my path that tested my patience and resolve and threw my own ignorance back at me. In Cuba I got used to having my feet cut out from under me. Yet just when failure seemed certain, a teacher would appear out of nowhere and open doors to a new understanding.

What drew me to the island was a convergence of music, dance, myth, and ritual, drawn from many diverse cultures and blended and re-blended over the centuries. From Africa came deep rhythms: powerful *yuka* drums and chants from the Congo, Arará rhythms from Dahomey, *orisha* songs from Yorubaland, and the fierce music and dance of the Carabalí. From Spain came flamenco, Gypsy melodies, and Andalusian folk music. In Southern Spain, Jews, who started arriving in pre-Roman times, had mingled with Moors, Gypsies, and Christians, and so did their music. Africans, free and slaves, lived in the mountains of Andalusia as early as the twelfth century. And Spain itself was Islamic over a thousand years ago, when the country was known as Al-Andalus and cities like Córdoba had 700 mosques.

Islamic music spread through Africa centuries ago, and it, too, arrived in Cuba. The influence is in the *montunos,* the improvised sections of *son,* Cuba's national music. Moorish rhythms and spiraling melodies, reminiscent of Sufi and Moroccan music, create an ecstatic tension. You can hear it in Santiago's carnival music, and it pervades rumba, the moaning vocals of which have Islamic rhythms in them.

Over the centuries Spanish, African, European, and indigenous cultures blended to produce an Afro-Cuban music that was primordial and poetic, steeped in Eros and drenched in mysticism. Africa and Spain had the strongest influence. But from France came the *contradanza* and from its former colony powerful Afro-Haitian rhythms. And much later, jazz, blues, and R&B fertilized and fortified the music, making it that much richer. In Africa, where rhythm is balance and bliss, its absence is depression. Cuba's music, if nothing else, is sublimely balanced.

Western notions of sacred and profane are not really relevant. At a jazz club in Havana one night, explosions of bebop horns and electric guitars, all building into climax after shuddering climax, suddenly gave way to chants of the Abakuá, a men's secret leopard society, and the "sacred" rhythms of the *bata* drums. At Casa de la Música, I saw the lead singer of Cuba's all-girl, twelve-member Chicas del Son go from a lusty bump-and-grind to the rapturous ritual dance of her *orisha,* suggesting that sex, rhythm, harmony, and divine resonance were one and the same.

I came to Cuba seeking rhythm, but what I found was something deeper: a culture whose radical roots reached way back and down into the mysteries of life and death. Music was a bridge between visible and invisible worlds. It was part of the genius of the people, and the genius was an aspect of spirit, a gift from the gods that wasn't complete until it was given back to the community and offered up again to those same gods. In the United States, with certain exceptions, we've mostly lost this ecstatic connection between rhythm and spirit, just as we've lost the larger dance of life amid the ceaseless strivings for material things and the denial of worldwide suffering.

Years before I began writing this book, I was using Afro-Latin percussion to perform myths and folktales in schools, prisons, community centers, and museums here in the United States. Virtually everywhere I went I was confronted with fear. For young people, especially those of color, who walk blindly into the future, the fear was real. Modern American life offers them no transcendent vision. Even children of privilege experience this rise of fear, the sense of hope betrayed, the difficulty of living a life that really means something. Their music, often full of anxiety, rage, and alienation, tells the story.

Yet in Cuba, a mostly black country with widespread poverty, the young people I met were not fearful. They looked remarkably like their counterparts in Oakland and Brooklyn, in Compton and Miami. They played in hip-hop, jazz, *son,* and *timba* bands, and they downloaded music off the Internet. Many were great musicians, whether they made their living that way or not. Most were also initiates of one or more Afro-Cuban religions that allowed them to ascend to higher levels of responsibility and knowledge. These young people—there is no other way to say it more simply—*knew* who they were, and they were confident of being able to take a place of importance within their culture.

"The United States has all this material wealth," Freddy Alfonso, a young percussion master with Los Muñequitos de Matanzas, told me while Cuba's great folkloric group was teaching and performing in Los Angeles. "But at the same time, the people here have nothing: no rituals for the young people, no connection to the ancestors."

Rhythms and rites that have been lost can be resurrected. Afro-Cuban music and mythology, which thoroughly changed Cuba itself during the twentieth century, is reshaping our culture far beyond the obvious ways suggested by the popularity of salsa and the spectacular success of the Buena Vista Social Club recordings. Tens of thousands of Americans, Europeans, and Japanese are studying *rumba*—the music and the dance—as well as jazz with Cuba's master musicians and dancers by either traveling to Cuba or doing weekend workshops and master classes when the bands are touring. Cuban musicians as different as Chucho Valdés and Omar Sosa are once again reinvigorating American jazz. And Cuban hip-hop bands—there are dozens in Santiago alone—have only just begun to be heard.

Rites of Rhythm is not an encyclopedia of, much less a collection of essays about, Cuban music. It's not a memoir, though the book contains elements associated with that form. Nor is it a work of academic scholarship that deconstructs what's already been written or pretends to uncover "new" knowledge. For that you must go elsewhere. Instead, what I have tried to write is a living history of music and folklore as it is now, my encounter with a vibrant culture that is constantly changing, imbued, I hope, with deep imaginative sympathy for the already vanished past and the unknowable future.

The night before I left for Havana, I couldn't sleep. Travel to Cuba seemed, by its very nature, unpredictable, even though I was visiting pursuant to a general license. I'd heard rumors that my phone might be tapped, that I'd be followed by the CIA or tailed by Castro's secret police. I thought about Jesse Helms, the bug-eyed senator who didn't want anyone visiting Cuba. And as my fevered psyche hovered between exhaustion and excitement, I was beginning to have my doubts about going there altogether when the alarm clock rang.

I showered quickly, ran a comb through my hair, and counted out $2,000 in twenties, tens, and fives, which I stuffed in a money belt with my passport. It was the first time I'd worn a money belt, and I felt vaguely nefarious, like a figure out of a Graham Greene novel. As I headed out to the airport to catch my flight, I wondered what would happen if I were to lose the crisp dead presidents that were my sole source of survival. On the plane to Cancún, I sat next to a roguishly handsome Mexican who drank rum and Cokes through the whole flight. He asked me where I was going, and when I said I was on my way to Havana, he gave me a wolf's grin.

"Oh, man, you stepped into something now," he said. "I was down there last year, my friend. You brought plenty of protection?"

"No," I said. "I'm going for the music."

Maybe it was the way I said it or the answer itself, but the Mexican laughed, as if he had just heard the most naive thing in the world. His dark brown eyes held me tightly in their gaze as he leaned in close and put his arm around me.

"Listen, my friend, you need to get yourself some rubbers. Because in Cuba," he said, and I could smell his rummy breath now, "the women are like men. They *rape* you."

I thought about this for a while. But my mind was still filled with wide-eyed wonder for the country where I was going. I had wanted to visit Cuba a few years earlier, but another book had made it impractical. So I carried the country's rhythms inside me and experienced their powerful, indefinable pull. I listened to Mario Bauzá and Chano Pozo, to Irakere and Chucho Valdés, to Celia Cruz and Celina González, to Los Muñequitos de Matanzas and Carlos Embale. I found field recordings of Santerían possession rituals, Arará drumming, and the haunting chants accompanying initiations into Palo, Cuba's adaptation of a Congolese religion that seeks nothing less than the transcendence of human death.

Already, in the mid-1990s, Cuban *son, rumba, guajira,* and jazz were gaining wider audiences in the United States. Everyone from the Rolling Stones and Madonna to the Spice Girls and Marc Anthony brought along Cuban-style rhythm sections when they toured. And virtually all the great Latin stars, from Panama's salsa pioneer Ruben Blades to Venezuela's Oscar D'Leon, were mining musical styles that originated in Cuba.

The first incarnation of salsa, the Latin dance music that Hispanics from Los Angeles and New York to Paris and Berlin now claim as their own, was merely a reworking of *son,* Cuba's national music. Yet the island's influence extended even deeper into America. The left-handed piano style that erupted in ragtime and the rolling rumba-boogie of the New Orleans piano great Professor Longhair are fundamentally Afro-

Cuban. Cuban musicians, settling in New Orleans and New York beginning in the early 1900s, lent their brilliance to the early evolution of jazz, influencing everyone from Jelly Roll Morton to Dizzy Gillespie to Duke Ellington. In the 1920s, Cuban jazz musicians were already jamming in New York.

After his collaboration with the Cuban percussionist/composer/dancer Chano Pozo and bandleader Mario Bauzá, Dizzy Gillespie, the cofounder of bebop, said that everything he played thereafter reflected the Afro-Cuban influence. Many of the bass patterns heard in today's hip-hop and classic funk were nicked from Afro-Cuban bands. One of the most common saxophone and bass riffs of fifties rock came from an obscure Cuban rumba recording, according to music critic Robert Palmer.

But Cuba's influence reached even further, across oceans. Cuban music has been the popular music of Senegal for a long time—just straight Cuban music that got Africanized. Early Congolese *"rumba"* bands took their cue from Cuba's Orquesta Aragón and Johnny Pacheco. Franco and Tabu Ley and groups like Kékélé created an ingenious Congolese *rumba* that had its heyday in the fifties and sixties but is still going strong.

The Afro-Cuban music I heard put me in mind of black spirituals, ring shouts, deep Delta blues, and the jazz of Miles Davis and Duke Ellington. Yet the rhythms were more complex and seemed closer to Africa. Cuba's rhythms are so powerful, so immediately recognizable anywhere in the world, that you merely have to hear a few bars of *son montuno,* or the three-two pulse of the clicking wooden clave sticks—*pa-pa-pa*-pause-*pa-pa*—to be instantly transported there. Clave (pronounced *clavay*), the repeated two-bar phrase tapped out on wooden sticks of the same name, is the basic pulse of all Afro-Cuban music. Though it comes from Africa, clave has Cuba's imprint on it, especially in the way it's heard. In Cuba, not only the music but silences in the composition have to be in clave. And not only the rhythms but the rhythms of the melodies have to be in clave—no mean feat when composing a jazz score or improvising with eight or more other instruments.

Afro-Cuban music is at once exotic and familiar. Exotic because it was composed by a mélange of cultures—from African, Gypsy, and French to Spanish, Afro-American, and Islamic—that blended and reblended over time, but familiar because it contains seed elements of blues, gospel, jazz, and other African art forms that forever changed Western music. Whatever else it was, Cuba wasn't a colony of the United States. As a turquoise '53 Bel Air, belching gas fumes directly into the car, took me toward Havana, I remembered some lines from Walt Whitman's *Leaves of Grass:* "You shall no longer take things at second or third hand/. . . nor look through the eyes of the dead/. . . nor feed on the spectres in books/. . . you shall listen to all sides and filter them through yourself."

I rented a room in Old Havana from a friend's family, who greeted me warmly, as if I was some long-lost relative. I dropped off gifts from America, took a cold shower, and flopped down on the lumpy mattress. It wasn't that late, and though I felt tired, sleep would not come. So I went for a walk and decided I'd get lost in the city. Out on the streets, it was warm and windless. I could smell the Caribbean before I saw it, a black sea with glistening swells that pounded the seawall and then broke over the Malecon, Havana's great ocean promenade, spraying a wild froth of foam into the highway. I walked along the Malecon, past a hustler, his eyes as restless as a madman's, who offered me women and cigars and, when I said I wasn't interested, followed me for a block with lower prices. I passed two young lovers entwined in a kiss, a hawk-faced man with sunken cheeks and bulging eyes, and an old woman, dried and shriveled, her breasts two yamlike flaps.

I headed back into Old Havana and passed near a table where four men played dominos. Under a doorway, a few women were gossiping and chattering like a jungle of parrots. I kept walking deeper into the darkness, turning down a street called Amargura—Bitterness—and some time later, on Solo y Triste—Sad and Lonely. I walked many blocks to the stony sound of my own footfall, and I wondered what kind of a city this was that demanded such profound consideration when exploring it.

That's when I heard the sound of drums, bells, and *chekeres.* I rounded a corner, followed the music to an open door, and peered inside. A middle-aged woman smiled and held out a bony hand, beckoning me in as if she'd been half expecting me. I lingered near the doorway for a while and then, when one of the musicians motioned me inside, I entered a room that had been almost wholly transformed into an altar. A likeness of Ochún, feline goddess of love, stood in the center. The *orisha*, as she is known in the Afro-Cuban religion of Santería, wore bracelets, held a fan made of peacock feathers, and had a five-pointed golden crown atop her head. The altar was aflame with burning candles and festooned with sunflowers and fresh fruit. A tangle of men and women, their bodies glistening with sweat, shuffled and swayed across a wooden floor, answering the musicians with pumping arms and shouting voices. By chance, I had stumbled upon a *toque*, spirit-possession celebration. One musician played a single conga while two others played *chekeres*, beaded gourds that, when tapped and shaken, created the hissing sound of ocean waves receding over loose rocks. Each *chekére* played a different rhythm as a fourth musician tapped out clave on the blade of a hoe. Unlike American blues or gospel, whose rhythms tend to be synchronous, the rhythms here, played simultaneously, crossed and recrossed each other in a dense, fluid flow. And over it all, a young singer spun songs in an African tongue. His voice came up from deep within his throat and reminded me of the groaning, otherworldly sound of Mongolia's Tuvan singers. Before long I found myself lost in the singer's cascading, raspy calls and the dancers' shouted responses. "He is an *akpwón*," a man next to me volunteered, cupping his hand to my ear and motioning to the singer. He poured a glass of *aguardiente*, fermented sugarcane, from a plastic jug and tipped it down his throat in one gulp before passing it to me. "He sings to Ochún."

More people arrived. A few wore all white, the sign of an initiate, and others, sons and daughters of Ochún, wore yellow, the *orisha's* favorite color. It might've been just another party but for the altar and the drumming and the purpose of the dancing, which was soon apparent when a middle-aged woman spun into the center of the room. As if lightning surged through her body, she stiffened and shuddered and danced in widening spirals as the *akpwón* approached her and chanted African words directly into her ear while another woman, her black hair thick as syrup, rang a bell in the other. The woman had another seizure and fell backward into the arms of two other women, who led her away to another room.

A man with large black hands and a gypsy's face was the next to feel Ochún's power. He trembled and then stutter-stepped glassy-eyed, like a boxer who's been hit with a sidewinder and reels from the blow. The musicians now focused their attention on him. The *akpwón* both praised and taunted the *orisha,* chanting directly into one ear as a bell was rung into the other. And the drummers responded to the calls with a renewed ferocity as the multitude kept the energy at a fevered pitch. The woman who'd first been mounted by the *orisha* returned, smiling, smoking a cigarette and drinking rum. A friend draped an arm around her and the two laughed. The music stopped, the drummers lit up cigarettes and drank. I walked over to the *akpwón,* who was wiping his neck with a towel, and introduced myself to Fredy Inocente Betancourt Esquijarrosa.

"Where did you learn to speak Yoruba?" I asked.

"When I was a little boy, I never thought of my Yoruba heritage. But when I turned sixteen, I was initiated with Eleggua as my saint. My mother is a *santera,* a Yoruba priest, and she was always initiating people in our house. She had a Yoruba dictionary, and I liked the music and rituals so much that I began studying the language and taught myself Yoruba. I have to know the exact words to sing, because when someone is possessed, I begin a conversation with the *orisha.*"

Francisco Elejalde, the eldest musician who'd played the conga, walked over. He had a broad face, high cheeks, and a wide nose. He wore overalls and no shirt, showing off a torso rippling with muscles which had to come from hard manual labor. He had just turned sixty, he said. I asked him what it felt like to drum to the *orishas.*

"When I play the drum, the music comes from a place deep inside me.

I feel the spirit passing through me and coming into the drum, and I feel like I'm deep inside the drum. There was once a way of playing the drums in Africa called *fuki-fuki*, a rhythm that had disappeared in Cuba. It was a language, a way for our ancestors to communicate with each other. Well, some people have the power to see spirits, and one such person came up to me one night after a *güiro*. This man asked me where I learned to play the drum like that. I said I didn't know. And then he told me, 'When you were playing I saw an old African drummer from long ago. Because no one plays that way anymore. It's that drummer who was playing the drums, not you.' "

By now I was tired. Elejalde, who lived in the outlying suburb of Parraga, promised to invite me to see a different kind of ritual, where the musicians would use consecrated *batá* drums. I wrote down his address and left. There were no cabs in sight, but when I saw a taxi bicyclette pedaled by a lean youth, I jumped at the opportunity. In years to come, I would stumble upon or be invited to many *toques,* as spirit-possession celebrations are called. *Toques* merge elements of ritual, myth, music, and dance within the framework of a party, and it was often hard to tell where ritual ended and theater began. Questions about the ceremonies lingered in my imagination.

How had *toques* changed over the centuries, or were these rituals no different from those I would've encountered in Cuba, or even Africa, 500 years earlier? I'd heard a recording of a ring shout, a black holy dance, from the Deep South. Were Cuba's *toques* purer versions of this tradition or wholly different? I wondered if a nonbeliever could ever be possessed against his will, overcome by the rhythms and the drumming. But mostly I thought about what it was in the sacred songs, dances, and beliefs of Cuba's African religions that allowed the people to survive centuries of slavery with their culture intact. Ruminating on that, I crawled into bed and slept the sleep of the dead.

When I woke up it was to a sound so bloodcurdling that I thought for sure someone had been murdered. Out on the street I saw the scene of the crime. Four men were huddled over the body of a pig that was still in spasms from the death blows. One man had a large knife in his hand, dripping with blood that ran down the street in runnels; another was carving thick slabs of meat while two others held the body and looked over their shoulders to see that the police weren't coming. A mongrel mutt on a nearby rooftop surveyed the grisly scene, yapping wildly. My head spun. The butchering of pigs on the streets, the power of *aguardiente,* and the rhythms of ritual Santerian music were already rearranging the synapses within my brain.

On Sundays, there is a *rumba* at Callejon de Hammel promoted by Salvador González, an artist/entrepreneur whose abstract murals adorn nearby walls. The event had become something of a tourist attraction, but it was still an opportunity to see some of the best *rumberos* in Havana. Since I had plenty of time to get there, I meandered along the Malecon and took side streets to Plaza de Armas, where the booksellers were hawking their wares. In Old Havana I found a Middle Eastern store that sold dried apricots, which I popped in my mouth as I passed men playing dominos in the middle of the street, oblivious to cars zooming around them. A stench assaulted my nose: the pollution of diesel fumes and putrefying waste. For breakfast, I bought *churros,* fried yucca, from a street vendor and *mamey,* a drink made from a tropical fruit to which I soon became addicted. I passed houses with Spanish balconies and Moorish arches and watched children play in a park.

Callejon de Hammel was jammed with tourists, mostly from Europe. By edging my way in toward the chairs, I managed to get one of the last seats. A few minutes later Clave y Guaguancó began to play. Two dancers moved into a thin sliver of open space, kicking off an erotic call and response. The woman, a secret smile on her lips, moved with fantastic arabesques, protecting her womanhood from the man's stabbing thrusts known as *vacunao,* and still later, used crossed hands to cover her breasts. The male dancer, perhaps in his fifties, was grinning, warming up to this sublime pantomime of Eros with a lusty woman.

The set was a pastiche of folklore. The musicians played three kinds of *rumba—yambú, columbia,* and *guaguancó—*and sang "Que Viva

Vannia Borges of Bamboleo performing at the Hotel Havana Libre.

Chango," the song made famous by Celina González, mixing *guaguancó* with rhythms normally played on the *batá* for Changó, the Yoruba *orisha* of thunder. Near the end, Clave y Guaguancó performed a song of the Abakuá, a secret men's society. It had lyrics from a Los Van Van song pasted into a chorus, and without the presence of the *íreme,* the leopard-masked figure that is a symbol of Afro-Cuban folklore, the power of the music was diluted.

Ever since I heard a recording of an astonishing Afro-*son* played on the *tres,* I wanted to talk to Papi Oviedo, one of the two *treseros* who'd performed it. A Cuban friend in Los Angeles had given me his phone number, and amazingly enough I reached him on my first try. I was invited over to his house.

Oviedo lives in a woebegone section of La Playa. His sister greeted me with a cigar in her mouth and led me past an altar to Ogún, her *orisha,* and outdoor cages housing roosters and chickens to a back room.

"My mouth is swollen," Oviedo said, giving me a warm handshake with his right hand and massaging his jaw with the left. "My teeth are bad and I have to see the dentist."

Tall and lanky, Papi Oviedo resembles his father, Isaac Oviedo, one of the greatest *treseros* in the history of Cuban music. Isaac had died, but fortunately not before his artistry was captured on CD. One song, "Coballende," stayed with me. It was a stunning example of how the *tres,* paced by clave, could be an orchestra unto itself. Its beauty made me think of all the old *treseros* who must've been forgotten, the way you forget some poignant detail in your life which, remembered later, gives you a glimpse into eternity. Papi told me his story.

"I started as a drummer in my father's band. Everyone in our family is musical, but even though I was a good drummer, I always loved the *tres.* And one day, I picked it up and began playing. My father heard me, and when he saw me playing, he said, 'I can teach you if you want. And you can learn from others, too.' That's when I seriously began listening to Arsenio Rodríguez, Niño Rivera, and Rodolfo Oviedo. There were many great *treseros* then, but all of them are dead now. The *tres* has always been a difficult instrument. It has just three sets of double strings tuned in unison, so fingering for chords is hard. You have to invest a lot of time if you want to master it. And I had the desire.

"My father was born in Matanzas and lived to be ninety years old. He developed a unique style of playing the *tres*, singing the same notes he played and freely improvising. And he got a very pure sound that was deeply African and Spanish. Sometimes he sang in Yoruba, too. In those days, all the great *treseros* had their own way of playing—not like today. Now all the *treseros* imitate Pancho Amat, who is very quick," Oviedo said, as his wife, Nieve, walked by and showed him two bags of giant shrimp purchased from a black market fishmonger.

I'd seen Amat perform with bands like Cubanismo. He played the *tres* like a guitar and freely wove in blues and even rock phrasing. His style was flashy, even virtuoso, but it lacked the deep soul that Oviedo achieved naturally.

"Pancho is an excellent musician," Oviedo said. "But he has deviated from the roots of the instrument. Right now, there are more *treseros* than ever. But few know the roots. Some of the students from the music schools, even Pancho Amat's, come to me, because Pancho doesn't teach the old style."

I asked Oviedo what the role of the *tres* was in *son*.

"The *son* without *tres* is not *son*. The *tres* carries the rhythm and melody in *son*. Later, when the piano became part of the *conjunto*, the piano played the *tumbaos*, the rhythms that created excitement. But the piano would accompany the *tres*. And the *tresero's* job was to improvise."

A rooster suddenly let loose with a series of shrill choruses less than a foot away.

"We raise them because they're good to eat and my sister, who is a *santera*, uses them in rituals," Oviedo said.

I asked Oviedo if he would play a song, and he walked up a spiral staircase and returned with his *tres* and a bottle of Santero-brand *aguardiente*. He poured both of us a glass. He smiled, revealing a set of large teeth, and played "Cuando Se Quiere de Veras," a gorgeous old bolero by

Trio Matamoros, followed by an instrumental *son,* dense with inverted chords and driving rhythms. At times he hit a doubled string so powerfully that the *tres* sounded like an electric guitar. The solo had all the intensity of the blues, but without the flattened notes that gave the American idiom its distinct flavor.

"In the old days, before the *tres,* the musicians would modify the guitar. They left the neck alone and changed the tuning. There were now three strings tuned in octaves, with a capo on the second fret. But gradually they redesigned a new instrument, with the treble string tuned to the same note but a different pitch."

Oviedo spent twenty-one years with Conjunto Chocolate and eighteen years with Orquesta Revé, an influential band that merged *changüí,* Guantánamo's unique folk music, with urban *son.* I asked him what he thought he had given to Cuban music.

"Students from Japan come to study with me, and I've played all over the world. I spent twenty-one years with Conjunto Chocolate and eighteen years with Orquesta Revé. I've kept faith with the old traditions. That will be the legacy I leave."

On my way out I lingered at the elaborate altar to Ogún and received a forbidding look from Oviedo's sister. I walked a mile or more before I found a cab that took me back to central Havana. There I had a dinner of fish, rice, and *tostones,* crispy fried plantains, at a *paladar* near the Havana Libre Hotel.

The last rays of golden sunlight were flooding the sky and reflected off the buildings like alpen glow. Near the Hotel Cohiba, a car caught my eye—a sleek black Cadillac, its dark fins and gleaming chrome sending beads of light scattering off the hood. The front grill stared at me like a shark's mouth. A knot of women hovered around the car. And why not? The black 1956 Fleetwood was less a car than a vision: a panther sprung loose under a nearly full Havana moon.

Walking up to it, I wondered who could own such a piece of heaven. Perhaps some wealthy businessman from Europe who lived in a palazzo, or a confidante of Fidel's, making a fortune in the black market. But in

Benny Moré at St. Nicolas Arena in New York.

Cuba, where truth is stranger than fiction, the story was more unusual than I could begin to imagine.

"It's mine," a sandy-haired Cuban said, emerging from a cluster of admiring men and shaking my hand. He bestowed a carefree smile on me. "My name is Eduardo Leal."

Leal wore khaki slacks, a pressed white shirt, a brown-and-green-checked blazer, and a striped tie. He looked to be in his late thirties. On his left middle finger was an intricately carved Masonic ring. Cubans, I would soon discover, believe in everything: Catholicism, Santería, the Kabbalah, and Masonic mysticism, to name just a few.

"Come inside and take a look," Leal said, as his driver and mechanic, a wiry, bespectacled Cuban with dark black skin, opened the door for us. "This is no ordinary car. It was owned by Benny Moré."

This last sentence momentarily stopped all conversation. In Cuba, Benny Moré (rhymes with *foray*) was a legend, a cross—if you can imagine it—between Nat King Cole and Elvis Presley, an incomparable singer, dancer, bandleader, and composer who revolutionized the country's popular music. His stardom reached its zenith in the 1950s, when he returned to his beloved homeland from Mexico, where he and orchestra leader Perez Prado had ignited *mambo* firestorms. By the time he died, four years after Fidel Castro marched into Havana, Moré's fame was widespread.

Nothing had changed since the day the Cadillac was taken off the Detroit assembly line and shipped to Havana, except for a new diesel engine, Leal said, "and this—" He flipped open the glove compartment to reveal a CD player. Seconds later we were listening to Moré singing one of his most famous songs, "Santa Isabel de las Lajas," an ode to his hometown. I let myself sink back into the plump seat. The interior was luscious and expansive, the spotless seat covers done in two-toned cream and parchment. The clock still worked, and so did the radio. The electric windows zipped up and down. I told Leal I was a writer and would like to hear about his car and take a ride in it.

"Come. Let's go," Leal said, motioning to his driver, Ernesto Garves.

Seconds later we were cruising down the Malecon, past taxi bicyclettes, strolling lovers, and gorgeous *putas* selling the only thing they had—themselves. The Fleetwood had become Moré's in 1956, when one Gaspar Pumarejo, the wealthy manager of Cuban television and a great fan of the star, bought it for the singer as a gift. From books and films I knew what Havana was like then: a cauldron of Afro-Caribbean magic and political corruption; a fabled city that rivaled—many would say, exceeded—New York City for excitement and decadence. At Havana's nightclubs back then you could hear *rumba, guaracha, son, mambo,* and Cu-bop, the island's own mix of hot Harlem jazz and hip-shaking Afro-Cuban funk.

Great singers could be heard all over Cuba, but none matched Benny Moré, who was born August 24, 1919, in Santa Isabel de las Lajas. The eldest son of a poor rural family, Moré was a descendant of Congolese slaves who had arrived in Cuba in the nineteenth century to work the sugar plantations. Forced to quit school at twelve because of extreme poverty, Moré worked the fields cutting sugarcane. Raised in the Yoruba and Congo religions, he belonged to Casino de los Congos, a fraternal organization that preserved Afro-Cuban folklore, myth, and music. Every spare moment was spent singing, playing guitar or congas, and absorbing the island's rich musical heritage.

Moré staged imaginary concerts for his own pleasure and had a small combo that played local dances. But in order to make it he had to leave his home and go to Havana, where he lived on the streets, barely surviving. Some nights he couldn't sleep he was so hungry. However, he had faith in himself and the music he sang.

In 1940, Moré won first prize in a singing contest in Havana. Soon he was performing with Miguel Matamoros, whose influential band backed him in his first recordings. By 1945, Moré was touring with Matamoros's group in Mexico. Three years later, he hooked up with Pérez Prado, the great Cuban bandleader and pianist who had also arrived in Mexico. With Prado's great band behind him, everything clicked. Benny Moré toured Latin America, his piercing voice heard on Mexican radio, and his fame spread and snared him a movie contract there. He became a star throughout Latin America. But he was still homesick and virtually unknown in his own country.

He returned to Cuba and had a chance to deliver a radio concert that was heard across the country. For Cubans, it was like Americans hearing Elvis Presley for the first time. Moré formed an orchestra in 1953, Banda Gigante, that finally allowed his full genius to emerge. As he sang, he created fabulous, often funny steps that mirrored the rhythmic complexity of the music and influenced the development of salsa dancing. But he drank heavily, lived fast, and fell into debt. On February 19, 1963, he died, reportedly of liver problems. His funeral attracted 100,000 Cubans. Some years after that, strapped for cash, Moré's widow sold his black Cadillac to Leal's father, Generoso Leal, who had begun working in the casinos back in the heyday of the Mob, when four crime families ruled Cuba and the country was virtually a criminal state.

"At that time," Leal said, "the Cadillac was just another classic American car. But we treated it like a diamond. We kept the car in perfect condition to honor Benny's memory."

"What's your profession?" I asked.

"I'm a psychiatrist," Leal said. I tried to imagine a session of psychoanalysis in Havana, a town where every Cuban feels the weight of a boot on the back of his neck and must hustle in the black market to survive. As if reading my mind, Leal shook his head.

"The main problem here is neurosis. It comes from stress."

I knew that doctors and even surgeons made a pittance in Cuba—$25 a month. Leal had to make much more from Benny Moré's car than his practice. The psychiatrist looked at me candidly, and he nodded.

"This is the most famous car in all of Cuba. The police regularly stop it. The people swarm around it wherever it goes. Celia Cruz once offered $500,000 for it. But the government said the car could not leave the country. It was too important."

"What about Fidel?" I asked. "Had he ever ridden in it?"

"I *wish* Fidel took a ride with me!" And we all laughed.

"Many great actors and singers loved Benny's music," said Ernesto, who besides being a family friend and flawless driver was a great mechanic, and thus highly prized in Cuba. "Nat King Cole played with Benny. I saw them perform together."

Moré was also reputed to be a *santero,* one of the high priests of Santería. Ernesto pulled into the circular driveway of the Cohiba so that I could take some photographs of the Cadillac. Sure enough, a crowd soon formed around the sleek Fleetwood.

More than any other performer, Moré was associated with Salon Rosado de la Tropical, an open-air amphitheater where average Cubans could actually afford to hear music. So I took a cab there, a rusted Chrysler with a diesel engine. We passed old decaying sugar mansions before reaching the club. Outside the entrance young women asked if I wanted company, and I was tempted more than once to say yes. I was steered upstairs into a secure area reserved for tourists, VIPs, and the hustlers known as *jineteras.* Meanwhile, down below, poor blacks and mulattos, who paid a peso to get in, formed a mob of revelers.

Around me were nattily dressed Cubans obviously not living in the peso economy. But the scene was boring, and I decided to throw my lot in with the rabble. I walked up near the lip of the stage where a coal-black *tresero,* his dreadlocked hair stuffed under a rainbow-colored hat, picked out heavily syncopated leads on his *tres.* Backed by a septet, he played fast, ringing leads that conjured everything from *son* and *changüí* to gypsy jazz and scorching blues. He danced as furiously as he played, and he played so hard he snapped a string, which made his playing even more frenzied until, seemingly overcome by the rhythms, he shook his head from side to side and sank to his knees, rolling on his back, tongue lolling out like some Afro-Cuban Jimi Hendrix.

Maybe it was the sound of the *tres* and the congas and the *bongó,* the sound of skin, wood, and metal that seemed to be the soul of Cuba; or maybe it was the rum I was drinking, but rhythm seemed to pour into my legs and arms like a physical force. Almost involuntarily, I started dancing, and a leggy woman showed me the steps to the *son*. After the set ended I looked for the *tres* player and found him, drenched in sweat, talking with another musician. He went by the name Cotó, and only later would I discover that he was one of the greatest *tres* players in Cuba, the nephew of Elio Revé, founder of Orquesta Revé, a famous band from Guantánamo.

"Where did you learn to play *tres*?" I asked.

"Before I owned a *tres* I used to go to the railway station near my home and sit there playing a *yagua*—a long hard leaf which I attached nylon strings to. I grew up in the easternmost part of Cuba—in Guantánamo, near an old sugar mill. My father was a great *tresero*. He died when I was eight years old, and he never had the chance to teach me. But the sound of the *tres* was left engraved in my soul.

"After my father died, my mother took some of the money she got and bought me a guitar. But I didn't like the guitar. Five days later, I took it to a friend of my father's and asked him to turn it into a *tres*. The *tres* is the most important sound in *son,* and that's because *son* had no piano to create rhythm."

Cotó promised to speak to me again and gave me a number. But as with many musicians in Cuba, it would take a long time to find him.

In Havana I often felt like a gumshoe in a cheap detective novel. With sometimes flimsy leads—an old phone number, a friend's address, or just a name—I hunted down people I thought might help me. For three days I tried to contact Helio Orovio, a musicologist whose work I'd read and respected, but nobody answered the phone. Finally, someone at UNEAC gave me an address in Vedado, and it was there I went the next morning. The building was an enormous mansion that had been converted into apartments, but none of them were numbered. I knocked at two or three doors before one opened. A tall, gaunt man with the splotchy, ravaged face of an alcoholic stood before me.

"I'm looking for Helio Orovio."

"There," the man said, motioning to a door across the hall. "But he's out. Come in. He'll be back soon."

The man, Edgar Carillo, showed me around a shabby flat that must've been spectacular in its day. Once upon a time Carillo was a television producer. But then came the revolution.

"My family's money was in banking and sugar. They left for Miami and I drank. Now, many people live here. You want some rum?"

A half hour later, a short balding man, whose crooked teeth stuck up like rusty nails, walked by.

"Helio, you have a friend," Carillo said.

When I told Orovio why I'd come to Cuba, he graciously invited me to sit on the terrace. He was in the midst of editing a new edition of his book, but he never let work get in the way of pleasure. I had bought a bottle of rum with me and that was all I needed for a calling card. For the next two days, the two of us talked about blues, jazz, *rumba,* Cu-bop, and more than a century's worth of encounters between American and Afro-Cuban music.

It was in New Orleans, while researching a series on the roots of blues and jazz, that I first learned about Cuba's musical link with the Crescent City. Free blacks from Cuba traveled to New Orleans in the nineteenth century, establishing musical connections between the two countries. And while Buddy Bolden had attracted lasting legend playing cornet in Storyville, no less an authority than Sidney Bechet insisted that Cuba's Manuel Pérez, a cigar maker turned jazz cornetist, was the better musician.

"Manuel Pérez established the first real vocabulary for the trumpet," Orovio said. "After that, the music traveled to New York City. There, violinist Alberto Iznaga played in big bands and composed pieces that introduced Cuban rhythms—especially *rumba*—to American jazz. A Cuban flutist, Alberto Socarrás, not only played in New York City big bands but

Arsenio Rodríguez at the Manhattan Center in New York.

also founded his own orchestra that played *son, rumba, guaracha,* and *boleros.* Unconsciously, but in an organic way, he began integrating the many styles into a new sound."

By the 1930s, Duke Ellington was using *rumba* in his recordings. And in the same period, Don Justo Aspiazu took a Cuban orchestra to New York. For the first time, Orovio said, Cuban singer Antonio Machin was heard in America. Most American jazz fans had heard Xavier Cugat, but the famous bandleader played only a watered-down version of Cuban popular music. By contrast, trumpeter Mario Bauzá would revolutionize the sound of jazz by merging it with *rumba.* It was Bauzá who introduced the *conguero* Chano Pozo to Dizzy Gillespie, setting in motion a profound exchange of genius. This was the era of bebop, whose chord extensions and angular, sometimes dissonant lines were fundamentally changing jazz. Into this pivotal moment came Pozo, who incorporated *rumba*'s rhythmic language and the conga drums into the emerging sound.

"Chano Pozo simplified and distilled the rhythms of the *batá* into the conga drum," said Orovio. "And that paved the way for Cu-bop. From that point onward, many American bands played jazz with Afro-Cuban rhythms and arrangements."

Back in Cuba in the late thirties meanwhile, the *son* from Oriente had already undergone profound changes in Havana. The five-beat *cinquillo* had disappeared, and the music was now played in 2/4 and 4/4 time. But already Arsenio Rodríguez, a *tresero,* singer, and composer, was forging the future of the music.

Born in 1911 in the village of Guira de Majicures in Matanzas, the fourth of seventeen children, Rodríguez was blinded at age eight when a horse kicked him in the face. But in his imagination swam visions of where *son* had to go. In the 1940s, Rodríguez laid the foundations for what would become the sound of salsa. He used multiple trumpets that played heavy Congolese rhythms formerly heard only on percussion instruments. And instead of the *bongó,* he used the conga drum, deepening the rhythms and creating a vocabulary for the latter that evolved into a complex rhythmic partnership between all the instruments in the *conjunto*. None of this, however, was done without resistance from the musical elite.

"I remember when a famous impresario in Havana heard Arsenio's septet and told him, 'You're crazy to use these trumpets and put these congas in your band,' " Raúl Rodríguez, Arsenio's brother, had told me one day in his Los Angeles apartment. "But my brother said, 'Well, if I'm crazy then so is everyone else. Because this is the sound of the future.' "

There were other innovations. Arsenio Rodríguez heightened the role of clave and expanded the structure of the *montuno* section, essentially reinventing the way *son montuno* was played. Moreover, in New York City, he exposed new audiences to the deep roots of Afro-Cuban music.

"In Matanzas," says Orovio, "Septeto Sonora Matancera's drummer, Valentin Cané, was already using congas. And Santos Ramírez, who played in Havana with Septeto La Llave and directed one of Havana's most famous *comparsa* groups, was also playing the conga drums in a *son* band even earlier than Arsenio. But Arsenio was the most important figure. He was a genius, and *son* attains a perfect balance in his music."

I had seen a cardboard sign in Vedado advertising a concert appearance by Los Van Van at Salon Rosado de la Tropicale. I asked Orovio if he was planning to go.

"Yes," he said. "We'll go together."

⊷◈⊶

When Fidel Castro seized power in 1959, he closed Havana's casinos and put countless musicians out of work. Those who protested soon found that the new regime had its own ideas about art.

"I told them, 'I m a musician. I don't want to carry a rifle,' " said Los Angeles—based *conguero* and composer José Caridad "Perico" Hernández, who played with Havana's Conjunto Casino before the revolution and left Cuba in 1964. "But the Socialists said, 'We don't need musicians.' And to punish me, they sent me to Camaguey to cut sugarcane for six years, far away from my wife and six children. I can never forgive them for what they did to us."

Yet for Cuba's black musicians, the revolution opened doors. Before 1959, institutionalized racism prevented musical geniuses like Irakere's Oscar Valdés from studying music formally. But afterward, musical theory began to be taught in the schools. By the 1970s, a generation of musicians was graduating with a high degree of knowledge of both jazz and classical music, and many had mastered the complex rhythms on multiple instruments.

I saw the result of that one night at Club Zorra y El Cuervo, during the opening weekend of the Havana International Jazz Festival. There, a young group of alumni of the National School of the Arts, Habana Sax, played a blistering set anchored by a shifting quartet of saxophones growling and howling over trap drums, congas, timbales, and bells. The music alluded to Duke Ellington's jungle band, bebop, New Orleans second-line parade band funk, Cuban *comparsa* music, and free jazz. The horn phrasings were spectacular, not hardened into any single style, with dizzying, multiplying melodic lines. And the underlying rhythms, a mix of jazz and shadings of hip-hop all organized by clave's timelines, gave the music an ecstatic buoyancy. This was jazz to dance to, and people did.

"We've studied jazz composition and harmony, but we've been influenced by *rumba* and Afro-Cuban religious music," the group's artistic director, Mara Nuñez Salazar, told me after the set. "But we like the rhythmic strength of hip-hop, a rhythm that came from the streets and isn't weighted down by theories and academic approaches."

It was obvious that Habana Sax was more concerned with exploring the many timbres, tones, and rhythms available through their instruments than making "flawless" music. Like other bands I would see, they had never lost sight of the dance that had once animated all jazz. Which made it hard not to compare this with jazz in the United States, where a young generation of jazz musicians had made a fetish of technique, hoping to insulate themselves from criticism. Freshly minted jazz musicians graduating from top schools played all styles and memorized the signature riffs. But precious few had any authentic voice, nor were they encouraged to develop one. In a real sense, much of American jazz education was based on mimicry, not originality.

By good fortune, Irakere and Los Van Van were playing the same night. Orovio planned to meet me for the latter, so I took a cab to Teatro Nacionale, where Chucho Valdés and Irakere blazed through a set that recapitulated a century's worth of Afro-Cuban music. From the pianist's long-fingered hands poured *danzón* and *bolero, rumba* and *son, comparsa* music and jazz. I heard echoes of Art Tatum and Erroll Garner, of Duke Ellington and Bud Powell, but those were merely voices filtered through an imagination that had its own original path.

When Irakere exited, Valdés's jazz quartet came onstage and played what amounted to a spectacular musical game. With each burst of rhythm, harmony, and melody that Chucho threw out, percussionists

Roberto Vizcaino Guillot and Raul Pineda Roque answered him back note for note on the skins of the conga drums and trap set. Or Guillot and Pineda would throw out their own complex phrases: spluttering rolls with wicked off-beats or tommy-gunned high hats, and Valdés would have to answer in time, in clave. The piano, after all, was simply the most complex percussion instrument yet created.

I felt sorry for the American trumpeter Roy Hargrove, whose duet turn with Valdés felt stiff. But once the concert was over, I hopped in a cab and headed over to Orovio's apartment, and together we headed to Salon Rosado de la Tropical. The club was mobbed, for this was the twenty-ninth anniversary of the group's founding, and the band had just started playing.

"Irakere was sensational," I told Orovio. "And I forgot to tell you that I saw this great *tresero* the other day, Cotó."

"Ah, Cotó? He's one of my two favorite *treseros* in Cuba. And he's crazy, too!"

I'd seen Van Van two years earlier in 1997, when they had arrived in the United States for a multi-city tour. In Los Angeles, they turned the Palladium into a riotous party, and the group was the runaway hit of the Playboy Jazz Festival. It was a success they replicated in six different cities. But Latin radio DJs, fearing reprisals by right-wing Cuban *gusanos,* scarcely played the band's music. And when Ry Cooder and his Buena Vista Social Club came along, no other Cuban band could compete with its startling success, fanned by a global media blitz.

Los Van Van were superstars in Cuba and had remained that way for more than a generation. However, I'd heard that there was deep dissension within the group, that drugs were ruining the band, and that its founder, Juan Formell, was the problem. Of course, no one would talk about it. Nevertheless, that night I got a glimmer of Cuba's dismal situation by listening to Van Van. The group, which had always epitomized the best of Cuban music, sang about *machismo* and money and the fast life. One set of lyrics talked about whose *orisha,* in a fantasy showdown, would be more powerful.

All around me, beautiful prostitutes and well-dressed *jineteras,* the winners in Cuba's new dollar economy, drank rum and partied. If my eyes met a woman's, she would zero in on me like a raptor, letting me know she was ready for business. Los Van Van's genius, to create a protoplasmically funky music that commented on social conditions, was what sustained the group over nearly three decades. But this night their message was loud and clear. The music they sang was cynical, even nihilistic. Cuba might fool tourists who came looking for authenticity and mystical rapture, but in the end, living there on the cusp of the new millennium was a terrible joke, an absurdity, with no more meaning than a game of dice played by two drunks. It was a dangerous message, and there was no hint of irony about it.

2. THE *SON* RISES ON SANTIAGO

lthough it was winter, a blast of warm air, a memory of summer, blew through the streets of Santiago de Cuba. As I walked through hilly neighborhoods I was rewarded with dramatic vistas of the Sierra Maestra Mountains on all sides. Santiago was more African than Havana. And I would always be able to tell I was there by the way people talked and carried themselves. Letters were dropped, words were slurred, and French and Congolese phrases, as well as African proverbs, crept into conversations. People moved with a languid ease, as if propelled unconsciously by lilting rhythms—the same rhythms, I liked to imagine, that formed the *son*.

Santiago is the spiritual birthplace of *son*, that sublime marriage of rhythm and melody and a sensuous dance like no other. Cubans take it for granted as their foundation, but it wasn't always so. In the beginning, *son* was a subversive force. And as it spread across the island, it became a dangerous music, a shout of defiance, a fluming of raw, mixed-race sensuality that disrupted the tight controls enforced by Cuba's light-skinned ruling class. The early history of *son* has tales of repression and harassment, of police destroying instruments and jailing "lewd" musicians. But they might as well have tried to dam up the Caribbean. For *son* was an unstoppable force.

Just as jazz and blues eventually transcended racial boundaries and changed white America from the ground up—its poetry, literature, youth culture, speech—so *son* embodied national character and amounted to nothing less than a distillation of Afro-Cuban identity. Historians, ethnomusicologists, anthropologists, musicians, and journalists have propounded theories about the origins and evolution of *son*. But I only understood something if I ran it through my own imagination. So I came to Santiago looking for fresh answers to old questions. I sought out the elders first, the ones who could remember the music as it used to be. One of these, Felix Varela, from one of the most famous musical families in Santiago, had a vantage point few could equal. "The *son* was born in the countryside here in Oriente and is the result of a mixture of the Spanish and the African," Varela told me one muggy afternoon when I went to visit him at his apartment, located in downtown Santiago, two blocks from Casa de la Trova. "The rhythmic part is mostly African; the melody is Spanish. But the *maracas* are of Indian origin, and the rhythms of the *tres* are African."

Varela, now sixty-three, has played all over the world and recorded on international labels. When the Smithsonian Institution wanted lectures and performances of traditional *son,* it turned to Varela. Many Cubans I'd met were obsessed with lineage, but Varela had reason to be proud. He came from two musical families that evolved the tradition of the *son:* On his father's side were the Varelas from Bayamo, near the basin of the Cauto River, and originally from Spain, and on his mother's side were the Mirandas, from Las Tunas, about 140 miles northwest of Santiago.

"But our family also had African roots, traceable to either the Congo or Angola. Wait," Varela said. "I will play something for you."

He walked into the next room and returned with a *tres*. The *tres* was invented sometime around 1870 in the hills of Baracoa, the musicologist Helio Orovio had told me, and was originally made from boxes used to

Felix Varela at his home in Santiago.

carry bottles of rum and strung with metal wire. The musicians had wanted to make an instrument with a unique sound that couldn't be created by the guitar, and had succeeded, for the *tres* was a singing, ringing orchestra unto itself. As Varela's wife poured me thick, sweet black coffee, Varela sat down a foot away from me and played a simple, haunting song about a slave who is euphemistically called a *nengón,* a word meaning Negro or black. His nasal voice had the plaintive pureness I would encounter often in Oriente, whereas his face, Hispanic but with much darker skin and some African features, had the Creole quality that defines Santiago, Cuba's most African city. The song, with its insistent, unvarying rhythm, had the flavor of *son* but lacked the clave, the chorus, and the harmonic and melodic complexity.

"My great-grandfather, Vicente Cutino, who lived to be one hundred and twenty-five, played this song. It's called *nengón,* and it's one of the first expressions of the *son.* There are actually two kinds of *nengón:* the one I just played on my tres and the one that traveled to Guantánamo and Baracoa. This second kind took on the characteristics of *changüí.* Listen," Varela said, playing a few measures of it. "It has no clave and its rhythm has the sound of *rumba.* It's blacker and more Haitian."

As early as 1870, in rural areas near Santiago, groups were playing *changüí* (pronounced *changwee*) on *maracas, tres, güiro*—a notched gourd that produced a scraping rhythm—and a large, two-headed *bongó,* whose skins were heated under a flame. Nene Manfugás, a *mestizo,* was reputed to have brought the *tres* to Santiago from Guantánamo and was the first person to play it there. But this was just a story, and who could say for sure?

Varela said that if we could go back in time, we would see that Africans, mulattos, and Spaniards were playing *changüí* along with two other forms of early *son, quiribá* and *regina.* Which form came first is hard to say, but no one disputes that somewhere around the dawn of the twentieth century, *son* took root in Santiago. At first, it invaded the carnival processions, but then, because of its melodic richness, it entered the music halls, cafés, and clubs. Initially, *son* had no verses: just a refrain, which was sung call-and-response. By the 1880s, the musical configuration of *bongó, tres,* clave sticks, *maracas,* and *botijuela* would have been a familiar sight.

Already, the *son* had the ability to provoke many moods. It was aggressive or romantic, playful or poetic. And because of slavery, the *son* carried a great lament and made it humanly possible to bear the weight of inhuman suffering, just as the blues made it possible for American blacks to carry the anguish and terror of four centuries of slavery.

The *trova* was likewise versatile. There were days in Santiago when, with time on my hands, I would grab some coffee and a pastry and go to

Casa de la Trova, on Calle Heredia. There, I would listen to the *soneros* and the *trovadores,* and watch the dancers and marvel at the splendid portraits of the legendary singers that the Santiagan artist Ferrer Cabello had painted and then donated to the city. The wall of canvases included José (Pepe) Sánchez, Ángel Almenares, Emiliano Blez, Miguel Matamoros, Ñico Saquito, Salvador Adams, and Sindo Garay. Together they formed the soul of *trova,* whose roots, like *son,* stretched back many generations.

The Cuban *trova,* sung by one or two vocalists accompanied by guitar, modeled itself on Spanish *canciones,* especially *boleros.* Elements of French *romanzas* and Italian opera found their way into *trova,* too. Pepe Sánchez, a handsome, dark-skinned mulatto who lived in the last years of slavery and died in 1918, is considered the progenitor of the sound. Like the rest of the *trovadores,* he was born into the bottom of Cuban society and his music tells of a simple life. The *trovadores* were barred from elegant salons and high society, so their music came from those who labored at sugar mills and farms. *Trova* was sung on the streets and in alleys and vacant lots. Sung for love, not fame. Sung for beauty, not riches. Sung for laughter.

What did the *trovadores* sing about? They sang of amorous secrets, futile regrets, and innocence lost; of patriotic duty, faithless love, and the quest for freedom. They conjured the mad, fanatic passions of the heart and recounted descents into an abyss of sorrow. Thus, Ángel Almenares, who claimed a wife had put a hex on him and paralyzed his arm, could write "Cajón de Muerto (Dead Man's Coffin)," an ode to death, when he was all of twenty years old.

The *trovadores* sang *boleros* and *bambucos, habaneras, criollas,* and *guarachas.* You could be starving, without even two pesos to rub between your fingers, but that could be the inspiration for a brilliant *guaracha.* What's more, the music could be hilarious. Ñico Saquito, the great *trovador* whose life spanned the last century, sang of half-dead peasants pushing ox-drawn fruit carts all day in the blazing sun for nothing, and of luckless marriages to evil, abusive hags. One of my favorite *guarachas* by Saquito, "Cuidadito, Compay Gallo," is about a lusty parrot who takes his pleasures in a rooster's harem and lives to regret it.

If *guarachas* were hilarious, even bawdy, the *boleros* were passionate, sentimental, and saturated with inexhaustible longing. The Cuban *bolero* was officially born in Santiago when "Tristeza," by Pepe Sánchez, was first transcribed. But no one could ever mistake it for the music of the same name that originated in Spain. Sung originally in 2/4 time—later, as it evolved, it went to a standard 4/4 signature—Santiago's *bolero* had a five-beat *cinquillo* rhythm. And like everything in Cuba, it was a mongrel mixture of Spanish and Italian melody and harmony with African rhythm.

"You want to know about the *trovadores*?" Antonio Fernández Arbelo asked, pouring me a glass of rum one afternoon. "Well, it was Pepe Sánchez who started the tradition of the Cuban *bolero*. Soon other young singers and guitarists started singing *boleros*: Clotario Blez, Sindo Garay, Alberto Villalon, Rosendo Ruiz, José Bandera."

Arbelo should know. His father was none other than the fabled *trovador*, Ñico Saquito. In fact, we were sitting in an upstairs room of an addition made possible by royalties finally paid out to Arbelo by Peer Music on some of his father's more than 560 songs.

In the neighborhood of Tivolí, said Arbelo, there were many descendants of blacks and mulatto masters and slaves. Before the Afro-Haitians arrived, Tivolí was inhabited by Cubans and some French. But after the Haitian revolution of 1791, with an influx of planters, slaves, and free blacks, the area became predominantly French-speaking. By then, the city was the main population center of the Afro-Haitian community in Santiago.

"Of course, the Haitians had a great musical tradition," said Arbelo, "which came in contact with the Afro-Hispanic culture of Santiago. Those traditions mixed, forming new styles."

Toussaint-Louverture, a charismatic Haitian slave, had led a bloody uprising that liberated Haiti from French rule and spread terror throughout Cuba, where whites lived in dread of the same thing happening. The Franco-Haitian influence was soon felt everywhere in the country. The French brought the *contradanza* and the *rigadoon,* as well as theater and an attitude of cultural superiority, while their slaves brought powerful drumming and the voodoo religion. In Guantánamo, this mix of cultures gave birth to the *changüí* and *guaracha.*

"My father is considered one of the great figures in the history of *son, guaracha,* and *bolero,*" said Arbelo, whose face echoed his father's crooked visage. "The *son* added a trumpet and a chorus—or a *montuno*—to the *guaracha.* To the *guaracha,* my father added *son* and Cuban *bolero.* Pepe Sánchez started the tradition of the *bolero.* He played guitar, because the *tres* was not yet invented. But soon other young musicians started writing and singing *boleros:* Emiliano Clotario Blez, Sindo Garay, Alberto Villalón." When he was thirteen, Saquito joined a group of singers who were already adults. They sang on the streets and during carnival. When the *comparsa* groups heard his tunes, they asked him to compose carnival songs they could sing.

"You see, the leaders of the *comparsas* saw my father was a great composer and singer, even though he was just a boy at the time," says Arbelo. "Already, he was hanging out with Rafael Cueto and Ciro Rodríguez, who went on to form Trio Matamoros. And in their group were other musicians, like Albert Arocha and Enrique González, who became legends, too. My father wrote hundreds of songs—at this moment I've recovered more than five hundred and sixty. He couldn't read music, but the songs came pouring out of him. Other musicians would transcribe his music. Sometimes the trained musicians would make slight mistakes. But when the notes were played back to him, Ñico would say, 'No. That's wrong.' Because the music was in his soul."

One day, I went to see Antonio Ferrer Cabello, who had painted Saquito and all the other great *trovadores.* I was told I could always find him at his gallery near the cathedral after 9 A.M. Sure enough, when I knocked on his door, the artist emerged, paintbrush in hand, wearing atop his bald head a straw hat with the top missing, as if a machete had sheared it off.

Cabello is eighty-nine years old and walks slowly, shuffling his feet. He has gentle, melancholy eyes and a child's radiant smile. From his studio I gazed at the square, the cathedral, the colonial museum, and the myriad layers of jumbled roofs that overhang the twisted streets, mingling faded blues and greens with the colors of clay, bone, and ash.

"I painted all the portraits that hang in the Casa de la Trova, but the walls of the *trova* are not big enough to hold all the great musicians we have," said Cabello. "Because Santiago is the cradle of the *trova*. It was born in this city and reached its zenith here."

The *trovadores* were those who sang in duos or trios, with guitars. When Cabello was a little boy, there used to be a place nearby his house where all the *trovadores* and guitarists would gather. There, they drank rum and played all night.

"I remember there was a singer called Palay who had a powerful voice. He was a cigar roller, too. Later, when I had a studio, the *trovadores* would ask me to paint portraits of those great ones already dead."

Cabello smiled wistfully at the memory, summoning it for a lingering moment into his mind's eye.

"So I asked the *trovadores* to sing the songs of those dead masters. 'Otherwise,' I told them, 'I would not be able to capture their genius.' "

Sindo Garay was a friend of Cabello's father, who told his son stories about El Caney, a small village, just outside of Santiago, where the *trovadores* would party late into the night.

"My father told me how Sindo was always with his guitar and the musicians would take a cart and push it all the way to El Caney, which was the perfect place to roast a pig and eat mangos," Cabello recalled. "Sindo was a modest man, very much loved by all who knew him. He had an inner goodness. The songs Sindo and the *trovadores* sang were profound. The songs they sang were living poetry."

The *trova* blended easily with *son*, though it wasn't as all-powerful. *Son* had the *tres*—an orchestra unto itself, African rhythm and tonality, Islamic and Jewish trance rhythms, and other secret ingredients that had blended over centuries, cooked into a tangy stew. I heard a range of *son* styles throughout Santiago. But while *son* was in no danger of disappearing, the young bands I encountered tended to rush the music, as if not wholly trusting that its beauty could be captured at a slower cadence. I was beginning to wonder if I would hear the classic *son* of Oriente, with its filigree of jazz, until one day I happened on La Estudiantina Invasora, a group I remembered hearing on an anthology years earlier.

Led by a trumpeter whose tone was pure and melting and whose majestic solos referenced the jazz of old New Orleans, the septet had a glorious sound. The percussionists held the group together. The *bongó* player dipped into a reservoir of subtle techniques, and his accents were placed marvelously, sometimes where you least expected them. The conjoined rhythms of the scraping *güiro* and the three-two clave were enhanced by the syncopated contrabass.

La Estudiantina played *boleros* and *guarachas* and *son-guarachas*. The music drew dancers, cheek to cheek, out onto the thin area in front of the stage. A gorgeous black woman in her late twenties, her molasses-colored hair falling like a banner, danced with a stick-thin man in his eighties who wore neatly pressed gray slacks and a baby blue guayabera shirt and glided with ease to the shaking seeds of the *maracas* and the full-throated singing. When the group played "Cajón de Muerto," singer Aristides Torres's voice cut like a knife:

Solo ambicion de fatiga yerto
cansado ya de fatiga guerras
y al acostarme en mi cajón de muerto
dormir en paz debajo de la tierra.
(My only ambition, exhausted
and tired of the enduring war,

is to lie down in my box of death
to sleep in peace underneath
the Earth.)

The song itself had a double meaning. The box could be not only a coffin but a powerful Afro-Cuban ritual of the same name, played on *cajones*—wooden boxes—for the purpose of calling down ancestral spirits. When the set ended, I ran into Pastor Panes, the young director of Sones de Oriente, another popular *son* band.

"Who is the trumpeter?" I asked.

"Inaudi Paisán."

"And the contrabassist?"

"Roberto Napoles." Panes smiled. "Roberto is the oldest working musician in Santiago. The music they perform represents a pure version of the *son*, everything played tightly."

I asked Paisán if we could talk, but he had to leave. His wife was entering the hospital. Napoles, however, gave me a broad grin. He was in no rush to go anywhere. "I didn't always play the contrabass. I started on the guitar when I was twelve years old," he said. "I'm ninety now. In the old days, the *son* bands used a *botijuela*, a primitive instrument made of clay. The *botijuela* was a ceramic jug used to carry oil. But the musicians cut a hole in the side to produce a bass sound made by blowing it and covering and uncovering the hole. The *botijuela* came from Matanzas, which was a great seaport. After that came the *marímbula*, which you sat on and had metal keys. But in 1932, the same year I founded La Orquesta de Chepín Chovén, I began playing the contrabass, which started being used about 1924."

When I told Felix Varela that I had finally seen a great *son* group, with a gifted trumpeter fluent in jazz, he smiled knowingly.

"Ah, yes. La Estudiantina Invasora. Most of the *son* bands at Casa de la Trova don't know the roots. They add things and change the music, sometimes without any knowledge of what they're changing. But Paisán is a great musician. In fact, Estudiantina Invasora was formed by my family back in 1928, and for many years it was one of the best *son* bands in Oriente. But it fell into decline and was in danger of disintegrating until one day I took Paisán aside and convinced him to join it. Paisán played with the symphony; he had studied jazz. Paisán is a master trumpeter, and now the group is sounding very good."

I heard music everywhere in Santiago. The fruit and vegetable vendors pulling their donkey-drawn carts through the streets had their own songs, *pregones,* that harkened back to the street cries of rural Andalucía in Spain. In Havana, *pregones* had disappeared from the streets. But in the East the vendors hawked tomatoes and tangerines, bananas and plantains, with singing voices that awakened your senses and made you taste the flesh of the fruit or vegetable. Sometimes the *pregones* were set to fragments of Yoruba or Congolese songs, and occasionally the *pregoneros* told musical stories that reminded me of a song I'd heard, "Pregón Santiaguero," about a vendor who was so charismatic with his songs and spiels that everyone instantly wanted whatever he was selling.

Nor was Santiago just the cradle of *son.* The city held other treasures for anyone willing to explore it. During the days and weeks I spent there, I took in a feast of mythopoetic dances and ritual re-creations. I saw Conjunto Folklórico de Oriente do an astonishing piece called *El Maní,* which drew on the music and dance of the *yuka, macuta,* and Palo traditions. *Maní,* a Congolese word, refers to a dance that is a savage battle between rival factions. A dozen or more half-naked male dancers fight each other with sticks. But what stuck in my mind was the image of an agonized warrior, in the throes of some dire spell, eating fire and then passing a flaming torch all over his body.

"In the Palo religion you work with plants. The *palero* distills a powder from the plants, and from that he casts spells," Milagros González, the general director of the *conjunto,* explained to me after the performance. "In this story, one of the dancers takes the potion and pours it on one of the most important warriors. The powder causes the warrior to seek out fires to break the spell—to burn it away."

One morning, at Teatro Heredia, I watched a performance by two of the region's best dance troupes, Danza Libre from Guantánamo and Danza del Caribe from Santiago. The former freely mixed Yoruba and Congolese dancing with a library of movements from modern dance, while the latter embodied the spirit of Martha Graham and modern ballet without sacrificing Afro-Cuban phrasing and movement. Each was backed by a group of virtuoso young percussionists whose drumming triggered the dancers' movements.

In Cuba, more than in most countries, dance embodies a living mythology. And Ballet Folklórico Cutumba, like all folkloric troupes, showed off its mastery of many legends and rituals. I'd heard a recording of the group a friend had given me years before I went to Cuba. But seeing the ensemble on two separate nights, with its more than two dozen dancers and musicians, was a treat. The group did a spectacular dance that drew on *gagá*, a version of voodoo that originated in Haiti and came to Cuba in the early nineteenth century when Haitian workers helped build the coffee and sugar production centers. Most Americans don't realize the vast cultural influence Haiti has exerted on Cuban art and culture over the course of two centuries. But Cutumba made it evident. The dancers did a glorious version of the maypole dance—weaving and unraveling, at lightning speed, colorful streamers—that was brought over by Haitian slaves but has come to be a cultural representation as recognizable as an Abakuá *írime* or the presence, during carnival, of the piercing *corneta china*.

Though descendants of the Yoruba arrived relatively late in Oriente, their music, dance, rituals, and myths were quickly adapted. Cutumba dipped into the seductions, betrayals, and fights of the Patakin, a selection of key Yoruba myths that made their way to Cuba. Comprehending the Patakin requires some knowledge of the myths; luckily I knew the tale of Ochún, Obba, and Changó.

In a long ago time, Ochún, the *orisha* of sweet waters, conned Obba, the legitimate wife of the *orisha* Changó, into cutting off her ear and feeding it to her husband on the pretext that it would make her, Obba, more attractive to Changó. But when Changó realized what Obba had done, he left her house forever. Changó, *orisha* of thunder and fire, had tasted death once upon a time by hanging himself, a dark secret rarely alluded to. His reckless obsessions put him at constant risk. When he became obsessed with Ochún, a consort of the warrior god Ogún, the two *orishas* fought an epic machete dance. This is the story Cutumba reenacted now. As the drummers pumped out waves of thunder, the dancers wielding the machetes moved at blurring speeds that could, with a small slip, have sliced off an arm or a head. In the terrifying climax, Ogún moved the machete's blade across his tongue. As he did so, I watched the dancer's eyes roll back in his head and saw that he had the glazed look of someone wholly lost in a trance. I looked for the dancer, Roberto Nordet, after the concert and found him sweating.

"Where did you learn to dance?" I asked.

"I never went to schools. My parents came from Haiti and had no money," Nordet said. "But when I was thirteen I auditioned for the Conjunto Folklórico and was accepted. My mother is a *santera* and I'm initiated as a *santero* and a *palero*. The religions, the dances, the songs, and the rhythms are all interconnected, all one. So in a performance I do a secular version of what would be sacred in another context—but details are altered slightly."

"When the machete went across your tongue, you appeared to be in a trance," I said.

Nordet nodded. "Sometimes when I dance, ancestors take possession of my spirit and I'm lifted to another level." Nordet lit a cigarette and blew out a stream of smoke. "When I perform Changó, I expel fire from my mouth, and when I perform Ogún, I have to handle the machete and run it across my tongue. Ogún is the *orisha* of metal and a very powerful, strong warrior. To move the machete across your tongue, you have to have incredible concentration."

The next morning I dropped by the home of folklorist Julian Mateo and told him about the performance.

"You know, Santería wasn't brought here until after it arrived in Matanzas," Mateo said. "It came later, in the early twentieth century, so the music and the folklore in Oriente is not so heavily influenced by the Yoruba culture as it is in Havana."

I had met Mateo, a former professor of art history and philosophy at the University of Oriente, one afternoon at a gallery adjacent to Casa del Caribe, a cultural center and research institute, where he was lecturing a tour group from *National Geographic*. Speaking impeccable English that had a slight Eastern European lilt to it (Mateo had lived in Czechoslovakia for years), he held the attention of twenty or more mostly gray-haired Americans with a discourse on everything from Congolese drumming to the origins of Yoruba divination. When he finished he was kind enough to give me a private tour.

"This is isn't really a museum—we call it a house or temple, because the people who built these altars were, or are, practitioners of the religions of eastern Cuba," said Mateo, indicating an assemblage of ritual objects. "Voodoo is a combination of Congo, Dahomey, Yoruba, spiritism, Catholicism, and Freemasonry; Palo is from the Congo and Angola and is widespread down into South Africa. Palo is about finding the balance of the world and channeling the forces of Nature."

All around me were altars. There were three to spiritism and one to the Congo religion, called Palo Monte in Oriente. Mateo told me that they believe in Nzambi, a god that is inside everyone and animates all existence.

We walked outside and there, on a patio, was a thatched hut that a priest named Pablo Milanes, a *houngan* of voodoo, built.

"Those who worship voodoo here believe that the *loas* come from under the ground and possess the initiates," Mateo said. Pointing to the pole outside the hut, he explained that it symbolized the axis upon which the *loas* ascend from below in the primordial waters and that there are two kinds of *loas: rada* and *petrol*. The *rada* are less terrible, but the *petrol* are violent.

My eyes focused on two throne altars to the twin female *orishas* Yemayá and Ochún. Why, I wondered, were these two rulers of the waters so omnipresent? "Ah," Mateo said. "That's because the majority of *babalawos* throughout Cuba consulted Ifa oracles with the casting of necklaces and determined that Yemayá and Ochún would predominate over the people of Cuba that year."

Musicians started arriving and Mateo greeted them warmly, introducing me.

"We're in luck," he said. "Kokoyé is performing at Casa del Caribe shortly, and you must see them."

As we walked to Casa del Caribe, we ran into Juan Bautista Castillo Mustelier, director of Kokoyé, which was founded fourteen years ago. Short and trim, he has the physique of a forty-year-old dancer but is actually sixty. His eyes were what I noticed first: a milky shade of violet.

"In my family, eye color changes with age," Bautista said. "I come from the countryside, near Caney. I began dancing professionally when I was twelve. I danced Tajona, a kind of *comparsa* that is native to rural Oriente."

Bautista's father was descended from the Yorubas, but the family lived adjacent to a community of Haitians. Bautista's mother was Haitian, too, and the religion he grew up with was mongrelized.

"The rituals, the gods, the spirits—everything was mixed," Bautista said. "We call it *espiritismo.*"

Bautista paused, borrowed a lighter from another musician he knew, and lit up a cigarette. I knew a little about *espiritismo,* a movement that came to Cuba via the teachings of Allan Kardec, a French academic whose birth name was Hippolyte Léon Denizard Rivail. Rivail published numerous scholarly books until his interests, late in his life, turned toward the mystical. He assumed a druid's name, Allan Kardec, and promoted spiritism, a movement that spread like wildfire through Europe and North America. Its fundamental belief—that souls of the dead could communicate through the living—jibed with the Yoruba practice of having an *egungun,* a shaman, conjure the spirit of someone who had just died during funerals. There were few *egunguns* in Cuba and probably none at all in Santiago. But French planters and Haitian slaves were avid devotees of Kardec's writings. Thus, *espiritismo* took hold in Santiago and has persisted ever since as a spiritual root.

"If the drumming and singing were strong enough to send a person into a trance, a Yoruba spirit might come one moment, and a Haitian spirit might show up later," Bautista said. Ever since he was a little boy, Bautista was immersed in a culture of ecstatic drumming, singing, and dancing. His grandfather was a noted dancer, and his mother was, as well. "She was a member of Sociedad de Negros, and she took me to celebrations where there were great African dancing competitions."

When Bautista arrived in Santiago, he danced the *rumba*—but in the Tajona tradition.

"Many people think there are just three kinds of *rumba*. But there is really a fourth style, and I introduced this style into the repertoire of Cutumba and Conjunto Folklórico de Oriente when I was the director of both those groups," Bautista said.

In Tajona, the force of the music powers the dancer into what is called the *jiribilla,* where he must create, very quickly and very powerfully, certain improvisations. The dancer reacts to the *repique* drum, which is akin to the *quinto* but comes from Dahomey. In fact, I'd seen this the night before at Teatro Martí: a spectacular eruption of dancing that seemed like a controlled convulsion.

"What about the machete dance?" I asked, remembering the glazed look in the eyes of the dancer in Conjunto Folklórico de Oriente who had whipped the machete around in dazzling arabesques. Bautista's violet eyes narrowed.

"You can only dance that if you are a *machete mayor*—a master. In the dance the performance can quickly turn into spirit possession. The lines can blur because it's a dance both incredibly powerful and extremely dangerous."

The three of us walked over to the bar at Casa del Caribe and Mateo pointed out Abelardo Lardouet, a thin black man with haunting eyes and a head covered with a multicolored, woven reggae hat.

"Abelardo is a *palero* and a singer. He's recorded the life and death of a *santero,* which you must hear. If you want to experience a Palo ritual, Abelardo's the one. How much would something like that cost?" Mateo said, not bothering to consult me.

"For $500, you would experience everything," Abelardo said as he stared deeply into my eyes.

"There are many animals to be sacrificed, and of course there are the musicians," Mateo said. "That's the standard price. But I warn you, it's not for the faint of heart."

I hadn't thought about commissioning a Palo ritual, though the offer momentarily intrigued me. I'd heard the unearthly beauty of Palo drumming and singing, and I knew a little about the religion. The foundation of Palo Monte, as it's called in Oriente, is the covenant between the *palero,* the high priest of the Palo religion, and a dead person. The dead person makes a commitment to serve the *palero* with sacrifices and music, while the *palero* makes a similar commitment to serve the dead person. *Paleros* didn't accept death; in fact, the old *paleros* who were close to shedding the mortal coil would instruct young *paleros* to put their remains in a *nganga,* a magical way of transcending death. I told Abelardo that I would pass on the Palo ritual. The truth was that I was not about to be responsible for the slaughter of animals.

Mateo had the blasé smile of one who would never go native, yet couldn't help admiring the rich culture that Africans had forged in Oriente. He poured himself the first of many glasses of rum and filled a plastic cup for me, as well.

"We're in luck. Tonight, Casa del Caribe is hosting the centennial of two mutual aid societies known as *cabildos*—Olugo and Isuama—and the *comparsa,* Conga de los Hoyos, as well as the society of La Tumba Francesa, which means we get to see them all perform."

As night fell, people began to drift in. A researcher at Casa del Caribe who'd spent years tracking Isuama's roots gave an emotional, somewhat histrionic tribute to the groups. And then, to the sound of a ringing bell and a roar of drums, Carabalí Isuama came onstage. It was a spectacular sight: Some twenty men and women, young and old, came out dancing.

Carabalí Isuama celebrating at Casa del Caribe.

An old woman, her eyes full of fire and secret joy, came out waving a machete with perfect precision, pumping her arms in time to the rhythms, jabbing the sword in the air, and swirling it in spirals. Other dancers reeled off the names of members of the *cabildo* who had died or reached the age of 100 as singers chanted. They sang about legendary black Carabalí warriors who fought fearlessly for liberty so that their children might be free:

Marchamos de Oriente a la Habana
Y peleamos sin rencor por nuestra libertad
(We are advancing from eastern Cuba to Havana
And fight without vengeance for our freedom)

Of all the *cabildos,* Carabalí Isuama's presentation stood out. When their members sang and danced, there was something both mysterious and dangerous in their music. Later, I went over and introduced myself to the director, a feisty fifty-five-year-old woman named Gertrudis González, whose *cabildo* name is Tula Carabalí.

"We come from Calabar, the southern part of Nigeria," González said. "I'm not Carabalí, but I grew up in a neighborhood in Santiago, in Los Hoyos, where many people are Carabalí. We have one *cabildo* for adults and one for children. We teach the children the songs, the dances, and the religious myths of our people. We have two hundred thirty people all told. And our oldest member is Pio Rosado, who you saw tonight. She's one hundred seven years old." I asked González if I could come by her *cabildo.*

"Yes, come. We're having our monthly practice Tuesday at six P.M."

The next day I walked up Moncada, past women selling herbs, past scrawny men hawking live turtles held upside down by their tails. Two chickens, each tied by one leg to a cage, stared at me as their owner quickly sized me up as a noncustomer and looked for a potential buyer. I turned a corner onto Carniceria Street and arrived at Cabildo Carabalí Isuama.

"I have been coming here since I was five and I'm forty now," Alfredo Bonet Leyva said, greeting me at the door. "My grandmother was the first queen this *cabildo* had after the revolution, and ours is the oldest in Santiago. It's officially one hundred thirty years old. The *cabildo* is where I learned to sing, dance, and play all the percussion instruments. Tonight, we have seven of our musicians. But other nights there are usually more members learning to play."

Cabildo director Gertrudis González, who I'd met the night before, came over and embraced me as if we were old friends.

"I'm glad you came," she said. "Tonight we practice our songs, our drumming, and our singing."

The seven musicians took their place at the back of the room. At a signal from the group's leader, they began playing powerful Carabalí rhythms. Eight women dressed in pink, white, and blue skirts, their heads in white turbans, came out and danced to the hurricane of cross-rhythms and clanging bells. One woman held the flag of the *cabildo,* while others shook *maracas* as they pumped their arms. The old woman I had seen with the machete at Casa del Caribe the night before now held a large black doll aloft in one hand. She smiled when our eyes met and beckoned me with her hands to dance, and I joined her. The rhythms swept through the room like a torrent now, and a chorus of chanting voices filled the room. Twenty minutes later the music ended.

My dancing partner introduced herself. "I am Dolores Rivera González," she said. "I have been a member of this *cabildo* for fifteen years. I'm sixty-five years old, but I feel like a young girl."

"Where did you learn these songs?"

"Here," Dolores said. "The songs we sing are in Yoruba, a language some of us grew up with at home and others learned." Gertrudis González presently joined us.

"There's an electricity, a force that passes among us all when we dance and sing," González said. "When we first start, we ask for help from the ancestors. Then, when we feel them inside us, we dance. And there are times when we become possessed."

The *cabildo* meeting was breaking up. I thanked both women for inviting me.

"I'm coming back for carnival," I said. "I hope to see you."

"You can't miss us. We have a great *comparsa,*" González said, referring to Carbalí Isuama's carnival procession.

I walked outside and headed down San Bartolome Street. I stopped a man and asked if he knew where the Tumba Francesa association was.

"It's on Maceo Street." He pointed me in the right direction and five minutes later I entered 501 Maceo.

La Tumba Francesa occupies a large room saturated with history. Faded photographs of the group's members and historical memorabilia adorned the walls. Five singers stood near an altar, and one of them called out a chant as five percussionists began playing the special drums.

One had a large frame drum, a *requinto,* hung around his neck, and another played a *catá,* a kind of a log drum, with sticks. Two other drummers played *bulas,* and another played a *premier,* a drum much like the *quinto.* Soon, furious Afro-Haitian rhythms became the backdrop to a startlingly incongruous, albeit spectacular, dance called *masón.*

I watched regal black and mulatto couples with haughty faces and stiff bodies engage in a couples dance that mimicked the ways of the French "plantocracy." Absent the African rhythms and costumes, I might have been at a palace ball in eighteenth-century France. But this is the cultural conundrum behind La Tumba Francesa. For later, if only for a brief time, three percussionists would slide their drums across the floor and sit astride them, daring—even taunting—a male dancer to match their ferocious improvisations.

What seemed like an aping of white French court society would turn deeply African. But then it would shift once more, giving way to the famed dance around the maypole known as El Tejido de las Cintas. Suspended from the maypole, red, white, and blue streamers hung loosely, and it was the job of the dancers to weave them together and then, without falling out of rhythm, to unweave them. An old man with cinnamon-tinted skin stood next to me, smiling, holding a shaker in his hand.

"I've been in this association eleven years," said Rafael Canet. "I live down the street. I'm not Haitian. But when I moved to this neighborhood, I liked the music and the people, so I joined the *cabildo.*"

After *masón* ended, a woman in the association overheard us talking and drew closer.

"I've been queen for four years," she said, introducing herself as Andrea Quiala. "I sing and lead the group. We did an imitation of the French court so that the whites could see that we blacks and mulattos could dance just as well as they did. But you should talk to Fabio Figueroa, over there. He's the choreographer and director of La Tumba Francesa."

I found Figueroa, a compact man with mischievous eyes, outside talking to a friend. "I was born in the countryside near here," the sixty-two-year-old choreographer said. "My wife was the niece of the president of the association. So naturally I joined. I was twenty-three years old when I became a member. We have been around a long time. The Tumba Francesa was recognized officially in 1862, in the days of slavery. But we had been around long before that."

Only one part was the dance of the slaves, done with percussion. The rest of it was the dance of the French. I had wondered if La Tumba Francesa was meant as pointed mockery of French plantation society and asked Figueroa as much.

"There's a mockery in what we're doing. The dances the white slave-owners did in those days were minuets, carabinets, and rigadoons," Figueroa said. "But the drums were from Dahomey, a region of Africa where many blacks were taken into slavery. The dance we did around the flagpole was brought to Cuba by a French general. The Cuban slaves from Haiti adapted it into their rituals. We call it the Weaving of the Stripes."

When a musician from Catalonia, who lived in Santiago, transcribed it, La Tumba Francesa was the first music from carnival that became a "higher" art form. Yet the music and dance brought up complex issues of race and self-acceptance. After the War of 1895, the first governor of Santiago tried to make the city a "whiter" place with the complicity of local Creole politicians. Officials tried to confine blacks to certain neighborhoods, and the press demonized anything having to do with African culture as "savage."

"This was the time that Cabildo Olugo disappeared. But the Cabildo Cocoyé immediately claimed they were not African," the sociologist Nancy Pérez said when I ran into her the next day. "It was just like Frantz Fanon said: 'black face, white mask.' So Cocoyé changed to Tumba Francesa and became an association to distance itself from its true identity. And the ironic thing is that the name they took for themselves—*tumba*—was African."

Some of the black women from Haiti that Pérez interviewed told her they were French, not black. And this was understandable. The Cuban schools never taught them African culture, never taught them anything during colonial times until after slavery ended.

"The truth is, the whites wanted to remove all traces of Africa from us. But you can't kill cultural identity," Pérez said. "I studied La Tumba Francesa in the 1960s. But I found that it has something that really doesn't fuse with Afro-Cuban culture. I don't see the mockery in it at all. To me, it's a classic example of how a culture can lose its identity in the face of oppression."

Dania, a sensational dancer from the folkloric group Kokoyé, had said she was eager to accompany me to Casa de la Musica and hear some *son*. But the band was mediocre, and after losing a few dollars to *rifa,* a local version of bingo, we left and headed for Casa de las Tradiciones. Even before we turned down the street I heard a riotous blast of *son*. We walked up the flight of stairs, paid a $3 cover, and entered an old Spanish house with two patios. I felt like I'd stepped into a party. Inside, a septet was playing a fiery *son* by Arsenio Rodríguez. The trumpets were screaming and a bohemian crowd of interracial couples—a blond woman from Sweden and her black Cuban boyfriend, a Cuban and her German beau—danced near the bar, in the halls, and off in private rooms.

"The bandleader is Finnish," the bartender told me. "He studied trumpet here for five years and finally married a Cuban girl."

A cigar roller offered me a handmade beauty, but I told him I turned green when I smoked cigars and he laughed.

"Not with these," he said.

Dania led me out on the dance floor, giving me pointers on how to move my hips and legs and chest independently. I was nearly getting the hang of it when the club closed. We walked through Tivolí and Dania told me a little of her life. Though she was thirty-two she still lived with her mother and had never married. I couldn't imagine this African Venus, with high, carved cheekbones and pendulous lips, not having a line of admirers.

"I can't believe no one ever proposed," I said.

A sadness crossed her face like a dark shadow. She looked away, I thought, so as not to cry.

"The men in Cuba are all womanizers. It's part of the culture here. But that's not what I want," she said.

We passed a cab, and I sent her home, sensing that she was expecting something that I could never give her.

The next morning, I walked up to Vista Alegre, a swank neighborhood where many of the city's most important people live. Julian Mateo had invited me over, and already he had an open bottle of rum in hand when he opened the door of his mother's house, located across the street from the Russian embassy.

"No," I said. "I had plenty last night at Casa de las Tradiciones."

"Oh, now that's the real Santiago. The tourists haven't discovered it yet."

"Some have," I said. "The Finns and the Germans at any rate." Mateo's mother, a spunky, gray-haired woman with boundless energy, set down a piping hot thermos of syrupy black coffee.

"If you want to see some films, I have fifty or so," Mateo said. "I've got films on voodoo, Palo, Santería, espiritism. One film has *everything*, nothing held back," Mateo said in a tone of fascinated revulsion. "Some Italian doctors asked Abelardo to preside over it, and they got more than they bargained for. Here, have some more *aguardiente*. Now, these doctors thought they were inured to everything. They'd done surgery, seen corpses, seen death. But they never saw anything like this before. They were shocked. And it wasn't just the sacrifices of all the animals, but the way they were opened up. A *palero*, a priest of Palo, *knows* anatomy; he knows where all the organs are and how to remove them. What happened? The Italian doctors finally stopped it. But I ate the raw heart of a pig that night and it was sweet. Now there's only one film I wouldn't care to see." Mateo shuddered. "I would never want to see it again. It would turn your stomach." I could only imagine what horrors would cause Mateo, steeled to all manner of the grotesque, such displeasure.

"What kind of ritual is it?" I asked.

"We don't know."

He rummaged through his collection for a good ten minutes before coming up with the film. "I think I subconsciously hid it away. You know, about five years ago there was a case in Santiago of a child who was sacrificed in a ritual of black magic. The *babalawo,* who was obviously deranged, was shot. It was a great scandal."

Mateo cued up the video and I watched a group of drummers ringed around a tall black woman. At some point, she made an incision in the neck of a goat and then crouched down, as the drums became stronger, and sucked the blood like a vampire. The goat seemed strangely calm as the woman lit a candle and poured the molten wax down her throat for a full minute.

"Now look," Mateo said. But I already saw what was happening. With a massive knife the woman was sawing the head off the goat, which she and a few others held tightly. It was a gruesome sight. But it would get worse. After twisting off the head, they cut off the goat's testicles and passed them around. A half dozen or more people then put the sex organs in their mouths and sucked on them.

"Disgusting," Mateo said. "We don't know what ritual this is. It's not Palo, or Santería or voodoo or *espiritismo.*"

As the woman took the goat's head and sucked the bloody stump, I involuntarily shuddered.

"None of the so-called scholars here in Santiago know what this is about. What's the intent of the sacrifice? Of course, it's an animal sacrifice, and blood is the vital principle of life. The *orishas* and the *loas* like blood. Perhaps they're getting virility from the testicles."

I'd seen animals sacrificed before. In Morocco I'd been at a *gnawa* wedding where a goat was decapitated. The memory of its head falling and the blood running everywhere still haunted me. Sacrifices, I knew, were part of initiations in most traditional cultures. Long ago, shamans went deep into the earth, into caves, to paint mysterious pictures of animals. They had to have experienced powerful, conflicting emotions connected with hunting, killing, slaughtering, and eating other living beings.

"A sacrifice is a sacred act, composed of awe and terror," I offered. "It creates a rupture in reality, maybe the kind of rupture needed to take someone into another state."

Mateo thought about that for a moment. "The primitive mind is a mystery. And mysteries," he said, "don't always have answers."

❧

When I'd first arrived in Santiago, I tried to visit Eliades Ochoa. But the leader of Cuarteto Patria was in Havana being treated for liver problems. I figured I wouldn't see him this trip until Raulito Campos, a musician who knew him, called me to say he was back. Campos would drive me there.

"When the doctors told him he had to quit drinking, Eliades answered, 'I'd rather die than give up rum,' " Campos said, as I leaned out the window of his blue 1983 Moskvitch in order to avoid inhaling the gas fumes that were streaming directly into the car.

"What? You don't feel good?" Campos asked.

"It's the fumes. They make me nauseous."

Campos, who looked a little like Stan Laurel but grimmer, sighed.

"Yes, the pollution here is terrible because of these lousy Russian cars we have." This in a tone of voice which spoke of yet sadder things in life.

These days, Eliades Ochoa is a superstar of Cuban music. One of the featured artists of Wim Wenders's film about the Buena Vista Social Club, the fifty-six-year-old musician's voice and face are recognized around the world. But he still lives in a modest house in Santiago, the city he was born in. The main wall of his small living room was covered with a large velvet painting of pheasants. When Ochoa finally came out,

Eliades Ochoa near his home in Santiago.

he was wearing his trademark black *guajira* hat. He looked a little heavier since I last saw him. His rugged face was set off by a natty little wisp of a silver-gray beard sprouting from his cleft chin.

"How are you feeling?" I asked.

"Agghh," he said, as if waving away a nuisance. "I mustn't drink right now. But as soon as that's over and the doctors say I can drink, you can send me a box of whiskey. And what brings you all the way to Santiago?"

"I've come to look for the roots of *son*," I said.

"Well, if you didn't come here you would never find the *real son*. It would take centuries. In Havana they form their own bands. They have radio stations and TV. But everyone knows that Santiago is the birthplace of *son* and *changüí*, of *quiribá* and *nengón*."

The competition between Havana and Santiago is strong, and even Ochoa, who has achieved renown despite Havana's dominance of the Cuban music scene, feels it. He remembers playing in obscurity when there was no Buena Vista Social Club, when pesos would be thrown at him in the parks and on street corners. And he remembers playing guitar as a twelve-year-old for Benny Moré, who came to Santiago in the late fifties and was having his shoes shined.

"Benny threw me some coins. He said all the good ones start out this way," Ochoa says, a sly smile on his face.

"Eliades always respected the tradition," Campos says. "He has always been loyal to the roots of *son*, without letting foreign influences in."

Both his parents played the *tres*, and Ochoa started singing on the street corner near his house when he was just eight years old. By then, Ochoa says, he knew in his heart that he wanted to be a musician.

"I sang the songs of Los Compadres and Trio Matamoros. But I also loved *jíbaro* music, which comes from the countryside of Puerto Rico. Those musicians played *aguinaldos* and their music spoke to me. The songs they sang were about the problems of the people. I learned the music from my father, who plays an *aguinaldos*," he said.

The life of a *son* musician was precarious and hard, but Ochoa refined his craft over decades. Good as he was, he sang on the streets for years, playing for a pittance, barely surviving at times. Then, in 1963, he got a break. A local radio station hired him to sing, and almost as soon as he began, the letters started pouring in, praising his voice. "I played on that station for seven years, and I received more letters than any other performer," Ochoa remembered.

In the 1970s, Cuban music had a small following. And even through the 1980s, the *trovadores* had little popularity outside their own confines. You heard them at Casa de la Trova, to be sure, but nowhere else, Ochoa says. Still, he believed in the music and kept playing *sones, boleros,* and *guarachas.*

In 1978, Ochoa became the leader of Cuarteto Patria, one of Oriente's most important groups. Long before the Buena Vista phenomenon, Cuarteto Patria was traveling to Spain, Mexico, and other Caribbean countries, popularizing the classic music of eastern Cuba. Now Ochoa could sing his *sones, boleros,* and *guarachas* by the likes of Miguel Matamoros, Ñico Saquito, Francisco Repilado, and Luis Marqueti. I'd first heard Ochoa in the late 1980s. His grainy voice sounded natural and was full of passionate intensity, but what further set him apart from the rest of the *soneros* and *trovadores* was the sound of the band.

"The people say I have a different way of playing from other guitarists. And I do. I use two guitars instead of a *tres*. And I don't use a normal tuning for the guitar. I have a special tuning that makes my instrument part guitar and part *tres*. I can't read music; I'm self-taught. But the music is inside my head. I hear it and arrange it. I use two guitars in my group, and both are tuned specially. On my guitar, one of the treble strings is doubled," Ochoa said, pulling his instrument out of the case.

I asked him if he would sing a *jíbaro* and he played one he had recorded.

"You see, I wanted to give it a sound that is part *tres* and part guitar," he said.

As we drove back to my place, Campos told me that his daughter's band was performing that night in the room above the Casa de la Trova. "You might want to see them. They all studied at the music schools, and they play very well. And my daughter plays the *tres*."

"I'll see you there," I said.

The weather was hot enough that I wanted to go swimming. The closest beach was Siboney, a thirty-minute drive. The beach was filled with locals mostly, and when I dove into the cool waters I happened to swim by two men conversing in French. When I asked the younger of the men if he was visiting, he said no, he lived here now.

"And what does a Frenchman eat in this city of pork, chicken, and plantains?"

Fabien—for that was his name—put his finger to his lips and whispered, "I run a clandestine restaurant—a *paladar*."

"And what do you serve?"

"We have chicken, fish, and lobster. I can cook the lobster with two different kinds of sauce if you wish."

The thought of any kind of French food made my mouth water. Fabien, who'd been a poorly paid gardener in France, now had a Cuban wife and a toddler in Santiago. I took his card and, after returning to my room for a cool shower, I walked over to his secret *paladar,* where I ate a one-pound lobster cooked with fresh tomatoes, wine, garlic, and onions. It was the best meal I'd ever had in Cuba, and with a beer it cost a mere nine dollars.

I walked down Aguilera Street and passed a *toque,* a spirit-possession party, and watched a man spit a spray of rum ten feet out into the street. Then I went to the Big Salon, a room on top of the Casa de la Trova, and saw Morena Son, one of three all-girl *son* bands. The group played classic *sones* like "Suavecito," and Niurca Cardona, the group's thirty-five-year-old lead singer and percussionist, danced sensuously as she sang. A few couples glided across the floor. When I looked behind me, Raulito was there, proudly listening as his twenty-nine-year-old daughter Aimée played a *tres* solo.

"I produced their CD," Campos said, "so I would know it came out right. But it's a hard life, I can tell you, to be a musician in Santiago."

"I come from a family of musicians," Niurca Cardona said after the set. "One day, I began playing the drums. I was an actor, but the drums called me. I played folkloric music. And then I was asked to join this group. For women it's hard to reach the place where men can go. Santiago is the cradle of *son*. There are many great *soneros,* but very few are women."

"It's a challenge for us to play *son* on instruments like *tres* and trumpet, which have been traditionally played by men only," Aimée Campos said. "But I studied classical guitar at the university. Because we are women, we have to play our instruments really well. But the men help us. They're our friends."

෨෧ඁ෧

One cloudless Friday I went to visit Guantánamo. The rains had fallen heavy that summer and fall, and the countryside was bursting with blooms. Fields full of sugarcane that seemed to last for miles gave way to mango and coffee plantations, and every now and then I saw an *anacahuita* tree, its stone-colored trunk shaped like a woman's body. As I entered Guantánamo I saw billboards with paintings of famous black generals and signs proclaiming the revolution. One read: "We have decided to fight for our freedom." Laid out in grids, Guantánamo has a woebegone feel to it, and its strange marriage with an American naval base lends a surreal flavor to what is essentially Cuba's version of a shipyard town, where total dependence on the military has shaped the evolution of the city. Prostitution has been a constant since the turn of the last century, when the marines came to stay. But appearances can be deceiving.

Culturally, Guantánamo is rich in history. The city didn't evolve until the Haitian rebellion that brought the black revolutionary Toussaint-Louverture into power and set the French planters and their slaves fleeing to the region. The French brought coffee plantations and the *contradanza,* not to mention an imperious attitude. A significant portion of the people of Guantánamo have French, Haitian, and Jamaican blood in their veins. Here, black Haitians are called *franceses,* as if to set them apart from other Africans in Cuba. And many Jamaican descendants speak a pidgin English.

I traveled to Guantánamo hoping to hear *changüí,* a music and dance that had originated here and had intrigued me ever since I first heard it in the early 1990s. But the city also had spawned three other kinds of *son: quiribá, nengón,* and *regina.* Some musicians and musicologists from other parts of Cuba considered the four forms to be cousins of *son,* regional variants. But to my ears each of the four styles seemed part of a definite progression. I'd been told a couple of great *changüí* bands, including Changüí a Guantánamo, would be performing that day. But when I stopped off at the local Casa de Cultura, a marvelous building with Moorish tiling and arched doorways, I was told the show had been canceled, with no reason given.

"So who in Guantánamo knows the most about the history of *changüí*?" I asked.

"Ramón Gómez lives not far away," the center's administrator said, writing down the address. "Ramón is the musical director of Universales del Son, and he knows the true history of this music."

I found him sitting in his T-shirt talking with some musicians in the cramped front room of his modest apartment, not far from downtown. He looked younger than his fifty-two years and has the handsome face that comes from Cuba's many blendings of different races. When I told him I had come to learn about *changüí,* he leveled a sunny smile on me.

By coincidence, Gómez had just finished an investigation of *changüí, nengón, quiribá,* and *regina.* He reached across the table, pulled out a typewritten report, and handed it to me.

"*Changüí* is the result of a mix of several cultures, of African, Spanish, and French music, as well as aboriginal. The *bongó* we use is the fusion of two *bokú* drums. The *bokú* comes from Africa, but in Cuba the drum was transformed. In Santiago, the *bokú* is small, but here in Guantánamo, we make the heads larger. We call it *bongó de monte,* and we heat the drum over a flame to tune it. Our *bongó* has a hollow, dryer sound, which is perfect for our music."

Gómez disagrees with those who separate *changüí* from *son*. All of the music in Oriente are different branches of *son*. Yet he believes there is a sequence. The oldest forms of *son*, Gómez believes, are the *nengón*, followed by the *quiribá*, the *regina*, and *changüí*.

"*Quiribá*, an embryonic form of *son*, was born in Baracoa, a city where many people have Indian blood," Gómez said. "How do I know that *nengón* and *quiribá* are the oldest forms of *son*?" Gómez smiled.

"Listen. There are two rhythms they have as the basis of their sound—the first, or tonic, and the fifth note of the scale. In addition, when you hear the *tres*, what it plays is not harmonic but melodic. But the other forms of *son* use harmonic devices, which shows they come later."

If you listen to it, *quiribá* is more developed than *nengón*. It's composed of four parts and has a different structure. All four early forms of *son* include the *tres*, but in the *quiribá*, the first two measures are for the chorus and the next two are for the singer.

"How does the *regina* fit in?" I asked.

"*Regina* was born in a region near here called El Salvador. It has four measures of the chorus and then a part for a solo singer. What the *tres* is playing is echoed by the chorus. So when you see a lot of difference in the vocal response to the *tres*, it's definitely not *regina*. As for *changüí*, it begins with the chorus, called *llamada al montuno*, but then it goes to *paso de calle*, which is what gives *changüí* its flavor."

Nengón was first played with a very primitive instrument called the *bajo en tierra*. As its name implies, this was basically a grill of sticks that could resonate over a hole in the ground. Musicians also used a *bokú* drum and a *guayo*, a gourd scraper. *Quiribá* has the same instruments and was played at fiestas, while *regina* used *tres*, *maracas*, *botija* (a jug), *bongó*, and *guayo*.

"*Regina* is the mother of *changüí*," Gómez said. "But *changüí* underwent transformations. The *maracas* came in the second transformation of *changüí*. And the *marímbula*—you are familiar with the *marímbula*?"

"Yes," I said, remembering the first time I'd seen *son*'s primitive bass, with its metal keys that used three or four notes to mark the harmony.

"Well, the *marímbula* comes in only after the third transformation of *changüí*."

"And where did the *maracas* come from?" I asked.

"The *maracas* were used by the Indians in sacred rituals. And the black slaves would've heard that and felt drawn to the rhythms," Gómez said.

In fact, the Indians were the first ones to run away from the Spaniards. There are many aspects of Cuban music and folklore that people think of as African but are in fact Indian.

"The *guaya* was an Indian instrument. And, for instance, the use of cigars in *orisha* ceremonies is Indian, not African," Gómez said. "The *chabalongo,* a form of divination with coconuts used in Ifa, was taught *to* the Africans *by* the Indians. In Cuba, we had Arawaks, Tainos, Siboneyes, and Caribes. All of them were musical. They had drums."

The first blacks that came to Guantánamo came as a result of the Haitian revolution. Before that, the area was peopled by Spaniards and Indians. When the English invaded Guantánamo in the eighteenth century and decided to attack, they knew whoever controlled the city controlled the Caribbean. The spy they sent to investigate said the town was a village of freed slaves. In 1871, General Máximo Gómez invaded Guantánamo. Because Guantánamo was not part of the insurrection, Spaniards controlled the region. But on May 26, 1871, after the battle of Mt. Libano, Guillermón Moncada, one of the legendary black generals of Cuban history, destroyed the Spanish troops and freed the slaves. The slaves, in their joy, were said to dance the *regina*.

"You see, that kind of music was already among the slaves. And after that, the music spread," Gómez said.

It was time to leave for the band's practice. I bought a bottle of rum as a gift for the band and we headed off to a rehearsal space located downtown. Once there, the other musicians began rolling in. Universales del Son, founded in 1993, was a kind of *changüí* supergroup, formed from the best musicians in other *changüí* bands.

Gómez pulled out his *tres* and, for my benefit, the band played in succession *nengón, quiribá, regina,* and *changüí.* It was like sitting in on a master class.

"The *nengón* and *quiribá* are strong in Baracoa, whereas *changüí* is strong in a place like El Salvador," said Gómez. "Until you get *changüí* you don't have improvisation."

I listened to the band play Ignacio Piniero's gorgeous "Suavecito." To play it, the *bongocero* alternated with a bell that pushed the rhythm. The musicians switched instruments. Now the *marímbula* player was on trumpet, while the *guayo* player went to guitar. The band played a *son* called "Sazonando," written by Luis Martínez. Gómez played one of two trumpets that soared above the rhythm section.

"The scraper has kept the same rhythm in all of these songs so far," Gómez told me when it was over. "When you hear the *bongó* playing in Septeto Habanero, it's the *bongó* pattern of *changüí.* It's all part of the *son.* The *son* contains everything."

The band took a break and rum was passed around, a splash poured for the spirits.

"Most of the *treseros* who live here have taught themselves," said Onil Revé, the group's *bongosero* and a cousin of Elio Revé, leader of the most famous *son-changüí* orchestra in Santiago. "Ramón is one of the first people to seriously investigate this music."

Night had fallen, and it was warm and windless. We walked over to Café Indiana, a central gathering spot, where I met other well-known musicians from Guantánamo.

"I want to introduce you to José Olivares Pérez, the *marímbula* player in Grupo Changüí," Gómez said. Pérez was tall and lanky, with leathery skin, bad teeth, and a squared-off face that hinted at Indian ancestry.

"I'm eighty years old and I *still* cheat on my wife," he announced in a booming voice that ended in a raspy laugh. "And I have played in the United States and France and Spain."

A stout singer wearing a black beret picked up a guitar and sang a *bolero,* the first of three songs, in a booming baritone voice. He sang a song about Che Guevara and "Petronila," an original *bolero* sung in the inimitable style of *trovadore* master Ñico Saquito.

"His name is Mario Zamora Delgado," Gómez said, leaning over.

When Delgado came over to our table, I asked him what inspired "Petronila."

"I wrote it after reading Boccaccio, and I decided to sing it in Saquito's style because he had such a great sense of humor. I'm a member of a musical family and grew up here with *son* in my blood. Benito Velásquez, my grandfather on my mother's side, was a famous *tresero*. He died when I was young. But I remember the parties. Luis Martínez, my uncle, was the greatest *son* pianist in Cuba. My uncle studied all kinds of music. He could've been a concert pianist—he was so exceptional. But in his lessons he would always break into *changüí* and *son*. I want to uphold the traditions. But I add sounds from Peru and Brazil and the Caribbean. It's very important to keep the roots. That's the foundation upon which to build anything else. But I want to enrich the tradition, too."

"And the song about Che?"

"Che is a figure, but not of this century. He is what man should be in the future. Because anything Che said he would do himself. He had the courage of his convictions."

I said good-bye and headed back to Santiago. I had another dinner of lobster at the French *paladar* and let myself get lost in Santiago. I had it in mind to visit Casa de las Tradiciones. But on my way there, I heard the steady thump of rap music. I followed the sound down the street and walked into Ateneo Cultural. There, in a scene that could've been lifted straight out of New York or Detroit, hundreds of youth were listening to Candyman, one of seven rap bands on tap that night. The women were dressed in tight slacks with tube tops and the men wore baggy pants, fake gold medallions, and backward baseball caps. Some had dreadlocks, and one youth had his hair in an astonishing spike motif that made him resemble a black Statue of Liberty.

Candyman's rappers nicked beats from old and new bands, and there wasn't a trace of macho posturing, violence, or misogyny in the lyrics.

When the set was over I found Luis González, the leader of Santiago's hip-hop association.

"There are twenty-two rap bands here in Santiago," González said. "As an organized group we began in 1998. But rap was here long before that. We follow the American rap scene and we're influenced by groups like Wu Tang Clan, Public Enemy, Tupac Shakur. We rap about Cuban identity, Cuban history, and social problems."

As we talked, more members of Santiago's hip-hop community joined us.

"This is just a small show," said Tomás Montoya, the president of Association Hermanos Saíz, a kind of UNEAC for those thirty-five and below. "We don't do much promotion. But the last show we had at an amphitheater drew three thousand people."

"The movement here is very strong, and has moved to the countryside, too," said González.

"Rap," said Montoya, "has influenced us for years. The words have the ability to communicate feelings that young people have which have no outlet in *son* or *trovador* music. Rap gives us freedom to mix words and beats in a creative way."

None of the rap groups used instruments. "Why?" I asked.

"The reason is we're not professional yet," said González. "In Cuba, that means passing a certain kind of test. And the reason is partly economic. A lot of us don't have the money to buy instruments, which are expensive."

On the radio, I had heard a song called "Maria Juana," by a Santiago rap group calling itself Marca Registrada. I asked Montoya if the title was a sly reference to marijuana, which was being smoked throughout Cuba.

Montoya arched one eyebrow and shook his head. "No," he said. "It's about a girl and love." But the way he said it left the answer in doubt.

It was late. I wandered along the harbor, which lay like a black mirror, and found myself wondering where all the slaves had entered Santiago. A historian I knew said there were no historical markers like the Bight of Benin, no shrines to that monumental suffering where one could linger and sense what had transpired. In fact, though slavery in Cuba was technically forbidden early in the nineteenth century, the slave trade continued illegally into the 1860s.

Somehow, without intending to, I ended up at Calle Heredia. I stopped in to look at a used bookstore up the street from Casa de la Trova. There were no diet books, no rows of computer manuals or endless shelves of pop psychology books on how to raise a healthy child. Some of the greatest Spanish poets were in cheap paperback translations that looked like they wouldn't last more than a month. I was ready to head to my room and crash when I bumped into Marino Wilson, Santiago's greatest poet, whom I'd first met at UNEAC a week before.

I told Wilson about my visits to the various *cabildos,* and we fell easily into a conversation about music, myth, American blues, and the distinctions between the black experience in the United States and Cuba. We went outside and sat on some stairs. Wilson is stocky, and his large eyes are intense and hold no illusions about life. I asked him if there was an Afro-Cuban aesthetic that influenced him and he stared at me before answering, as if he were somehow measuring the depth of my purpose and passion.

"As a poet I receive the spirit of Africa through a Cuban prism. But it's not transmitted through a prism of oppression, which some would have you believe. American blues was born in the South, where historical conditions were quite different for Africans. Even after the Civil War, American blacks suffered terribly. And that suffering went into their blues. But Cuban *son* developed *after* the Spanish lost control of Cuba. There was no longer any slavery in Cuba, and the *son* reflects that. We can't forget that Cuba suffered through two wars of independence in the nineteenth century. But by the beginning of the twentieth century, those struggles were over. The *son* was mostly an ode to love and joy and triumph."

We could just hear the sounds of *son* drifting toward us from Casa de la Trova. "In the Delta blues and black spiritual music," I said, "you hear a lament of the soul. The poetry and sorrow is in the music *and* the words."

"True," Wilson said. "But in Cuba the suffering of the slaves went into the drumming and the chanting, which was sung in African tongues—in Yoruba, Carabalí, and Congolese. The Africans who were enslaved here kept their rituals and drums and chants. That's where the poetry and lament is. That's where the art is held." A taxi bicyclette stopped before us and the young driver offered us a ride. Then two women, one a mulatto and the other a pure-blooded African with bluish-black skin that shone in the night, walked up with the predatory gaze of raptors and made their pitch until I shooed them away. Wilson's eyes followed them as they sauntered off.

"If music, poetry, and theater make themselves the direct reflection of politics, then when the system fails, the artists are left without anything of value. When economics sends everyone into poverty, we have to take refuge in art. Man is capable of giving up many things, but not art. If all that's material fails, what's left but to create? That's why we still weep before Hamlet and tremble when we see Orestes or Oedipus onstage. They tell us what it's like to suffer into truth."

Wilson stood up abruptly and shook my hand. He looked tired. He picked up his attaché case and I watched him disappear into the darkened night of Santiago.

3. MATANZAS: THE CRADLE OF AFRO-CUBAN CULTURE

Get in! Quick," Alberto said as I squeezed into the wretchedly uncomfortable backseat of his Lada, a cruel joke of a car that Russia had brought to the tropics along with communism. His sidekick, Luis, thin and full of pent-up anger, along to cut the boredom, looked at me as one would appraise a slab of questionable meat being sold at a butcher's shop.

"What are you doing in Matanzas?" Alberto asked.

"I'm talking to musicians."

"You better be careful," Luis said. "The place is hot. They would love your money."

Alberto laughed, obviously amused by the thought of me being shaken down. But just then, he swerved into an alley and made the first of three secretive stop-offs for black-market gas.

"The police and soldiers are everywhere," Alberto said as we finally hit the highway. Soon, Havana gave way to a countryside dotted with bony, humpbacked cattle, thatched huts, palms, and an occasional ceiba tree. On the dashboard, Alberto had an altar, if you could call it that, composed of a cross, a royal crown, and a photograph of a naked *mulata*.

"That's my girlfriend," he said, putting his fingers to his mouth and transferring a kiss to her womanhood. Luis laughed and opened up the first of many bottles of beer that he would fling out of the window into the verdant meadows. I asked if polluting wasn't illegal.

"No problem. Fidel will have someone clean it up," Alberto said.

"And what do you think of Fidel?" I asked. In the rearview mirror I saw Alberto's eyes darken. He spit out the window.

"Fuck Fidel! Just like he's fucked the Cuban people!"

"Just like his brother Raul fucks the young soldiers!" Luis chimed in, with venom in his voice.

I was just imagining Fidel's brother, head of the Cuban army, bedding down his favorite young recruits, when Alberto demanded that I crouch down and hide in the backseat. A handle—there was only one for the car—was passed back to me and I hurriedly cranked the window up as the car slowed down. A stone-faced soldier approached the car but then waved it on, and Alberto and Luis breathed a collective sigh of relief.

"We get caught taking you, all my money goes to that muthafucker," Alberto said, spitting out the window and jamming a tape of wretched Latin disco in his cassette player. After that, conversation ebbed until we got to Matanzas.

Founded at the end of the seventeenth century on the site of an Indian village called Yacayo, Matanzas is saturated with the spirit of millions of Africans who arrived with shackles across their backs. The slaves came from the Congo and Yorubaland, from Guinea and Cameroon, from Senegal and Burkina Faso, from Dahomey and Sierra Leone, from Benin and Gambia. Those unaware of the city's roots cannot possibly know what they are traveling through when they come to this city that doesn't have the concentrated architectural splendor of Havana. The food is nondescript, the people poor, and even the best guidebooks have little to say about the place. There are no high-end tourist resorts, no chichi beaches. But Matanzas is the great spiritual center of Afro-Cuban culture.

The name itself means "slaughter" in Spanish, and some believe it's here that a mass murder of Indians happened as the Spaniards sought to clear the land for slavery. Cuba's three indigenous peoples—the Tainos (a branch of the Arawaks), the Siboneys, and Guanajatabeyes—did not last long. Some ran away into the mountains, fleeing from Spaniards who hunted them down with dogs. Others killed themselves by eating dirt or sucking the poisonous sap of the cassava. Diseases finished off the rest.

Bartolome de las Casas, the priest who accompanied Columbus on his conquest of Cuba, witnessed this holocaust. Spaniards thought nothing of murdering the Indians for sport, slicing off parts of their bodies to test the sharpness of their blades. Eventually they found some gold. The Arawak men worked the mines, dying by the thousands. The Arawak women slaved in the fields. Families stopped procreating; mothers drank herbs and aborted babies.

"To justify this destruction, the Spaniards devised many charges against the Indians," Hugh Thomas writes in *Cuba: The Pursuit of Freedom,* his epic history of the island's encounters with colonialism. "They were said to be homosexual and promiscuous, shiftless . . . they were cannibals, had no system of justice, were lazy, cowardly."

Only later would the Africans come, ironically at Las Casas's recommendation. The Africans were used to brutal labor. And the Spaniards were used to the African slave trade. In the 1800s, when Cuba was the slave-trading center of the New World, Matanzas accounted for 50 percent of the country's sugar. That's when hundreds of thousands of slaves, mostly Yorubas, were imported to work the sugar plantations—a job so dangerous and exhausting that many died as young men. It's been estimated that some 400,000 Yorubas were brought to Cuba in the mid-nineteenth century. Some resisted. There were slave uprisings in those years, but Spanish retribution was swift and brutal. The rebels were either mutilated or executed and order was restored, but the powerful knowledge the many African tribes brought with them sunk deep roots.

Many slaves joined *cabildos,* mutual aid societies for those from the same African region or "tribe," and some joined secret societies, like the

Mongo Santamaria at the Los Angeles Sports Arena.

RITES OF RHYTHM

Abakuá, which became pockets of resistance against the Spaniards' barbarity. The *cabildos* were underground in the days of slavery; afterward, they were forced to adopt a Catholic patron saint. But while they outwardly might worship St. Barbara or Our Lady of Charity, their true spirits were aligned with the African gods that lay "behind" the Catholic icons: Changó, the Yoruba *orisha* of thunder, and Ochún, the *orisha* of rivers and lakes. Olodumare, the king of the Yoruba *orisha* pantheon, found his closest counterpart in Jesus Christ, and Yemayá, the goddess of the sea and mother of mankind, had her equivalent in Our Lady of Regla. The Spaniards thought they were building a spiritual and colonial empire that would last forever. But in Matanzas, as in the rest of Cuba, the *cabildos* survived to transmit African art, ritual, and mythology to new generations of blacks. They not only gathered together, under one roof, ancestral knowledge that had been fragmented in the terrors of slavery, but also brought other nations' traditions into their fold. Thus, the *cabildos* rewove cultural and spiritual identities while thoroughly subverting the Spaniards' intent to create "good" Christians out of "savages."

"Matanzas has never lost the culture of the ancestors—what the slaves brought here from Africa. It's the legacy we received, which helped us survive as a people. We have seven *cabildos* in Matanzas, more than any other city in Cuba. We have Iyesá and Arará, Brinkama and Olokun," Israel Berriel, a musician with Los Muñequitos, had told me a few months earlier, when I'd seen the group perform in the United States. "We are the cradle of Afro-Cuban culture and spirit."

I had a phone number for Francisco Zamora "Minini" Chirino, the leader of Grupo AfroCuba, one of the great folkloric ensembles in Matanzas, but first I had to deal with Teresa, his manager. Alberto and Luis dropped me off in front of the apartment/office and sped away.

"We'll go to Minini's in a few minutes," Teresa said crisply. "But first I have to deal with a problem." Her apartment had a fine view of the lively street below, and I listened to a vendor musically hawk his plantains. A few minutes turned into an hour, after which, without any explanation, Teresa returned and said: "Come, let's go. I bet you're hungry. We can all have lunch."

Minini lived less than a mile away. His wife, a statuesque African woman in her fifties, met us at the door and beckoned us into their modest apartment. Behind her was Minini, dressed in a black-and-silver sports outfit and wearing a rapper's gold chain necklace and a Yankee baseball cap. He had high, flaring cheekbones, bronzed skin, and fierce, flat, angled eyes, generously lidded, that put you in mind of an ancient Mongol warrior—the effect being the result of a paternal Chinese grandfather. He looked at me as if I was some strange and surprising animal.

"Digame," he said, after we were introduced.

His apartment looked like a folk art museum, jammed with altars to the *orishas* of Santería, the Yoruba religion that came with slaves from Africa. Each altar—to Oya, the *orisha* of graves, to Changó, the god of thunder, or to Ochún, the goddess of love—contained the specific instrument used to summon them in ritual: bells, seed pods, *maracas,* and, in one case, a weird wooden toy. Seeing my eyes fall on it, Minini picked it up and cranked its tiny handle, causing a high-pitched whining, grinding sound.

"This is called a *matraca,*" Minini said. "It's meant to call down Babalú-Ayé. He's the *orisha* who cures sickness and disease. Tomorrow is his special day, and there will be *toques* in his honor."

Everyone was hungry, and we left to go eat. But even before we sat down at a nearby restaurant, I noticed a change of attitude come over Teresa. When drinks arrived, she looked at me with calculating eyes.

"So how much are you going to pay for this interview?" she asked. The question caught me off guard. I was expecting to pay for the food, but I had never expected to pay for an interview.

"The only gift I can offer," I said, turning to Minini, whose eyes were now hidden behind dark sunglasses, "is my interest in your knowledge and the promise of it appearing in the book I am writing. But I cannot pay for interviews even if I had the money, which I don't."

Teresa eyed me suspiciously. A tense moment followed. Then Minini smiled and raised his glass of beer, and I raised mine.

"Salud! To your book," he said. And for the next few days, Minini was my constant companion, telling me stories, teaching me rhythms, taking me to see his friends, and patiently explaining many an esoteric mystery along the way. He talked fast, in machine-gun bursts, crowding his words together, gaining momentum and then coming to an abrupt silence. When he finished, he withdrew into himself, like a bird of prey, alert and watchful. But every word was important and carefully thought out.

Minini conceived of Grupo AfroCuba in 1957 when various musicians, who were part of a carnival *comparsa*, founded a band that played *rumba*. The group's reputation for virtuosity soon spread, as Minini focused his attention on all the Afro-Cuban sacred and secular music that could be heard in Matanzas. He learned to play the music of the Arará (from Dahomey), Palo (from the Bantu), and Abakuá, who came from the Calabar region of Africa.

"The slaves who came here came from Nigeria, Angola, Tanzania, Togo, Dahomey, and Benin," he said as we drove toward the workshop and gallery of Rogelio Mesa, a master instrument builder who had made Minini a set of consecrated *batá* drums necessary for initiations. "The Yorubas and the Arará were the strongest tribes. Many, many came. But the blacks who came from the Congo were the ones who most maintained their identity. The Africans knew who they were. And the people, no matter what tribe, would pay great respect. So if Yorubas heard a king of the Congo had arrived, they would go and honor him."

We had arrived. Rogelio Mesa's face lit up when he saw Minini, and the two embraced as I wandered around the spacious gallery, a high-ceilinged nineteenth-century building that had once been a warehouse but was now filled with drums of all shapes and sizes, as well as paintings and carvings. One that fascinated me was a drawing burned into leather of slaves in African costumes dancing in front of the governor's mansion in Matanzas.

Mesa came over and explained its significance. The drawing was inspired by a similar picture Mesa had seen in a museum. The painting had been done in 1880 and depicted a January 6 gathering called Día de Reyes, or the Day of Kings, when slaves celebrated the emancipation of one of their own.

"The slaves would dance in the streets, and on that day a pregnant mother might celebrate having her newborn child freed. All the *cabildos,* the social clubs for the slaves, celebrated Kings' Day. It was the only day of the year they were free to openly wear their ceremonial garments and dance and sing the music of their ancestors."

In the drawing, a *nanigo,* a fantastic hooded and masked figure, held a wand and did a strange dance watched by a throng of revelers.

"That's an *íreme,* a member of the Abakuá," Minini said. "The *íremes* are the spirits of ancestors. But now I want to show you something."

We walked over to a bench where three drums lay, each shaped like an hourglass. Mesa picked one up.

"These are the *batá* drums. When I make them, it starts with cutting the trunk of a cedar tree. I look for a tree with the diameter of the drum to be carved—one with no knots. From that one trunk I make all three *batá* drums. And since only one trunk is used, I can make all the drum's walls as thin and light as possible."

Like any instrument builder, Mesa was both scientist and artist. For the past seven years he'd carefully studied the way drums create tone, pitch, and timbre, the way wood and skin resonate. The largest *batá,* the *iyá,* the middle-sized *itótele,* and the small *okónkolo* look different from most drums. Played on the lap, they sound different, too, talking together in a dense, syncopated conversation that's both richly rhythmic and melodic. One devotes a lifetime to playing them, mastering their *oros,* or calls.

"The *bataleros* must know all the rhythms," Mesa said. "Because the drums have the power to bring down the *orishas.*"

"When the *orisha* possesses an initiate, the person is purified," Minini explained. "And some people have been healed by the music. I have seen it. One day a cripple came to a *toque* we played. He walked in on crutches. But later, when he was possessed by Yemayá, he dropped the crutches and danced like a normal person. When Yemayá let him go, he was back to being a cripple."

According to Yoruba mythology, *batá* drums emerged in the fourteenth-century kingdom of Oyo-Ile, soaked with the aura of Changó, the fourth king of the empire and their god of thunder. Changó, whose flaming gaze can set houses on fire, made the first *batá*, learning the secret sounds through studying the mysteries of lightning and thunder. Only those initiated into the secrets of Aña can play the *batá* at sacred rituals. A consecrated set of *batá* drums, *ilu Aña*, is only built when it's determined, through divination, that an initiate is allowed to receive it. Oracles and *orishas* are consulted and the wood is soaked in *omiero*, an herbal infusion that includes everything from rainwater and river water to honey and powdered eggshell. The *omiero* suffuses the drums with divine power. Other rituals include an animal sacrifice, the attaching of an amulet, sacred inscriptions, and the infusion of *aché*—a Yoruba word that roughly translates to "spiritual force." In the end, says Mesa, an older consecrated set "gives birth" to a new set.

Mesa built other Afro-Cuban drums. But the demands of the *batá* were the most rigorous. And while he had the authority to build the drums, he could not complete the process of making them sacred, which involved secret rituals that were closely guarded.

"You have to be initiated in Aña, the *orisha* of the *batá*, to perform the sacred rites that consecrate the drums," said Minini, who underwent the initiation many years ago. "A *babalawo*, who rules over divination, a *santero* [a priest of Santería], and the drummer being initiated must be present. And the drumhead must be taken off again." Minini walked over to a set of conga drums and started playing a *rumba* that had an obviously different feel to it than the *rumba* I'd heard in Havana. When I mentioned this, Minini smiled.

"People in Havana will tell you that *rumba* began there. But it was Africans in the dock area of Matanzas who developed this music. *Rumba matancera* is the oldest style of *rumba*. We use two *tumba* drums and a box to play it. And we're the only ones in Matanzas to do it this way."

Grupo AfroCuba de Matanzas was scheduled to perform in nearby Varadero, Cuba's most famous beach resort, the next day. So I decided to tag along. Some twenty members of the troupe arrived at the Caribbean Grand International Hotel, including Grupo AfroCuba's fabulous dancers, Minini's wife being one of them. Minini sang *rumba* as the dancers, dressed in white and yellow, moved against a green-blue ocean. Other dances followed, the drumming full of hidden rhythms and floating melodies. When Minini sang, his voice sounded as deep as the waves, full of ancient pain and old sufferings that refused to leave, a reminder of the days of slavery that were not so long ago. A short while later, the group played *batá-rumba,* a style of music that Minini trailblazed—a phenomenally complex gumbo of cross-rhythms that tap all the sounds of Matanzas.

After the gig, Minini sat down and drank some rum. "Our goal," he said, "is to keep the legacy of our ancestors alive, while enriching it with our creative interpretation." The sun, a bloodred ball, began to sink below the horizon. Some French tourists walked by, rhapsodizing about the beach, how perfect it was.

"The music and the rituals are part of our religion," Minini said, as we watched the waves crash against the shore. "It's been transmitted from fathers to sons for generations. I have taught it to my children and they will teach it to theirs. This will never die. Nothing can stop it."

That night I had an invitation to attend a mass in observance of Babalú-Ayé, the god of smallpox and contagious diseases. Minini himself couldn't make it, but the family hosting it were friends of his and he gave me directions.

"The house where it is happening, the people there lost a relative four days ago," Minini said. "So it should be powerful."

In Nigeria, Babalú-Ayé, who is syncretized with the Catholic St. Lazarus, was known as Obaluaye (King who owns the Earth) and Omolu (the Lord's son), among other names. I'd seen representations of

A dancer from Grupo AfroCuba performing in Varadero.

him all over Cuba, as a frail old man leaning on a knobby, wooden staff. Stories abounded. Long ago, in mythic time, Obaluaye had scattered sesame seeds in the soil of an enemy and left them with smallpox. According to Afro-Cuban legend, Babalú-Ayé was vain and handsome and his favorite pastime was seducing as many young women as he could. But Olodumare, the ruler of the *orishas*, put a restriction on his virility, which Babalú-Ayé violated. His punishment was that his once-beautiful body was disfigured, covered with leprous sores. Babalú-Ayé tried to heal himself, but he eventually died and would've remained in the ground but for the supplications that Ochún, the *orisha* of fresh waters, made on behalf of all the women who missed the god.

Olodumare finally gave Babalú-Ayé life again. But he would never be the same. The sores on his body remained forever and people ridiculed him. The former womanizer became the *orisha* of pestilence and leprosy. And though he had great compassion for the sick, his wrath was terrifying. Like the Greek Furies, who hunted down those who broke the rules of society, Babalú-Ayé punished evildoers.

A cab took me to the wrong street and so I walked a few blocks to the home where the mass would be held. Thin clouds stretched across an inky black sky but didn't obscure the icy moon. I soon found the house, but before I could actually sit in the room where the *toque* was to start, I had to undergo a ritual. Eduardo Cardenas Villamil, a sixty-four-year-old *santero,* led me to a small room with an altar to Babalú-Ayé. He picked up a rooster that lay on the floor, its legs tied with rope, and brushed the animal across the circumference of my body. Then he asked me to lay prostrate before the altar as he intoned Yoruba words. I had arrived with a slight headache, but as I stood up I was stoned, as if I'd smoked a pipe full of mushrooms or hashish.

I walked into a room and sat on a bench with about two dozen other people. On a small table was an altar to the black Virgin of Caridad. Villamil sat nearby and led off the chanting with a *maraca* in his hand, which he shook to count out time. The singing was beautiful, and for perhaps an hour I felt waves of peace. At one point, a woman shuddered, apparently possessed. An older woman, wearing a white skirt, a red and white turban, and black and white beads around her neck then approached me out of nowhere.

"You will have trouble when you return to your country," she told me, placing burned corn in the palm of my hand. "People who say they were your friends won't be anymore. They will betray you or use you. And then, because you are not protected, you will die."

Suddenly, most of the room was focused on me and the woman. I looked deeply into her eyes, which seemed fierce and bloodshot, like two dark cherries floating in a bowl of milk.

"I'm protected," I said. "Don't worry."

But she didn't give up. Later, when the mass was over, the woman offered to give me a *despojo*—a cleansing—that would protect me from my awful fate. She looked through me, as those whose thoughts are not really with you are wont to do. And when I politely declined, she walked away disgusted.

I was not so naive as to think that my presence would have no effect on the people and rituals I encountered in Cuba. But it disturbed me to think that a sacred ritual was being used to exploit fear and generate some small profit. Of course, I was being naive. Even in the 1940s, Cuban novelist and musicologist Alejo Carpentier was lamenting the tendency of Cuba's blacks to create a charade of their customs for "some coins." But who could blame them? In the 1990s, as significant numbers of Americans drifted into Cuba in search of "authentic" teachers and spiritual elders, cash in hand, many Cubans, suffering from desperate poverty, saw ways to profit.

"The sacred and profane need each other in order to define what the other is," Katherine Hagedorn, an initiated *santera* and scholar of Afro-Cuban Santería performance, told me. "They're constantly drawing on each other's powers so they can evolve. But now the boundaries are blurrier than ever. Art is about the search for authenticity. But if Americans are in such need of the authentic, maybe it's because their own culture is so inauthentic. So in Cuba, a place lacking in material resources, the people create what it is they think Westerners want."

But it was worse in the United States. Some of the *toques* I'd been to in California had shocked me. Large amounts of money were tossed around freely and people fell into phony trances. A friend who was scheduled to become a *santero* saw his initiation presided over by gangsters who issued death threats when he fled the ritual that was supposed to celebrate his ascent.

"If you're a fanatic, they'll eat you" was the way Long John Oliva, a Cuban-born *rumbero, santero,* and *palero,* had put it. When I told Jesús Alfonso, the great percussionist and musical administrator of Los Muñequitos de Matanzas, about the incident, he nodded gravely.

"Unfortunately, due to the arrival of more Americans, the influence of United States materialism has begun to creep in. The people in Cuba are very poor, and some of this is coming from their desperation. But another part of it is shameless greed. Los Muñequitos and other elders in Matanzas are trying to stop this exploitation, but it's hard," Alfonso said.

Among the great folkloric groups of Cuba, Los Muñequitos occupy an exalted position. The first time I heard the group perform live in 1993, I came away stunned. Their concerts in the United States, which presented a pastiche of all Afro-Cuban folkloric music, included reenactments of Abakuá rituals and presentations of the Patakin, a body of *orisha* stories that rival Greek mythology for its mythic power. All of it was superb. But the way the group played *rumba,* led by Alfonso's majestic *quinto* solos, was unforgettable. The *rumba* has a foundation rhythm, but the Muñequitos manage to create a sublime symphony based on the form, each drummer able to carry on multiple conversations that convey both transcendent beauty and an aching melancholy.

"*Rumba* originated in Havana, but trade between the two cities brought it to Matanzas and we took to it with a passion," Alfonso told me one afternoon. "Eventually, we developed our own style. And it was passed down from father to son."

Alfonso is tall and bears a passing resemblance to the actor Laurence Fishburne. His wife, Ana, is the senior dancer in the troupe, and a son Freddy plays percussion. The Muñequitos' drummers and dancers have students all over the world, and a regime of performances, master classes, and workshops, from New York and Los Angeles to Paris and Japan, kept everyone busy on the road. Yet there was no danger that Alfonso would leave Matanzas.

"The *orishas* came with us from Africa. And the rites and rituals and initiations that our ancestors brought with them enabled us to survive all the terror. Matanzas is the most powerful center of African culture in all of Cuba," Alfonso said. "When the slave traders came to Africa they took whole nations of Yorubas and sent us to Cuba. In those days, there was lots of intertribal warfare in that part of Africa, and the victors would sell the losers. Of course, fights were instigated by the Spaniards to divide us."

Alfonso's life story is archetypal. His ancestors were powerful leaders and religious figures who had come to Cuba as slaves during the nineteenth century, and his grandfather, Florencio Alfonso, was one of the foremost authorities on Yoruba folklore and culture. Florencio Alfonso spoke Yoruba fluently and founded a school to preserve the language, rituals, and spiritual customs of his people. When visiting Nigerians, who spoke Yoruba, needed a translator, they were referred to Florencio.

Jesús Alfonso was born into a family where Yoruba was the primary language. And the instinct for preservation ran deep in the family. When Alfonso's great-grandmother came to Cuba as a slave, she refused to take a Spanish name.

"Her Nigerian name was Madelé," Alfonso said. "And that's the name she went by. Nowadays, the kids in Matanzas speak a pidgin version of Yoruba, dropping syllables, but we speak it as it was spoken in Africa by our ancestors. Even now, the Muñequitos speak Yoruba better than Spanish. It's still the mother tongue."

Alfonso poured each of us a glass of rum and swallowed his in a single gulp. He continued.

"All the great musicians in Matanzas know each other and are part of one big family. I was seven when I began being initiated as a *santero*. And a lot of what I learned was by watching. I would show up at my uncle's house and tell him what I knew. And he would say, 'Sh. You're not supposed to know that.' We would play the rhythms we heard on shoe boxes. And all the adults would say, '*Mira*, that's our legacy.' The old masters watched us develop and at a certain point they would say we were ready for more knowledge. I remember at parties or festivals, around midnight the adults would tell us to go to sleep, because at that point, sacred rituals would usually begin. So you see we were being secretly rewarded. One thing the elders told us was, 'Don't be greedy. The religion, Regla de Ocha, if you're really part of it, is not for money.' In America, it's all about money. But in Cuba, the religion is a calling."

If you listen to any Los Muñequitos recording you will hear a selection of Abakuá music. That's because Alfonso and many of the musicians are members of that secret society. To play the music is to be part of a powerful fraternity of men whose roots go far back into Africa.

"Anyone can be a *santero* or a *palero*," Alfonso says. "But to be an Abakuá is to be part of a very exclusive group."

I had picked up bits and pieces of Abakuá lore over the years by talking to initiates and reading accounts of their rites. Founded by slaves around 1835, the Abakuá had principally come from the Ejagham peoples of southwestern Cameroon and southeastern Nigeria, who had an astonishing ideographic language and a spiritual system for returning the spirits of dead ancestors. Among the Ejagham slaves coming to Cuba were members of the leopard society, called Ngbe, who, according to Africanist and art historian Robert Farris Thompson, developed into a powerful force over hundreds of years. The Ngbe put on festivals with messengers who wore conical, raffia-edged masks during rituals. In Cuba, the masked dancers came to be known as *íremes* or *diablitos,* and the rituals were protected by initiates who were willing to die rather than reveal the secret practices of their society.

There were Abakuá lodges, or *potencias,* in the cities of Havana, Regla, Guanabacoa, Matanzas, Marianao, and Cardenas. I'd seen representations of the Abakuá ideographs, known as *anaforuana,* in paintings and on the floors of patios in Matanzas. Some were done in white, symbolizing death, and some were in yellow, representing life. But as powerful as the art and pictograms were, Abakuá music is what attracted me to the society.

I'd first heard a snatch of Abakuá music without even knowing it, on

Íreme at an Abakuá ritual.

a version of "Manteca," performed by Dizzy Gillespie and the fabulous Cuban *conguero* Chano Pozo in a 1948 recording. But the Abakuá influence on Cuba's popular music was far-reaching. Los Van Van used Abakuá rhythms throughout their songs, and on "Danza Nanigo," Chucho Valdés found a way to infuse jazz into Abakuá, creating a mesmerizing hybrid. Pancho Quinto and Tata Güines, two of Cuba's greatest *congueros,* were initiates of Abakuá who introduced the rhythms into mainstream Afro-Cuban music.

The Abakuá first landed in Havana. They arrived as a unified tribe, but officials quickly outlawed the members from congregating together. Forced to go underground, the Abakuá fiercely guarded their rites and rituals.

"The tragedy of the Abakuá is that in the nineteenth century, a high official of the Spanish government wanted to join the society, but the Abakuá elders refused. The soldiers wanted to enter the temple, but the Abakuá wouldn't allow it," said Alfonso. "Whenever the Abakuá held a ritual they would post sentries all around the area. And the sentries were instructed to defend the area even to their death."

When the Spanish official was refused admittance into the Abakuá society, the Spaniards retaliated by spreading the rumor that the Abakuá ate children and were devils. The army was brought in to penetrate the societies, and many Abakuá were killed.

"This happened up to 1931," Alfonso said. "Until then it was underground and just to be an Abakuá was a crime."

In the Abakuá songs the Muñequitos sing about the group's indomitable spirit in the face of oppression. In the War of Independence, thousands of Abakuá fought for freedom. They were fierce warriors, known and feared by the Spaniards for their bravery, and they endured a two-year-long initiation. Among outsiders, they had a reputation as hotheads. But a history of vicious persecution and state-sponsored violence would leave any group riled up. I asked Alfonso to sing a lyric from a favorite Abakuá song. Suddenly, a sadness passed across his face, a memory, it seemed, of some deep sorrow, as he sang words that translated to:

So we are the brothers under the sacrament
and by our god, right here
we will die for our faith.

"I'm sorry, I get very emotional talking about this," he said. "And that's because many of my friends and relatives live with that same conviction, as the ancestors did. Many Abakuá were sent by the Spaniards to prisons in Africa as punishment. Many died there in captivity. But those who came back, they possessed even a stronger knowledge and became our teachers."

Ever since I'd heard one of his early CDs, I had wanted to spend time with Roberto Fonseca, one of Cuba's great young jazz pianists, but somehow I had neglected to bring his phone number. I called Chucho Valdés, who had been married for a time to Fonseca's mother. Valdés knew the street Fonseca lived on, but not his phone number, so I went door-to-door asking people where the pianist lived, until I found his address. A dense gray sky had lowered over Havana by now. When I knocked on the door, a woman told me Fonseca was out.

"Do you know where he went?"

"The studio."

"Which studio?"

"Egrem."

Egrem was *the* studio in Havana. I caught a taxi there and explained to a security guard with a blank expression why I was looking for Fonseca. The guard told me to wait. Ten minutes later, a young British woman from World Circuit Records came down. Fonseca was recording upstairs, she said, and if I could be quiet, I could come listen.

Upstairs, in a fabled studio that had produced countless masterpieces of Cuban music, I was in for a surprise. Fonseca sat at the grand piano behind the glass window. Surrounding him were ten members of the Buena Vista Social Club. Three trumpeters—Luis Alemañy, Alejandro Pichardo, and the peerless Manuel "El Guajiro" Mirabal—were in the back. The sensational *conguero* Miguel "Angá" Díaz was in the center of the room, close by *tres* legend Papi Oviedo and the *timbalero* Amadito Valdés. Next to me, smoking a cigarette, was a weary-looking Nick Gold, who had produced most of the Buena Vista Social Club recordings, along with his engineer Jerry Boys.

The musical director, Demetrio Muñíz, standing behind Fonseca, conferred with some of the musicians. He looked over the score and raised his hands, signaling the start of a take. Whispering stopped, and then the room was alive with the sounds of a magnificent *son* by Arsenio Rodríguez, sung by Lázaro Villa Morgan. When the moment for the piano solo came, Fonseca, wearing his trademark black derby, looked up, half smiled to himself, and took off. His solo was full of spectacular jazzy riffs based around the *montuno,* each anchoring chord triggering a cascade of runs that ingeniously touched on the melodies before reharmonizing everything.

"Well, what do you think?" Gold asked Fonseca when the song was finished. He lit up a Marlboro, fell silent, and tapped his leg impatiently, blowing out a long stream of smoke. Muñiz looked at Fonseca, and the two were of one mind.

"*Nearly,*" Muñiz said, smiling. "But let's try again."

"Well, then get it fucking right!" Boys yelled in jest.

"Okay, try it again," Gold said.

This time Fonseca improvised an even more intricate solo, echoing the trumpet lines but dense with rhythmic riffs called *tumbaos,* which pushed the music. I heard echoes of Lilí Martínez, the keyboard genius in Arsenio's *conjunto,* whose solos were pure lyric invention that could never be improved upon. Fonseca tilted his head up and smiled. A moment later, Anga grinned and shouted "Ya!" as he jabbed both fists in the air. Both solos had outstanding features, but minutely different tempos, preventing a fusion of takes. As everyone took a break to ponder what next to tackle, I asked Gold what inspired this recording.

"The whole project is a tribute to Arsenio Rodríguez," Gold said. "We always wanted to feature Mirabal's brilliance. He played beautifully on previous projects we did. But we didn't want to become some production line pumping out the Buena Vista brand. Anyway, I loved Arsenio's work. More than a great songwriter and bandleader, he was a force of nature, a creator of new rhythms and sounds and ways of expressing music. It hit me that this was the right vehicle for showcasing Mirabal. We've been here for ten days, and this is the second session we've done. We've already got way too many songs. But where do we stop? Arsenio was a genius."

Fonseca only had a short time to spare but was eager to spend more time later in the week. So we went next door to Egrem's patio bar to talk.

"This CD is a tribute to all the old master musicians of Cuba who know the secrets of the music. Many people don't know that *son* is the most difficult music to play, and that's because its simplicity requires invention and soul. I studied jazz for many years, and I have my own jazz band. But for me, the Buena Vista Social Club has been the best school of music I've had. The musicians I'm playing with helped evolve the *son*. And the sound they get no one has been ever able to achieve. No one has come *close* to it afterward."

When I told Fonseca that a lot of musicians in Havana had dissed the Buena Vista music as simplistic, he smiled knowingly.

"I know a lot of young musicians in Cuba who look down on this music, and there was a time when I thought it was old people's music, too," he said. "But what the young musicians don't know is that this is some of the most complex music to make *because* of its simplicity. To make people dance, to make them sing—that is *something*. And this is what most of the young bands can't accomplish. Yet these old masters have been able to rattle people's hearts because they love the music. The young musicians can't understand this, but the old ones know the secrets. Genius is doing more with less."

Fonseca gave me his home phone and told me to call him later in the week. As I walked downstairs I ran into Amadito Valdés, another Buena Vista alumnus and one of Cuba's great *timbales* players. Thin and gangly, Valdés has the face of a stork. He leveled an open smile on me when I asked if we could talk. And when I told him I'd just come from two weeks in Santiago and an immersion in the roots of *son,* the smile deepened and he nodded his head.

"Arsenio Rodríguez was the greatest figure in the evolution of *son.* The way he orchestrated and composed was completely original. He was from Matanzas, where *rumba* was born. He brought the congas into *son.* He used three trumpets instead of one. But do you know what horn was first used in *son* here?" Valdés asked in the voice of a teacher who has a trick question.

"No idea," I said, eager to know the answer.

"Clarinet. Before the *son* musicians had a trumpet, the clarinet was used in a group led by Nene Emris. This was in 1927. And do you know who that clarinet player was? It was Amadito Valdés, my father."

Valdés, who is fifty-five now, chose the *timbales,* the lead instrument in the rhythm section, over horns and has helped take the instrument into new territory, expanding its rhythmic and melodic possibilities. When he isn't touring the world with the top Afro-Cuban bands, he might be recording with avant-garde American jazz musicians or Congolese *rumba* bands.

"You can see the way the *timbales* have evolved in rock, Latin jazz, and pop that are not Cuban. The *timbales* have gained a new vigor in the last twenty years, and that's exciting. Our music has never been static, and I think the mission for us is to mix with other music of the world, like rap and jazz and funk, and create a richer sound." As Valdés left the studio, Anga walked by. I asked if we could meet and he scribbled down his phone number.

"It's best to reach me in the late morning," Anga said. "Then we can talk."

I wanted to see Peruchin, the son of the great pianist of the same name. It was a weekday, and only a few dozen people showed up at La Zorra y El Cuervo in La Rampa. The band had a smooth sound, an intelligent, seamless melding of Afro-Cuban rhythm and bop. Peruchin had actually started as a guitarist, and I could hear the influences of Wes Montgomery and Joe Pass, two influential American jazz guitarists.

"From them, I learned phrasing, time, tone, and harmony," Peruchin said between sets. I mentioned that I had just come from hearing Fonseca recording Arsenio's music with the Buena Vista Social Club. Peruchin arched one eyebrow.

"Look," he said, "for me that music is nothing new. It was the music we heard as children, classic *son* and *guaracha* and *boleros* that all the old musicians played forever. But Ry Cooder, he has promoted it well."

That was a sentiment I would hear often in Havana. To be sure, part of it was envy. But there was also legitimate concern that the Buena Vista recordings were crowding out other great Cuban music. By now, I was tired and about to leave when some black-and-white photographs on the wall of the club caught my eye. I asked the bartender if he knew who shot them.

"Two different photographers, and one of them is right here," he said, pointing down the bar to a handsome man, dressed nattily in gray slacks and a pale blue shirt. "His name is Juan Cuadras."

I introduced myself to Cuadras and told him that I was looking for other musicians to talk to.

"My friend, I know all of the musicians in Havana. I program the jazz here and have been photographing the city's musicians for twenty-eight years. At my house, I have rooms full of negatives. Many of the musicians are my friends. This weekend will be great. Roberto Fonseca is playing here, and so is Diakara, Oscar Valdés's group. Canela, an all-girl group, which mixes jazz and merengue with salsa and reggae and hip-hop, is also playing."

A jazz bassist at the Teatro Nacional.

I took Cuadras's card and said I would call him, never suspecting that he would be one of the most important people I would know in Havana, a person who could, like Eleggua, open doors to other worlds.

The next morning I took a walk to Old Havana, toward the National Museum of Music. I had plenty of time to meander before meeting up with Anga. So I walked past houses with slummy weeds, past buildings that had collapsed or partially collapsed, making renovation difficult. I bought tangerines from a fruit vendor, stepped over mounds of seeping sewage, and stared down two mangy dogs that growled from the depths of their throats at my coming.

Santiago was open and warm, a languid, tropical city akin to New Orleans; the music and the people had won my heart. But Havana, with its harried pace, often arrogant attitude, and solipsistic view of itself as the epicenter of Cuban culture and art, reminded me of New York. All the same, the city was bristling with life despite a forty-four-year trade embargo. Parts of Havana had changed remarkably since my last visit two years earlier. The terror attacks had closed more than twenty hotels, but I counted at least four five-star hotels being built. Old Havana was as gentrified as Nantucket in some places. UNESCO and the Cuban government had renovated many of the historic buildings and now tourist shops were selling such dubious items as giant cigar sculptures and poorly made *bongó*.

A friend in the Ministry of Culture had given me a thumbnail sketch of Havana's hidden cultural problems. The sex trade was still a growth industry, though prostitutes were not as numerous as they were in 1997, when I'd last been there. Drugs were more prevalent, though virtually no one would talk about it. A dancer I knew told me that some of the city's pop musicians were using drugs, which were either brought in by foreigners or smuggled in by the bands themselves. And though Castro and the socialists had brutally suppressed homosexuality in the early days of the revolution, the gay scene was strong. In La Rampa and a park near the Capitol, transvestites and transsexuals were openly on parade. And a friend of mine in Los Angeles, who'd lived in Cuba for many years, told me that men's magazines were openly advertising gay excursions to Havana.

I turned onto Capdevilla Street and walked inside the National Museum of Music, a mansion formerly owned by Francisco Pons, a sugar baron who built his house in 1905 and hosted soirees with all the famous figures from Havana's cultural elite. Here were enormous rooms devoted to the polite parlor instruments of eighteenth- and nineteenth-century Cuba. But what drew my attention were two exhibits of old percussion instruments: Behind one glass case sat a set of worn *rada* drums brought to Cuba by the Haitian slaves after their revolution had sent knives of fear into every planter in Cuba. Centuries-old drums of Congolese origin, some made from barrel staves, were covered with thick ox hide stretched over their mouths, tempered and tuned in their day by fire. I lingered over a massive, intricately carved Arará drum and its neighbors—*yuka* drums, *repicadors,* and *pailas campesinas,* the forerunner of the *timbales.* Many tribes had come to Cuba, and this room struck me as a shrine to their spirit and musical genius.

I walked to the spectacular new Museum of Fine Arts, which had opened in one of Havana's most splendiferous buildings, the former home of Spain's elite Centro Asturiano. Fully restored, the museum held five floors' worth of art, going back to the colonial period. I stood transfixed before a painting of a colonial aristocrat by the Spanish artist Sorolla. Staring at this face, with its stiff mien and arrogant eyes, I couldn't help wondering what thoughts went through this man's mind when he saw Africans dancing and playing their drums. Could the aristocrat have ever conceived that one day the Africans' "savage" music, religion, mythology, and cosmology would not only survive but overtake his own?

I left the museum, munched on a delicious guava pastry, and headed to Vedado, where Angá lived. With his somewhat squared-off head, sleepy eyes, and olive-brown skin, Angá bore some of the traits of Cuba's

Indians. At forty, he stood between the older generation of percussionists, who created the rhythmic language of Afro-Cuban music, and the younger percussionists, who were taking the *tambores,* as the hand drums were called in Cuba, in new directions. I had heard him perform in many situations: on *descarga* outings and in *timba* bands, behind famous *soneros* and with Irakere. He'd played with hip-hop groups like Orishas, funk bands, and French DJs, and he'd backed American jazz musicians like Roy Hargrove and Steve Coleman. In every case he put his mark on the music. From his hands came swells of popcorn-popping rhythm and hidden melodies, with nuanced color and perfect tone that seemed to lift the musicians around him to another level. He was eager to talk about his art.

Angá began playing the drums in art school in Havana during a time when only the classical style of percussion was being taught. To hear the great Afro-Cuban drummers, he was forced to go straight to the masters: El Niño Alfonso, with Irakere, and the greatest of them all, Tata Güines.

"With Tata, it was like father and son. What I took from him was his musical style. I never actually took lessons from Tata, but we would talk and I would ask him how he used his hands. The way he hit the drum created a pure tone, and I wanted to achieve that bell-like sound."

Anga studied the history of percussion, too. Chano Pozo was the first revolutionary. He introduced the conga into jazz and thereafter the conga drums became a powerful ingredient in Afro-Cuban music. By contrast, Patato Valdés had a soft, melodic approach, and tuned the congas to the piano.

"With Armando Peraza, it was his incredible sense of rhythm, and he played the *bongó* beautifully, too. Candido had an incredible musical sense. He played with Machito and he knew exactly where to put the accents and how not to interfere with the other instruments," Anga said.

For eight years Angá played with Irakere, which had the greatest musicians in all of Cuba. And when the percussionist was there, it was like being in school every day.

"We were creating the foundation of Afro-Cuban jazz each time we rehearsed or performed. And we knew the evolution of our instruments. The young percussionists today unfortunately are not spending the time to listen to the old masters. And you cannot play the instrument with genius unless you know its history. That's because each of those old masters had a different method by which they were able to swing and lift and drive a band."

Angá listened to pianists, too, because piano was the ultimate percussion instrument. And no one played it with more authority than Irakere's founder, Chucho Valdés, who Angá says "transformed the piano into a set of drums."

I asked him whether there was some performance that stood out from those days. "When we played 'Misa Negra' that was for me a spiritual experience. And we all had to be conscious of that. All of us had to use many colors to express a lot of ideas. And every time we played that composition we were really invoking spirits from the ancestral world."

Angá recommended I talk to Enrique Pla, another of Irakere's drummers. But when I dialed the number it was no longer in service. Back at my room, however, there was a message from Omar Sosa. I'd had dinner with Sosa, one of Cuba's young visionary jazz pianists, two months earlier, when he had come to Los Angeles to play a concert at the Getty Museum with the percussionist and arranger John Santos. When I happened to mention that I would be in Havana in the second half of December, Sosa, who grew up in Cuba but now divides his time between Spain and the Bay Area, gave me a conspiratorial grin.

"That's when *I'll* be there. My mother lives in La Playa and you're welcome to stay with us. I have to see my *babalawo* and my godmother and make some parties for the ancestors and the *orishas,*" he said.

I dialed Omar's number. His mother, Maricusa, picked up the phone and told me to wait.

"Welcome to Havana, my friend. Listen," Sosa said, "we're having a *cajón de muerto* later today. Come around two P.M., okay? It will be great to see you." Since I'd never been to a *cajón de muerto,* a celebration for the dead, I was excited. I flagged down a cab and rode out to La Playa, where Sosa was staying with his mother. It was a small place, humbly appointed. A pot of soup was boiling on the kitchen stove, full of gristled meat.

"What's happening?" the thirty-three-year-old pianist said, giving me a warm hug. "Has Cuba been treating you okay?"

"As well as it can," I said. "But I'm pretty ragged."

Sosa was dressed entirely in white, with loose-fitting pants that put me in mind of the men I saw in Morocco. His head was shaved but for a patch of hair center and top, from which a dreadlocked tail grew out. He wore the beads of a *santero,* including those of Obatalá, his *orisha.* But he also wore an unusual necklace with abalone, animal teeth, and claws. When Sosa saw me look at it, he smiled.

"An Indian shaman from the rainforest of South America gave this to me—in a gay club in San Francisco where I was performing. In exchange he wanted a necklace I had. He said it would protect me and, so far, it has. Come, I want to introduce you to some friends," Sosa said, leading me to three drummers who were members of a group called Abure Okanani. But on the way there a woman walked up next to him and smiled. "And this is my wife, Shirma," Sosa said, putting an arm around her.

"Today, we're going to play a *cajón de muerto*—a *toque* we're offering to the ancestors, ours and yours," Leonel Argüelles said, shaking my hand. Tall and lean, Argüelles had long, tapering, nicotine-stained fingers and a disarming smile.

His brother, Roberto, more muscular, sat next to his *cajón,* a wooden box that would soon explode with sounds. He lit a cigarette and, opening a bottle of rum, took a swallow. He turned over his box and spray-spit a mouthful of the alcohol into the instrument's chambers. Turning the instrument upright again, he poured some rum on the floor.

"That's for the spirits," Sosa said.

I asked Roberto what the Yorubas believed about ancestors.

"In our religion, Regla de Ocha, every person in the world has an ancestral spirit, *egun,* that watches over you. A *babalawo* can determine who that is by divination. And by working with you, he can determine who is watching over your children as well." Guests arrived. The room was soon packed with young and old, friends and family members. Maricusa Sosa introduced me to her younger godmother, Marcia Escalina, a plump, beautiful woman with a radiant smile. The two women casually took their place on the floor in front of the musicians and began dancing with others as the two Argüelles brothers pounded out a river of rhythm on the boxes. I'd heard *cajones* played many times before, but not in a sacred context and not at this level of intensity.

When the *akpwón* launched into a piercing chant, in Spanish and Yoruba, urging the ancestors to come to Earth, into this very apartment, his verse was immediately answered by a hoarse-voiced chorus of those assembled. The drumming, the dancing, and the singing were like a spell that kept time, wavering up and down like the wind moving over the face of a lake. At some point when my eyes were on the drummers, Maricusa Sosa spun out into the center of the room and shuddered, dancing involuntarily, it seemed. Her whole body convulsed. Then, as if spent, she fell backward into the arms of two other women who were watching closely. They pushed her upright and held her lest she topple again. In the close darkness of the room I felt a humming presence move through the room.

Outside, along an exposed window grill, neighbors and children watched. This small, drab house was the Afro-Cuban equivalent of a church, and the *akpwón,* drummers, and dancers were preacher, choir, and congregation. Now Marcia Escalina's dance grew bolder. Her face, a blending of Indian, Spanish, and African bloodlines, seemed lit with an inner beauty that radiated love. She rocked and swayed, eyes closed, her arms rising above her head and moving like branches blowing in a strong wind.

Three times the moon came
three times the stars came

Equis Alfonso on the streets of Havana.

oh what a beautiful moon
and it leaves at dawn

The *akpwón* sang, and the room answered him with fifty voices. Then, without warning, Escalina shook, as if struck by seizures. The musicians, noticing her ecstasy, shifted their attention. The *cajones* cracked melodic thunder, and the *akpwón*'s voice gently taunted her, making the dance that much stronger, until a few minutes later, stumbling and falling, Escalina was caught by two other women before she could hit the ground. As she passed by me, her eyes and face had the intoxicated, blissful look that women get after a powerful orgasm. When the music came to a close, I asked Leonel Argüelles how he knew when to stop playing.

"After the spirit has departed we can tell," Argüelles said. "When the *egun* come down and inhabit a person, we feel that energy and play more powerfully. But eventually that energy dissipates."

Escalina walked by me, her face still flushed. I asked her what it felt like to be the vehicle of ancestral spirits, and she looked deep into my eyes.

"The *egun* come to free me and help me. Inside me it's a spiritual presence. One of my *egun* is a Gypsy woman, and I felt her tonight. Another is Congolese and another is a Cuban Indian. All these spirits are watching over me. But I also feel the spirits of my own ancestors, my grandmother and grandfather. The drums awaken the ancestors.

"When I was born, the spirit of a nun visited me and I felt her presence. Even as a little girl, I saw spirits. I have very strong spirits. My *orisha* is Oddua, the king of the dead. I am a receptacle for dead spirits—it's a gift I have. Tomorrow we're going to have a *toque* for Yemayá at my house, and I want you to come," she told me.

"I'll be there," I said. I was tired and needed sleep. But a block away, I heard the crack of the *cajones* resuming and the voices rising. And even when I was out of range, the songs echoed in my mind.

The next morning I paid a visit to Oscar Valdés, the cofounder of Irakere and the leader of his own group, Diakara. Pogoloti, the section of San Marinao where Valdés lives, is renowned for its great musicians and deep spiritual history that stretches back into the early days of slavery. But I wondered why one of Cuba's foremost musicians would choose to live in a squalid section of Havana.

Valdés is sixty-five, powerfully built, with the physique of a heavyweight boxer who refuses to get old. His head, shaved bald, is massive and circular. His enormous arms and thick, bulldog's neck are the result of working out regularly on gym equipment at his house. He greeted me with a warm smile and led me up to his air-conditioned studio. On one wall was a large faded, black-and-white photograph of Irakere. Behind me were all manner of drums, from *timbales* to *batá,* but my eyes fell on an unusual set of four drums.

"These are used in Abakuá rituals—and I made them," Valdés said. "There's an Abakuá temple here, one of three in Havana. The Abakuá are my favorite group, even though many of them are wild, even dangerous. I was involved with a lot of them as a young man and I still get invited to their events. They also come to me when they want their drums fixed."

Though musicians now enjoy some of the highest standards of living in Cuba, it wasn't always so. Valdés faced enormous obstacles growing up black in Cuba before the revolution. After slavery, there was another form of racism.

He told me that he was a musician but was never able to study music at schools because of the poverty he came from and the institutionalized oppression. But with the revolution all that changed.

"With all of its problems," Valdés said, "the revolution still opened doors for blacks. My children have all gone to music schools."

Irakere was the first Cuban group to use jazz phrasing and arrange the brass instruments over complex Afro-Cuban percussion. But the story went much deeper than that, and I was eager to hear Valdés explain his own involvement.

"My role as a musician has been to recover the lost rhythms of Africa that were revived and reimagined here in Cuba and fuse them organically with jazz. I always had it in mind to use all the great percussion instruments we had. With Irakere, Chucho and I created a fusion. We were bonded by religion and both raised on the music and rituals of the *orishas.* We're both *santeros,* both sons of Changó. We grew up steeped in Cuba's unique African music. But we felt that a true Afro-Cuban jazz had yet to be forged. So from the beginning, our mission was to find a form that could contain these rhythms. And finding that form wouldn't have been possible if it weren't for jazz and the harmonic freedom it offered."

As he spoke, Valdés's long, meaty hands sliced and arced through the air, as if playing invisible rhythms. His knees moved together rhythmically, too, sometimes knocking like clave sticks.

Today, dozens of bands here in Cuba play jazz and add *batá* drums. But Irakere set the standard and worked in a completely different way. The group took the folkloric rhythms and *orisha* chants and adapted Chucho's compositions to them. Though difficult, the results were extraordinary, especially the rhythmic combination of the *batá* with a full jazz orchestra.

"Chucho is a musical genius and I was a connoisseur of Afro-Cuban folklore. But you have to realize that the *batá* drums are extremely difficult to master because their rhythms are in opposition to each other and each *orisha* song has a different rhythm. So the challenge was to create Afro-Cuban jazz that flowed naturally out of these rhythms. To do that, every musician had to possess deep knowledge of the music."

With Diakara, Valdés was following the same impulses that inspired him with Irakere, but he considered the music even more complex.

"Now, for instance, apart from playing the traditional Afro-Cuban rhythms, I'm improvising new rhythms on the *batá*. So when I play *chacharo-kefun,* even though I don't abandon the basic structure, I'm adding new ideas," Valdés said. "Musicians are like doctors: we always have to be educating ourselves, keeping up with the latest developments."

With each passing year, Cuba's percussionists have been evolving their instruments and opening up new rhythmic possibilities. The great *congueros* had transferred the awesome techniques and complexities of trap drumming into the conga drums. The list of innovators was endless. But Diakara had a *conguero* who had raised the bar even higher. I'd caught part of a set by the group a few nights earlier and saw nineteen-year-old Bobby Angel do something I'd never heard before. On

"Manteca," the Afro-Cuban classic, he launched into a sonorous ten-minute conga solo that recapitulated every idea the band had played. From his hands came jabbing horns and loping bass riffs, speed-of-light rolls and multiplied beats. In his solo was melody, rhythm, orchestration, and improvisation.

"Bobby was one of my students and I worked with him in a special way. I did with him what I did with El Niño in Irakere. For me, right now, Bobby is the greatest *conguero* in all Havana today."

I asked Valdés why he chose to live in Marinao when he could easily afford a better neighborhood. He smiled benevolently, as if he were anticipating the question. "People ask me why I built my home in this run-down area, but I *like* Pogoloti. I was born and raised here. I'm a character in Pogoloti and people look out for me. They see me as someone to look up to, and they respect what I've done and love me for who I am. Pogoloti hasn't been exploited. Here eight of every ten people you meet have been initiated into Regla; and I'd say four of every ten people you meet practice Mayombe, our name for Palo. People here don't sell the sacred beads on the streets as they do in Guanabacoa. We keep the traditions alive here for the next generation. I only wish that we had a school or a temple of arts and culture where all the young kids could learn their roots and history. But there's no institution in Cuba to sponsor such a thing. The money is not there."

"Who were your teachers?" I asked.

"Rafael Somavilla, a great Cuban pianist, and Guillermo Barreto, the husband of Merecedita Valdés, were both mentors and teachers. And Walfredo de Los Reyes, a Cuban musician who lives in the United States, was a teacher, too."

"Walfredo lives in San Francisco," I said. "I plan to talk to him later this spring."

"Please give him my regards when you do," Valdés said, and I walked out into the glare of the street.

The night before, a friend in Havana called to tell me that Pedrito Calvo, the famous singer in Los Van Van, was rehearsing this afternoon for an upcoming solo album at Egrem. I'd heard through the grapevine that Calvo had a bitter parting of the ways with Juan Formell, Los Van Van's founder, and that the band, Cuba's most popular group for more than two decades, was embroiled in business difficulties with its American label. Only two founding Van Van members were left in the band.

I took a cab to Egrem and was escorted to a room adjacent to the one I'd been in with the Buena Vista Social Club. There, Calvo was rehearsing with a new fifteen-piece band that included twelve musicians and three backup singers. With his black, brush mustache, gold earrings (three on his right ear alone), and designer ensemble of Tommy Hilfiger overalls, red shirt, and baseball cap, Calvo looked as roguish as ever. He looked trim and fit, at least ten years younger than his actual age, which was sixty. He had five horns in his band, but unlike Van Van, no violins or keyboards. The group whipped through four songs that sounded tight: a classic *son,* a *timba,* a new song, and a new version of an old Van Van favorite associated with Calvo, "Candela." When the singer told the musicians that they would have to rehearse again tomorrow and Sunday, a groan of disappointment went up. But Calvo only smiled, toweled the sweat off his neck, and, when I introduced myself, invited me to have a beer next door at the patio café.

Formell had been shrewd to choose Calvo as a vocalist and dancer. His swaggering dance style and macho look compensated for his average voice and became part of the raunchy street sensibility that Van Van projected. In Cuba, he was a superstar. But he was also the father of many illegitimate children by myriad women. Not surprisingly, as soon as we walked out onto the street, Calvo was swarmed with fans, some asking for his autograph. When we finally sat down to talk, however, the aura of fame dissipated. Over beers, Calvo told me a short version of his life in music.

"I grew up in Guanabacoa. That's where you find the Abakuá, the *santeros,* and the most powerful *babalawos.* But I was never attracted to

Compay Segundo, Rubén González, and Omara Portuondo of the Buena Vista Social Club at the Karl Marx Theater.

that. I wanted to be a singer. I was very poor growing up. I used to sing in a Baptist church and I joined the choir and would sing angelic songs. Yet because of poverty I had to quit school and work when I was just twelve years old. I used to sell mangos and guavas on the street. I cleaned cars, I repaired shoes.

"I first started singing professionally in 1957, and my biggest influences were Benny Moré, Lucho Gatica, Vincente Valdés, Pacho Alonso, and Panchito Riset. Even with Van Van, I had a solo career going, too. I sang *boleros* and I was always interested in the old *son* long before the Buena Vista Social Club made it popular. With Van Van, I created a style of my own. There are greater singers, I know. But I had the ability to reach an audience and make them sing with me and dance. That was my gift, and I know I am lucky to be where I am."

Calvo's eyes darkened when I mentioned his split with Van Van. He weighed carefully what he was about to say.

"We played all over the world. But after all those years of hard work, I felt I wasn't being recognized. I gave my life to Van Van—for love, not money. There was no money in those early years, and even later we had hard times. But when Van Van became famous, money blinded people. And all the affection for the music disappeared."

I told Calvo that I had seen Van Van perform last at Salon Rosado de la Tropical and was greatly disappointed. The group that had penned the biting "La Habana No Aguanta Mas" (Havana Can Take No More) was cranking out drivel. The lyrics to the songs I heard were worse than weak.

"Our musicians are terrific but our lyrics are lousy," he said. "There are too few poets around these days. To write lyrics of power requires a certain level of cultural knowledge, and the market doesn't ask for more. Most of the young musicians want to be virtuosos on their instruments, not lyric geniuses. Pablo Milanes and Silvio Rodríguez reached for that level once. They showed it could be done. But nobody cares anymore."

Two of Calvo's children, Nairyn and Pedro Calvo, Jr., walked up to our table and their father gave them hugs.

"These are *my* singers," he said proudly. "In this band I'm using two trombones and two saxophones. I've written two new songs for the CD, and I'm singing *guarachas, boleros,* and *son.* Life is good. When I go to bed I can hardly sleep, I am so excited to get this record out of me. We have incredible musicians here in Cuba that deserve an international audience. But there's no promotion. I don't think Afro-Cuban music has yet reached its zenith. But because of the blockade against us by your country and the fact that the big record labels are not in Cuba, we can't get exposure."

I took a couple of photographs of Calvo outside the studio. And only when he took off his cap, exposing a bald pate, was I reminded of how old he was. Before leaving I stopped by Egrem's CD booth. "Llora Como Llore," a *rumba* sung with incendiary passion by the late great Carlos Embale, was playing. I listened and marveled at Embale's voice, an instrument of exquisite power.

"If Carlos were alive, nobody could touch him," a small, wiry man standing just to my right said suddenly. "Compay Segundo would be poor and the Buena Vista Social Club would be obscure."

"I would have to agree," I said. "And who do I have the pleasure of speaking to?"

"My name is Marco Ermino Díaz. Maybe you have heard me play. I am on a recording called *Rapsodia Rumbera,*" he said.

I'd heard the recording, one of the great *rumba* discs of all time. "It's one of my favorites," I said. I'd been trying to track down the great percussionist Pancho Quinto, and I thought Díaz might know his whereabouts.

"I was with him yesterday," Díaz said. He gave me Quinto's address and wished me luck. Then I left to go find Juan Cuadras.

Cuadras, I was discovering, was an intriguing figure: a seasoned journalist, a respected photographer, and an astute folklorist. He also had something perhaps no one else in Havana had: an actual address book filled with accurate phone numbers for many of the city's great musicians. I suspected that my half dozen messages, taken by his sullen wife over three days, were not getting to him. So I had finally decided to drop by Cuadras's apartment unannounced. He lived just off the Malecon, close to the American Interests Section, hard by the rallying spot the Cubans dubbed Anti-Imperialist Square. I rapped loudly on the door and it opened.

"*Pase*," a mischievously smiling Juan Cuadras said, greeting me with a cigarette dangling from his mouth, as if he had been expecting me all along. "I just photographed Chucho Valdés over a number of days in an attempt to capture a psychological portrait of him at work," Cuadras said, showing me a fistful of film rolls. "But I have to develop these and that takes time."

Cuadras disappeared into a back room and came out with a pouch. When he tilted it over, out poured negatives and prints: Isaac Oviedo and Benny Moré, Miguel Matamoros and a teen-aged, impossibly young Celia Cruz.

There were photos of Abakuá rituals with raffia-costumed *íremes* and stray shots of street musicians.

"Here's a woman possessed by Oyá, the *orisha* of the cemeteries, and here's a young conga player," he said, showing me a slide. "He's just a kid but already he plays like a young Tata Güines. And I have old photos, too, gifts from friends. Look. Isolino Carrillo, one of the legendary composers of *boleros,* including the unforgettable 'Dos Gardenias Para Tí.' This is the last photo taken of her, because she died shortly afterward. Or here. Arsenio Rodríguez, blind and with his *tres.* And here, Arsenio *before* he was blind. Do you know who this is?" Cuadras asked with an impish delight. He was talking fast now, machine-gunning his already rapid Spanish, madly puffing his cigarette and taking me through Havana's musical past.

"It's Lilí Martínez, Arsenio's great pianist. Did you know that he was a musician who thought that everything he played was terrible? And Lilí Martínez thought he was ugly, too, though you can see he's not."

Cuadras was the most open person I'd met in Havana, so I wasn't surprised to find out he wasn't from the city. He had grown up in Santiago de Cuba, where his father was president of the Carabalí Olugo.

"The *cabildo* was my education. There's so much people don't know.

The Haitians, not the Yorubas, introduced the *batá* drums to Oriente. In Haiti, there were many Carabalí slaves who played *batá*. And the Calabar region of Africa is where the Abakuá Society originated. From Santa Clara to Santiago you cannot find the Abakuá, only here and in Matanzas.

"In Santiago, the black slaves inherited a rich musical tradition. Many gained their freedom in the nineteenth century, and they absorbed influences from Spain and Islam for centuries. *Guanches* blacks, from the Canary Islands, were brought into slavery from Spain. And when they got to Haiti, they came in contact with French culture."

"What do you know of the spiritists in Oriente?"

"The spiritists were persecuted by the Spanish Inquisition, which considered everyone who practiced it to be a witch. But the slavemasters loved the spiritists. They went to visit them for everything from impotence to infertility. As a result, the spiritists were treated specially. In one way or another, all the musicians in Cuba draw their power from ancestral realms. They've all been initiated and possess a deep knowledge of secret worlds. Sixteen *babalawos* originally came to Cuba in the days of slavery. They bought their incredible knowledge of Ifa from Africa. I could take you to a *babalawo* who could tell you everything about yourself. They would know your past, your present, and your future. But right now I have an appointment to make."

I had arranged to meet Carlos Alfonso, the leader of Sintesis, at his house in Mirimar, and was pleased to be greeted by his son, Equis, a musician and producer in his own right.

"My father will be along in a moment," Equis said. "Please make yourself comfortable."

I waited in the living room and stared at walls covered with paintings and prints by a who's who of famous Cuban artists, including Mendive, Zaida Del Río, and Gustavo Acosta. A few minutes later, Carlos Alfonso bounded in, a middle-aged man with skin the color of ginger rind and receding hair dyed a punkish yellow-white. Alfonso is a major figure in Afro-Cuban music, a visionary musician who has voiced strong and unpopular views against the socialist regime. He founded Sintesis twenty-five years ago, when Havana had real rock bands and musicians were eager to explore their roots and use their imaginations to create hybrid art forms. Under Alfonso's direction, Sintesis spliced Santerían *orisha* chants with rock, jazz, and funk. In an era of soundalike Buena Vista knockoffs, Alfonso had strong views on where Cuba's music was going.

"I'm a revolutionary in the whole sense of the word. I'm not a member of the Communist Party or the Socialist Party. But how can it be revolutionary to dwell in a culture that existed before the revolution? Musical innovation is threatened when everyone wants to be Compay Segundo. The women of Cuba are intelligent and strong. Yet every time I tune in to a music video of our artists, all I see are sculptured, half-naked *mulatas* and men smoking cigars and drinking rum—which is nothing more than a colonial cliché. The truth is, Cuba has all kinds of cultures. The other night, a thrash band called Tendencias performed. They were from Piñar del Rio. And though I don't particularly like thrash, they were very good."

When I asked him to talk about his musical roots, he smiled.

"My life in music took strange, fateful turns. My grandfather, who lived with us, was a drunkard. But he played the violin and harmonica. Well, I used to steal his harmonica, which he would set in the fuse box, and I taught myself to play it. I grew up on classical music and opera. But when I was fourteen I discovered that this was not the only music in the world. That's when my family moved to a very poor neighborhood called Mantilla," he said.

"Mantilla was far from everything associated with culture. But it was there that I first heard Afro-Cuban spirit-possession music. On both sides of my house lived *santeros* who held *toques* all week long. I would hear people scream when they were possessed, and the drumming was astounding. The spaces where the *toques* were held had dirt floors.

Mantilla was primitive. But when I listened to that music, it awakened me to another world."

Alfonso had ambitions to study music formally. But the harsh economic realities of Cuba dictated that he go to work and earn money. Eventually he took a test and discovered he had an aptitude for electronics. A scholarship to a school in Havana brought him into the city, and his life forever changed.

"That's where I encountered the magical world of Vedado. I heard rock and roll and started to play in a band that did covers of the Beatles, the Rolling Stones, and the Beach Boys. I managed to graduate and took a job as an electrician. But all I really wanted to be was a musician.

"One day I auditioned for the National School of the Arts. The admissions committee didn't think I had a chance, so they ridiculed me and hit the keys of the piano with their elbows and asked me to call out the notes. But I knew every note and they had to admit me."

At art school, Alfonso studied vocal music and the history of the choir. But he admits to being a bad student.

"All I really wanted to do was explore rock and roll and Afro-Cuban folkloric music. But the school was only interested in enforcing a rigorous pedagogy." When he founded Sintesis, Alfonso had a vision. Over Santerían chants and the rhythms of *batá* drumming, he overlaid rich, vocal harmonies. Underneath it all was rock, *boleros, son,* and hip-hop. He's grown up on everyone from Pink Floyd to Bob Dylan to Crosby, Stills and Nash. But in his imagination, the Beatles, especially John Lennon, reigned supreme.

Alfonso remembers the day Lennon was assassinated: a day that left him stunned, wounded, and searching for answers. Lennon's idealism had resonated deep within his soul, and his music had influenced a generation of Cuban rock bands.

"I had to do something for Lennon that would endure," Alfonso said. From that conviction sprang an annual John Lennon memorial concert, held every December 9 in a park. The concert soon became a pilgrimage destination for Cuban and international fans visiting Havana. And because of Alfonso's love of Lennon, a life-sized bronze statue of the slain rock star was commissioned a few years back.

"We got the statue commissioned without any sponsorship. And when Fidel came to the unveiling of the statue two years ago, on the twentieth anniversary of his death, I started crying. Wait. I want to show you something."

Alfonso disappeared and returned with a photo. He handed me a color snapshot, already faded, of him and Castro at the statue's unveiling.

"We had a huge crowd," he said, his searching brown eyes moist with the memory. "The memorial concert had been going strong for ten years, and I was amazed at what it had become."

Alfonso believes in the Cuban revolution and that music must be a vehicle for expressing the views of the masses. His own songs have candidly addressed social issues and been critical, at times, of the Castro regime. So far officials have not tried to silence him, though the government has not always been pleased.

Equis, Alfonso's twenty-nine-year-old son, walked into the room. He threw back his mane of long, thick, tightly wound dreadlocks. I had heard he just finished recording a hip-hop homage to Benny Moré, so I asked if I could hear it. He smiled and came back a few minutes later with the disc: *Homenaje a Benny Moré*.

Equis had blended Moré's own timeless *boleros* and *sones* with drum loops, techno beats, thumping bass lines, and old-school hip-hop rhythms. "Castellano" had wicked horn breaks that wove in and out of the *son*'s soaring melody, with Moré's exquisite voice weaving in and out. "Dulce Desengaño" was a blend of *bolero* and samba, and the big band horns of "Devuelveme El Coco" lurched into bubbling *timba,* viscous rap, and machine-gunned bass and drum music, cut and spliced with Moré's gorgeous voice.

A *rumba* unleashed at blistering speed, then gave way to free jazz and flowing raps before turning into a spirit-possession ritual. And on "Se Te Cayó el Tabaco" (My Cigar Fell Down), wicked conga drums accompanied Alfonso himself, singing a duet with Moré, backed up by the rest of

Sintesis. The music had loose-jointed rhythms, a sense of sonic wonder, and many rhythmic surprises. It put me in mind of Edgard Varèse, the Wu Tang Clan, and Miles Davis.

"I studied classical piano from the time I was seven years old," Equis said, lighting up a cigarette. "And I did that for fifteen years. But afterward I began to play with jazz and, later, rock bands. I was like a sponge, I soaked up everything: Charlie Parker, Sonny Rollins, Herbie Hancock."

"You must've listened to *Bitch's Brew*," I said, "and all the electronic experiments Miles did."

"Yes, yes. Definitely. I listened to a lot of Miles, especially *Tutu*. And when I perform live I use the rappers from a great hip-hop group here in Havana called Free Hole Negras. The record is finished but we're still waiting for a release. But I can burn you a copy," he said, and a few minutes later he came back with a disc for me. Now, of course, Carlos Alfonso wanted me to hear a few songs from Sintesis's new CD.

"Conmigo En El Clave," a duet with Chucho Valdés, melded Cuban jazz and funk, and a composition called "Fifty-Fifty" opened with Tata Güines playing a phenomenal solo on the congas that encompassed a half century of innovative Afro-Cuban percussion before giving way to a river of *rumba,* rap, jungle funk, and rock. So much of Cuban music was awash in trite, meaningless lyrics. But on "Un Poco Mas de Fé," a tribute to the thunder *orisha,* Changó, Pablo Milanes and Alfonso spun lyrics of poetic beauty.

"I'm not here to re-create old fifties music or re-create the past," Alfonso said as he escorted me to the door. "In Havana now, there are thousands of musicians trying to be the next Buena Vista Social Club. But where's the vision behind that?"

Since I'd first met Roberto Fonseca a couple of weeks earlier, he'd holed himself away to compose, recorded part of a CD for another label, and rehearsed for the upcoming American tour with the Buena Vista Social Club. The few times we'd made up to meet, our wires got crossed. But I finally caught up with Fonseca on a Thursday night at Club Zorra y El Cuervo.

A couple of dozen people showed up for the set, which started around midnight. But after hearing him play, I had no doubt in my mind that I was watching the country's most exciting young jazz pianist. Though he's just twenty-six, Fonseca plays with the soul of an old master. Backed by a trio of musicians that included a baritone saxophonist, the pianist leaned in over the piano and softly sang out the notes he improvised on the keyboard in the manner of Keith Jarrett or Glen Gould. On "Xiomorra," a *rumba,* he ingeniously sprayed the room with sharp, kaleidoscopic bursts of melody and rhythm, transforming his piano into a *quinto.* And on "Soledad," he used an old-fashioned *son montuno* to sketch a haunting meditation on loneliness. The music, which began with a spare, poignant melody, soon wandered into a dense thicket of rhythms: driving, melodic passages set against keening flute, giving way to discordant ruminations and oblique runs that conjured the light inside the darkness of enforced solitude.

"Not many people write about loneliness. But loneliness is a constant companion when you're a traveling musician," Fonseca told me between sets. Then he reached down into a bag and presented me with a copy of *No Limit,* his latest CD, recorded on a Japanese label.

"How much do I owe you?" I asked.

"Nothing," Fonseca said, arching one eyebrow and giving me an impish smile. "A gift."

We made plans to meet for dinner the next evening, and the following day I listened to *No Limit* and marveled at its wonders. Like his one-time stepfather, Chucho Valdés, Fonseca reaches back to the ancestral ground for inspiration, the realm of art where origins refer to sources, not uniqueness, and no one is anyone else's ancestor. Yet how he uses the radical roots of Afro-Cuban rhythms is unique.

Where Valdés is often florid and dazzling, Fonseca's style is more sparsely lyrical. His rhythmic sense is flawless, and his solos possess a startling logic and clarity that arises from that foundation. On "Kowo Kowo," a piece dedicated to Changó, hip-hop and deep, sonorous *batá* drumming collide in a dance that paves the way for Fonseca to drop dissonant notes between the cracks in the music before launching into a stunning blues solo. "Yemayá" floats on the wings of an *orisha* chant before becoming a burning *son montuno*. And "Aggayu" was a deliciously funky *descarga*.

I met Fonseca in the lobby restaurant of the Habana Libre Hotel, where he was already seated and wearing his trademark black-cloth derby cap. When I noticed the yellow and green beads of Orunla, the *orisha* of divination, I asked Fonseca what role the religion played in his art and life.

"I hope my destiny is to be a *babalawo,* because Santería has let me see the music from inside the source. In each *toque,* a simple rhythm or dance is taken to its highest expression. My grandmother, Onelia, was a *santera* and she used to take me to *toques* in San Miguel del Padron, a neighborhood close to Guanabacoa. It was and still is a stronghold of Afro-Cuban religion. And hearing the sacred Yoruba music and seeing the rituals they came from and the effect they had on people had a profound influence on me. The first music I composed, when I was ten, a mix of African music and jazz, was the result of those experiences with my grandmother," he said. "I come from a very musical family. My mother began as a singer and my father studied percussion. My brothers introduced me to music. The eldest, Jesús Valdés, plays the piano. Emilio Valdés plays drums. And an older brother, Chuchito, has a band. I began playing piano when I was eight, but I was already devoted to music when I was four. I saw my brothers playing and that made me want to learn everything."

From ages eight to fifteen, Fonseca attended an academic school that required four hours a day of music study. Some weeks, he was forced to study music all day long. At school, too, he learned how to interpret and approach classical music. But the scholastic rigors intensified when he turned sixteen and went to study at Escuela de Nacional de Música. "From that point on, we were taken deeper into music: into composition, orchestration, direction," he says.

His tastes are omnivorous. He loves jazz, blues, hip-hop, techno, and ambient music for their experimental nature.

"Blues has the same internal beauty that *son* has, a deep feeling. The first thing I ever played was a blues in the key of F. And jazz I love for its freedom," he said.

After 1989, everything Fonseca wrote explored the genius of Afro-Cuban music. He mixed classical music and jazz with the folkloric music, and he studied the *batá*.

"The *batá* are both rhythmic and melodic. And what impresses me is how the rhythm and the melody are connected. The rhythms are so complex that they cannot be transcribed. That is, there are beats that cannot be measured. And this is incredible."

His brothers and sisters exposed him to James Brown and P-Funk, to Marvin Gaye and Busta Rhymes, to Prince and D'Angelo.

"For me right now, the most exciting music is to mix hip-hop drums and bass with the deep rhythms of Afro-Cuba," says Fonseca, who produced a CD for the Cuban hip-hop group Orishas.

A song I'd heard on *No Limit*, "De Que Vale," a weird, spiky mix of *bolero* with drum and bass, intrigued me. Where did the inspiration come from? The question made Fonseca laugh.

"It had never been done before, because the two musics have a great contrast. *Bolero* is calm, whereas drum and bass is electric. My mother sings on this, and with her voice it came out beautiful. I know it's crazy, but I had to do it."

The waiter came and I ordered ice cream with rum and asked for the check. Fonseca said that in a few weeks he would be in Los Angeles, performing at UCLA's Royce Hall with the Buena Vista Social Club and Ibrahim Ferrer. The anticipation made his heart soar.

"It's difficult to create this music—to improvise as the old masters did, just over two chords," he said. "You listen to Mirabal play trumpet and every note is where it must be. My parents always told me to listen to the great *soneros*, to how they sang. And I did. The first time I performed with the Buena Vista Social Club I said to myself, 'I could die tomorrow.' Because it was a dream come true. And many musicians will never have that happen to them."

When the check came I reached for it, but Fonseca grabbed it first and shook his head.

"Not to worry. My treat," he said, throwing two $20 bills on the table, marking the first time anyone in Cuba treated me to dinner.

✺

On my way to Marcia Escalina's house, where the *toque de santo* for Yemayá was being held, I passed a goat's leg on the street, the matted fur still on it. I smelled the unmistakable odor of animal blood, which made me walk faster. The same musicians that had played the *cajón de muerto* were on hand, only this time they had the consecrated *batá* drums, three hourglass-shaped drums that had the power to call down *orishas*. An *orisha* dwelling within the *batá*, Aña, gives the drums their sacred inner power.

The *batá* rhythms are a kind of codex, offering pathways to the realm of the spirits. Many of the greatest drummers in Cuba have spent endless years mastering its demanding language. If you conceive of rhythm as the cosmic principle of balance, then the *batá* rhythms constitute a sacred path to achieving that.

"I carry the rhythm and the other two *bataleros* talk to each other," Roberto Argüelles said, showing me the largest *batá* drum, the *iyá*. "You're going to hear us call on the twenty-one *orishas* and play the *oro seco*, the sacred rhythms that we would not perform if this were a folkloric performance."

Soon, the rhythms of the *batá*, a language in tones that sounded remarkably like human speech, were reverberating through the house. The Yoruba language has three different pitches: high, middle, and low. An alphabet-based language is hard-pressed to capture those sounds. But the drum's tones are perfectly suited. The congas can produce the tones and modulations of Yoruba speech, but the *batá* can capture the language the *orishas* speak. I looked at the altar, a vision to Yemayá. On it stood two candles, a blue-and-white embroidered cloth, a blue and white cake, sweets, two bottles of rum, flowers, coconut shells. How was it, I asked Maricusa, to see her son coming home and having sacred *toques* to honor the dead and the *orishas*.

"Ah," she said. "He's just fulfilling his obligation. These are rituals that were promised."

In time, the music grew powerful. The *batá* seemed to come from a deep place, a world without beginning or end, a cosmos roiling with change. *Iyawoces,* initiates, who entered from the street, bowed down to the *bataleros* and kissed the drums. Some threw a small offering of money into a coconut shell. At a certain point I saw Omar move out in front of the *bataleros,* his arms pumping heavily. His dancing grew more fluid, his head shaking to the dense exchange of rhythms. The drummers, sensing some change of energy, played more powerfully now, until suddenly Omar reeled with a small tremor. At that moment, a young man arrived, bowed before the altar to Yemayá, and shook a rattle in her honor. When the drummers shifted to Yemayá's rhythms, the man started dancing with her trademark wavelike movements. "He is a strong son of Yemayá," a woman next to me whispered. "Watch."

The *akpwón*'s voice came from deep in his throat, pleading now for Yemayá to set herself in the head of this *iyawo*. The man momentarily spasmed, as if jolted with electricity, and then spun like a Sufi. The *akpwón* grinned, as if waiting for this moment fulfilled the intense work of playing each and every rhythm precisely. His words were now a dialogue with Yemayá that would last more than an hour. The drumming grew freer, and all the people, formerly clustered around him, now gave him a wide berth to dance. I watched a group of kids peer in through an iron grill as the *akpwón* chanted:

Yemayá, you're the one
The one who rules the sea
Above and below

In Cuba, sacred music was the means by which rituals were created and sustained. Many *toques* had excellent drummers. But I had never heard the *batá* played with such intensity before. The rhythms seemed to be flowing into my right ear, while melody, pitch, and timbre seemed to enter strongest in my left ear. The overall sensation was euphoria, a lightheaded feeling that made my toes tingle. But that was apparently nothing compared to what was happening to Yemayá's son. As he danced, various people prostrated themselves before him, and his eyes rolled back in his head.

Transformed into an *iyawo* of Yemayá, he whirled round and round. Soon he was escorted into a back room, as the drumming continued and the *akpwón* kept up the furious singing that triggered the chorus of voices. I followed him back and saw him attended by a flock of women who dressed him with a blue and white hat and skirt, the colors favored by the powerful *orisha*. A spiritual "transvestite," he drank water held out in a coconut shell by Omar Sosa, who periodically dabbed his head with a towel.

"Listen," Escalina said, suddenly appearing next to me. "He will talk to the people here about their problems and help them. Yemayá will talk through him."

One woman began asking him questions as another, older woman interpreted the jumble of fast-flowing words that spilled out of his mouth, a patois of ancient Yoruba and Spanish. Various initiates asked questions, and Yemayá, like some Delphic oracle, gave back answers, occasionally laughing out of the side of her mouth. Escalina looked around the room carefully.

"No one can smoke here in this room, because Yemayá would eat the cigarettes," she said. "And we can't have cockroaches, either, because Yemayá would eat those. She would think they were *chicharrones*—fried pork skins—which is one of her favorite foods."

Eventually it was my turn to ask Yemayá a question. I realized I had none. Yemayá's *iyawo* gave me a warm, sweaty hug.

"You keep coming to Cuba to do research," he told me in an androgynous voice. "But you need to investigate your ancestors. Only one is with you. First, you must do spiritual research. Don't give up your path. You should wear the beads of Obatalá. Then seek out a *babalawo* and he can tell you your *orisha*."

He gave me a sweet girl's hug and went back to dance with the crowd. And I, of course, wondered if what I had witnessed was real or just theater. If real, life was stranger than fiction. But if it was theater, it was nevertheless good theater, and theater sprang from ritual. Maybe the tyranny of life as it is could never match the worlds that the human imagination could create. A *toque* without a possession—real or imagined—might be like sex without an orgasm, disappointing to all. Perhaps this theater of possession was all the inevitable result of so many "inauthenic" Westerners seeking an "authentic" spiritual experience in a country where most people were barely surviving. Or it might be a case of initiates acting like they're possessed in the hope of becoming possessed. At any rate, thoughts like this swarmed my head when I noticed Omar's wife, Shirma Guayasamin, nearby, taking in everything that was happening.

"Are you in the religion?" I asked, though I already knew the answer from the expression on her face.

"No, I am not in the religion," she said, shaking her head emphatically and giving me a smile full of irony that said this would never be her world, but it was part of the price of being married. A few minutes later I saw Omar.

"So what do you think?" I asked.

"To return here is like returning to the ground of my being. It's not just my blood family, but the ancestral family, the spiritual family. To hear this music is like a blood transfusion. And because I'm not living here, I have to drink it and savor it and let it enter me."

It was my last day in Havana and I had yet to catch up with Chucho Valdés. Despite the fact that we had a close friend in common—Perico Hernández, who had grown up with Chucho—and Valdés had promised to meet with me, every time I phoned him he had something pressing to deal with and put me off. I had all but given up on the idea of talking to him in his hometown when I bumped into Juan Cuadras, the photographer.

"Wait," Cuadras said. "Come to my apartment. I will call Chucho for you." Back at his apartment, Cuadras picked up his phone and was soon chatting away with Valdés, whom he simply called "maestro." They talked about an upcoming Chucho performance at Club Zorro y Cuervo and a series of photos Cuadras was taking of Valdés. Then he made his pitch.

"*Oye,* Chucho, I have a friend here, an American author, who needs to talk to you. He's doing an important book on the music of Cuba. Can you see him? Yes? *Bueno.* I will tell him."

Cuadras came over to me with a beaming smile. He put his hands on my shoulders.

"What would you do without me?" he said. "Chucho says he'll see you tonight at ten P.M. He knows the history of all the music." Cuadras drew me a map of Miramar and told me where to find the maestro's house.

"Is this the home of Chucho Valdés?" I yelled from outside, stirring up dogs left and right, who began howling antiphonal choruses. A tall gate surrounded the house, and I could not make out any address. But soon an upstairs window opened and a voice called down.

"And who wants to know?"

I identified myself and a minute later Valdés walked out, dressed in blue jeans, a beige sweater, and a tan velour cap. He looked both ways down the street and then unlocked the gate with a key, apologizing for having to screen me from the window before coming down.

"Unfortunately, there are thieves, so we need all this security," he said, giving me a warm handshake and then resecuring the gate.

As befits an artistic colossus, Chucho Valdés lives in a sprawling house in Miramar, a once elite neighborhood that boasts more than its fair share of mansions but now looks a little scraggly, its glamour days surrendered to a threadbare beauty. In the living room, Valdés told me to make myself comfortable, pointing to a sofa. "Please forgive me. I have to finish an important conversation with some people." With that, he disappeared into an adjoining room outfitted with a grand piano and paintings that artists have given him over the years, mostly portraits of himself. I waited and looked at a wooden altar full of swords and listened to snatches of *danzón,* which Valdés plays with lightning speed. Perhaps thirty minutes later, Valdés and two other men walked out, still talking animatedly about changes in a score and the critical commentaries of a well-known Havana musicologist. Valdés looked over at me and arched his eyebrow.

"I'll be right back," he said, escorting them out the door. Ten minutes later he returned.

Valdés is somewhat stoop-shouldered in the way that some very tall people are. His legs are like stilts and his massive hands have graceful, tapered fingers. He seemed tired—it was late after all—and he gave me the gentle, ironical, world-weary smile of an artist who never had enough time to spend with music, the one thing he'd rather be doing more than anything else when all is said and done. We went into his studio and Chucho sank back into a couch.

"Though I'm a jazz musician and composer, I've always studied the roots of Afro-Cuban music," he said. "It's the only way to know what I'm doing and it's often told me which direction I should go. For me it was always important to identify all the important elements that make up the music, and to know the history. To make a fusion, you have to understand the individual components."

In the past thirty years, Valdés's search for those components has taken him in unusual directions. American jazz fans know him as the founder

Tata Güines at the Teatro Amadeo Roldan, Havana.

and composer behind the incomparable band Irakere and, more re-cently, as the dazzling pianist–leader of a fiery quintet that's pushed Afro-Cuban jazz into new realms. Like Art Tatum, Valdés has rein-vented the piano, made it speak a new language. Like some spiritual master, he contains all the music of Cuba, and on any given night it comes pouring out of his hands.

"Chucho is the most important musician in Cuba today," Roberto Fonseca told me. "He broke all the rules and he took all the music to an-other level. Everyone wants to play like Chucho, but only he knows where Cuban music is going."

Like all geniuses, he had a remarkable childhood. His father, Bebo Valdés, was a brilliant pianist, composer, and arranger, and was for many years the pianist with the prestigious Tropicana Orchestra.

"Through my dad, I met Nat King Cole and Buddy Rich and Stan Getz and Sarah Vaughn. I saw them play live in Havana, and that was the luck of being born in my family," Chucho said.

But the luck turned with the revolution. In a move that shocked the family, Bebo Valdés fled the country in 1961 without his family and went to live in Sweden, never to return. I asked Chucho to recall those days, the anguish and abandonment he inevitably felt. He paused a moment, and then said his father's departure had no effect on him.

"My father fell in love with a Swedish woman and left," Valdés said. "I don't have any bad feelings toward him. I was already an adult and a professional musician." (Later, close friends of the musician assured me that he was devastated by his father's abandoning the family. "Chucho was *destroyed* inside when Bebo left. A father leaves his son and family—it's a blow you will remember for life," Perico Hernández, an L.A.-based percussionist who was a childhood friend of Valdés, told me. "That's why he became so driven to be a great musician.")

To do that, Valdés realized early on that he would have to play an-other, equally far-reaching role, as an explorer of near-vanished worlds.

"In my work and art, I've had to search for lost rhythms. Musical traditions have been lost everywhere, even in many parts of Africa. But during this century, Cuba lost a huge wealth of folkloric music, and with Irakere, one of our main goals was to recover what had been lost. We had to go out and make drums to create the music we wanted to play."

I was reminded that *Irakere* is a Yoruba word that translates to "forest," but more precisely connotes an area in Africa where the best drummers lived and competed. So the word itself hinted at the group's mission.

"When Irakere began, African instruments within Cuba were already being modernized. I saw the *batá* drums being made with plastic parts. So one of our tasks was to build authentic instruments. We knew we wanted to use the original *batás*. But after studying Afro-Cuban folklore, we also made *yuka* and Arará drums. It's not that they didn't exist, but only the master musicians had them. So we had to research, with the elders, to learn the ways the drums were constructed," he explained.

I'd seen a set of the oldest Arará drums in Cuba—in Havana's Museum of Music. Made of a dark hardwood and carved with twisting snakes in relief, they seemed like monumental works of art, imbued with a magical power. In Havana, the Arará, who'd arrived as slaves beginning in the seventeenth century, had a strong presence for more than 200 years. Groups of Arará drummers and dancers would gather and perform at religious celebrations and festivals.

At the Afro-Cuban festival of the Epiphany, celebrated for more than 200 years beginning in the seventeenth century, the Arará, would be side by side with the Lucumí and the Congolese slaves, their faces ritually scarred since childhood, their bodies adorned with shells, crocodile and dog teeth, and glass beads. All through Havana, Arará rhythms and chants could be heard at the funerals of slaves who came to Cuba from Dahomey. But by the end of the nineteenth century the Arará culture was disappearing.

"The Arará had their own drums and their own language. They came from Dahomey, where Benin, Togo, and Ghana are today," Valdés says.

"Here at home, I have Arará drums, and their sound is very dry, very deep and beautiful. But in the first half of this century, the Arará culture virtually disappeared. Their associations and *cabildos* where they developed their traditions were gone.

"From the beginning we rescued traditions. But we always did it with the idea of taking the music in a new direction. The creativity lay in innovating within the tradition and taking everything to another level entirely."

It's hard to believe that Valdés is sixty. But music keeps him young and searching for new muses. I'd seen him twice with his jazz quartet and each time had been mind-blowing.

"With the quartet, I'm trying something different. Irakere's foundation was Afro-Cuban. But the quartet is playing Latin jazz. In Irakere I was more a conductor and composer. But with the quartet I'm back to being a pianist."

For a colossus, no one direction satisfies. Over the past couple of years, Valdés has upped the ante and sought out the most complex of palettes: the symphonic. "The meeting I just concluded while you waited was with two leaders of our orchestras. What I'm working on now is a distillation of everything that's consumed me in the past thirty years. I've reached back to the sixteenth century and tried to create a music that takes in the whole history of Cuba—from slavery to *son* to jazz. I've written an opera that includes the drumming of slaves from Africa, Spanish guitars, *danzones,* lyric singers, and African spiritual music. I don't have to imagine what the music of the slaves sounded like four centuries ago, either, because that music is still with us, passed on from generation to generation."

If anyone could pull off such a work it would be Valdés. When he composed *Misa Negra* (Black Mass), he fused jazz and *son* with Afro-Cuban cult music and created a work of symphonic power that retained its spiritual identity.

"*Misa Negra* was my attempt at narrating an African mass with all the parts. It's sung in Yoruba, and when we call to the spirits, the music we play is the embodiment of that realm of spirit. I grew up saturated with Yoruba culture on both sides of my family. And the way I play the piano has a lot to do with the power of African percussion as it evolved in Cuba," he explained.

"Cuban identity has two roots. It should have had three, but the Indians were exterminated. Well, I've done my best to keep all the African traditions alive. But my great-grandfather was a Spaniard. So their rich music is part of me, too. All of us Cubans are mixed, and this has been good, because it's assimilated the best in each culture."

I looked at my watch and saw that it was 1:00 A.M. Valdés looked bushed, and so was I. But I had one more question.

"You're a *santero*," I said. "And almost all the great musicians I know are in the religion. What is the appeal of that path?" Valdés smiled and looked at me with total calm.

"All the initiations are roads to peace," he said. "They let you know who you are and why you're here."

We shook hands, and Valdés walked me outside.

"You're a friend of Perico's?" Valdés asked.

"Yes," I said. The two musicians had grown up together and had remained friends, recently appearing together on an American recording called *Del Alma*.

"When you get back to Los Angeles, tell him I love him."

I promised I would and walked out in the night, where I soon flagged down a cab.

5. THE TREE OF RHYTHM: CUBA IN NEW YORK

Sons look for blessings from their fathers, expecting to receive admiration, knowledge, and acceptance. A handful get unconditional affection. But sometimes there is a curse instead of a blessing, a wound in place of love.

Juan-Carlos Formell has lived inside that curse. When he was a month old, his parents—Juan Formell, the future founder of Los Van Van, and his wife, the famous cabaret singer and dancer Natalia Alfonso—took him to his paternal grandmother, Maria Cortina, who lived on the outskirts of Havana.

"My parents gave me away—they didn't want me," Formell says in a voice still tinged with disbelief at the memory these many years later. "They kept my younger brother, Samuel, and my sister, Elisa, at the house and treated them with love. They got to go to concerts and lead what looked like a normal life. But when I confronted my parents about this, they never explained why they wouldn't let me live there."

Moon-faced and husky, with dark olive skin and gentle eyes, Formell looks less like his parents than his grandfather, Francisco Formell, a well-known conductor and arranger for Ernesto Lecuona. He sits in the living room of the Harlem brownstone apartment he shares with his

American wife, Dita Sullivan. The two exchange knowing looks that say "there are things that will never be understood in this lifetime."

"In Cuba you don't ask why," Formell says. "Living there is like having a metal vise around your head that's always clamping down tighter and tighter. There's no cause and effect, no inner life that gets regularly examined. The individual comes to realize that he or she has no power over his or her life."

"So people engage in magical thinking," says Sullivan. "Or they live in total denial."

"I loved my grandmother. She was born in 1904 in Oriente, and so she saw Cuba evolve over a century," says Formell, who's thirty-seven. "She told me stories of Cuba in the old days. But I never gave up asking my parents why they abandoned me. The only answer they gave, which was no answer, was that my grandmother needed me."

Even so, the time Formell did spend with his parents, on weekend visits, created a lasting impression. He remembers listening to the famous musicians who congregated there, singers like José Antonio Méndez, Compay Segundo, Omara Portuondo.

"These were the people singing *filin* and this was the music I wanted to play. So I would sit in a corner with a little guitar I had and I would practice."

Though his parents could've easily afforded to give him the best lessons, Formell received no instruction. But he was a natural musician, and he taught himself to play the guitar by age seven. A year later, Formell was put in a school near his parents' house, which meant he had to get up at 5:00 every morning to be able to attend classes.

"It took me an hour and a half each day to get there," Formell says. "I couldn't understand why my father would pick up my brothers while I had to make this long journey and be away from my family. It made no sense. But that was my fate."

One night, when he was eleven years old and on a weekend visit, Formell decided to ask his father to drive him to his grandmother's house.

"I was exhausted, I remember, and my mother said I couldn't wake my father. But I told him I wouldn't live any longer with my grandmother. And that brought on a huge fight. My father took me to my grandmother's house and gathered all my things and brought me home. One year after that, my parents were divorced. And of course, I felt it was my fault."

Fresh from divorce, Formell was abandoned yet again, shipped off this time to a boarding school, a common practice in Cuba, located on the Isle of Pines.

"The school was like a prison," says Formell. "We were forced to work the citrus harvest up to ten hours a day in the orchards; as children, we were basically used as slave labor. That was my education. Meanwhile, the teachers were beating many of the students and there was never hot food. I could only go home once every month for four days to visit my family—in this case, my grandmother. So like many prisoners, I looked for the opportunity to escape."

In March 1978, Formell snuck off the school grounds. He made his way to the sea and hid in a boat as a stowaway. Once in Havana he managed to contact someone at the Ministry of Education. There, he denounced the school's abuses.

"I wasn't an unusual case. Most of the students in Cuba are sent to schools like this, where we were indoctrinated. You see, there's not enough food in Cuba to feed people. So the parents send the children away, thinking they're being fed properly, so that they can have enough to survive themselves.

"My father was the kind of person who never wanted to know what was going on. But when my grandmother called my father and told him I had run away, he was enraged. He came over and we had a big fight. And at one point he took my guitar and broke it over my head."

He tells me this in a calm, matter-of-fact voice. "I must've cried myself to sleep that night, but worse than the physical blow was the loss of the guitar, which I loved," he says. "For guitars are not easy to come by in Cuba."

I ask Formell if there's a song he's written that directly addresses the pain he suffered in his family, the dark burden that weighed down on his young heart and spirit. But he shakes his head. There's a song, "Flores," on his first CD, *Songs From a Little Blue House*, that speaks of wounds. But it's the woundedness, he says, that all Cubans have suffered:

Flores de mis amores:
Rosas de un cruel jardin.
Azucenas de mis dolores
de Cuba traigo yo aquí.
(Flowers of my loves:
Roses from a cruel garden.
Lilies of my sorrows
I bring here from Cuba.)

Scorned by his father, Formell, then fourteen, nevertheless burned with ambition. To become a great musician, he knew, he had to pursue serious training and focus on one instrument. He settled on bass, an orchestra unto itself, and searched for the best teacher he could find. Perhaps it was just another bitter irony that he was led first to Orestes Urfé, who happened to be his father's bass teacher. Urfé told the young musician that he was already "too old," that his time was over, that his calling was no calling. But rejection didn't deter him. Formell spoke to faculty members at the National School of Music, who directed him to another teacher, Andrés Escalona.

"Andrés played first bass with the symphony and was a virtuoso. So I went to meet with him, and when he heard me play he saw that I had a spiritual hunger to learn. And because of that he accepted me as a student.

"I went to my father and said I had made a decision to study bass. And since I was the same age he was when he had decided to study bass and his father had helped him, it was his obligation to help me. And this time my father said okay. He even bought me a bass and initially paid for lessons. But soon Andrés didn't even want money. He became my mentor and I began sleeping over at his house and learning not just how to play music but how to think about music. I began learning about the history of music and its theory. And Andrés's wife was a great teacher, as well."

After one year of study with Escalona, Formell took an examination at the National School of Music. The faculty was astonished at what they saw. Formell's playing and knowledge had advanced to such a degree that he was placed with students four years ahead of him.

His passion for music, he realizes, was an obsession. He studied and played day and night, wearing a hole in the floor on the spot where he practiced at his grandmother's house. And at the same time, he began writing songs that burst in his head. Between the ages of fifteen and sixteen, he wrote more than forty.

"I wrote *sones, boleros, filin*. My imagination was on fire," he says.

"Can you play one of those songs?" I ask.

Formell picks up his guitar and plays a lilting *son* that reveals his sweet, rapturous voice, shot through with longing. His fingers run up and down the neck of the guitar, finding complex chord inversions that support the melody.

"That's the first song I wrote," he says. "But long before that, I was experimenting. I was blending *son* with *filin*. For me that hybrid was a natural sound. And later I mixed in elements of *changüí*."

While he was at the National School of Music, Formell worked with the great Cuban jazz pianist Gonzalo Rubalcaba, who was the same age. When he graduated he took work wherever he could find it. Word of his talent spread, and like all ambitious musicians, he sought ways of traveling outside Cuba. An opportunity came in the early 1990s when Charanga Habanera's David Calzado asked him out on a European tour. In Cuba, every person has to apply to leave the country. But as Formell was about to board the airplane, he was pulled aside and told that he had to stay behind.

"Why? Because I had practiced yoga in Cuba," Formell says. "In practicing yoga, I was seeking to be a better, healthier person, to develop my purer self. But the Cuban government considered the study of yoga to be a political act. And once it was learned that I couldn't tour with Charanga Habanera doors closed to me. Other bands wouldn't work with me because none of them wanted the problems I might bring."

Formell struggled. For a time, he performed with the legendary Cuban jazz pianist Emiliano Salvador. But his career was going nowhere until 1992, when Joseito González, the leader of the popular group Rumbavana went to bat for him and got Cuba's state security to allow him a onetime exit visa.

"Joseito told me that if I decided not to return to Cuba to let him know beforehand. He said he wouldn't denounce me to the authorities. Actually, the thought of leaving Cuba permanently then never entered my mind. I had always been politically neutral. But once we got to Mexico, a free country, I woke up and saw reality. In two weeks I was aware of all the lies I was forced to live with. And all the repression we had to endure. As musicians, we were robbed by the government, which took ninety percent of the money we made. We had no artistic freedom to say what we wanted. And I knew that I had a mission to inform the world about the reality that was Cuba."

Formell stayed on tour with Rumbavana for eight months. But by then he had made up his mind to leave and told González of his decision. It was February then, and Formell worked his way up to the border town of Nuevo Laredo. There, he contacted a black market "coyote," who promised to spirit him across the border.

"I had to give him a couple of thousand dollars. But instead of being dropped off in the United States, I was taken to a huge garbage dump in Nuevo Laredo and told to wait. I stayed there several days, but no one ever came."

With the few hundred dollars he had left, Formell hired a Mexican to take him to a point where he might attempt his own escape—swimming across the Rio Grande River.

"It was February 11, 1993, and I remember walking out to the edge of the river. I looked at the black waters and I decided I couldn't wait another day. I'd been in the navy and knew how to swim. But I didn't know how strong the current was. I was never a follower of the Afro-Cuban religion, but at the moment I jumped in, I called on Ochún and that calmed me. Somehow I made it across. I felt as if I was really free and I bought a bus ticket. But after ten minutes the bus was stopped and everyone was asked for identification. I said I was Cuban and didn't have any papers. They said they could bring me back to Mexico or put me in jail. And I told them to put me in jail."

Formell spent three months in jail until an aunt in Queens bailed him out. He took a bus to New York City and stayed with his aunt. In New York he met two other young Cuban musicians who were in a band called Baroson. For a couple of months he played bass with the group.

"That's when I met my wife," he says.

Sullivan, who had lived on and off in Cuba during the 1980s and married a Cuban in 1990, is forty-two. But when she first met Formell she had no idea who he was.

"We ran into each other in a restaurant and the only reason we talked was because I heard he had a phone number of a friend of mine, a musician, who had recently gotten out of Cuba," she says. "When I asked him for the phone number, he told me to call him. And we ended up talking for hours. He came over to my apartment with a guitar, which surprised me. I played him my favorite salsa records, and he played me some of his songs, which at that point weren't very strong. But I really liked his company. I wasn't looking for romance. I was in the midst of a divorce. But everything happened quickly." As Formell's de facto manager, Sullivan admits she knew little about the music business in the beginning. And her caustic, blunt way of dealing with people—including journalists, whom she deems unfriendly—hasn't made her popular in some circles. She and her husband are fervently anti-Castro and critical of much of the music flowing out of Cuba lately. Yet Sullivan does have a deep knowledge of Latin music. She's written on Latin music for the *Village Voice* and had lived in Cuba on and off through most of the 1980s. But what she saw happening in New York was dispiriting. The Cuban

Celia Cruz, the queen of salsa, at the Los Angeles Sports Arena.

musicians who immigrated to New York in the early 1990s had no venues to play at, though any band from Cuba had entrée to New York clubs as early as 1991. Meanwhile, the vibrant salsa scene that had flourished since the 1960s, kept alive and enriched by countless brilliant Puerto Rican legends, was effectively gone.

"You have to realize that New York had a great salsa community up into the 1980s. And the premium place was the Village Gate," says Sullivan. "There, on a Monday night, you could see two amazing salsa bands, perhaps one from New York and one from Puerto Rico. People came from Europe and Japan, and great jazz musicians would drop by to jam. The Village Gate was the only place in New York where Latin and American audiences mingled, and the musicians who hung out and jammed there—Tito Puente, Hector Lavoe, Ray Barretto—were the best in the world. Even in its golden period, salsa was ignored by the mainstream media. But when the Village Gate lost its lease, the whole scene virtually collapsed."

Formell got a job playing bass with a group called Latin Legends that included Ray Barretto, and took other gigs that came his way. And he continued writing songs, though none of them fit into the rigid commercial categories that Latin music had fragmented into.

"I wasn't part of any scene. I wasn't writing salsa and I wasn't composing jazz, though there were elements of jazz in my music," says Formell.

Luckily, he got money through a songwriting deal and used it to form a band called Cubalibre.

"Juan-Carlos needed to have a group that would play his music and draw on the great young Cuban musicians living here in exile," says Sullivan, who is fiercely ambitious for, and protective of, her husband. "Cubalibre played at a SoHo club called Boom. And they debuted at S.O.B.'s, a show that got reviewed by the *New York Times*. But nothing came of it. This was the end of 1994, and no Cuban bands were coming to the U.S. The Buena Vista Social Club was years off. We had no money, no support."

"No one was interested in the kind of music I was creating," says Formell. "A whole generation of great Cuban musicians were living in the New York area—David Oquendo, Oriente López, Dafnis Prieto, Yosvany Terry, Horacio 'El Negro' Hernández, Pedro Martínez, Charles Flores—but once you got here it was as if you didn't exist. All the articles in the media were about how great the musicians in *Cuba* were, how important *that* music was. But the Cuban musicians here were forgotten."

Then came a break. In 1995, Pepe Horta, a Cuban living in Miami who had started the Havana Film Festival, opened Café Nostalgia.

"Pepe wanted me to bring a group down to play at the café. So I went down to Miami and stayed with my friend, the Cuban conga player Wickly Nogueras. Well, Wickly's day job was selling flowers, and one day I happened to accompany him. In Cuba, once upon a time, the street vendors who sold things like flowers and fruit used to sing *pregones,* improvised songs. But the *pregones* disappeared with the elimination of commerce. Well, that's what Wickly was doing as he walked into shops he visited. He sang *pregones* and his singing inspired me to write songs that functioned like that, awakening the senses. From that experience I began writing the music that appeared on *Songs From a LittleBlue House.* We played those songs at the café for a month and a half."

"I fell in love with those songs," says Sullivan. "But I begged Juan-Carlos to play them on guitar instead of bass. We had fights about it because it was a risky move. We had to always struggle against the limited expectations of Cuban audiences. People didn't want to hear Juan-Carlos playing guitar in a band—a band without a pianist, no less. So I convinced him to pull out of the Latin bookings. Instead, he began to perform in Greenwich Village, at a small place called the Zinc Bar, where mostly American audiences came. And they had no expectations."

It was at the Zinc Bar, in December 1996, that Juan Formell came to see his son perform for the first time in New York City.

"Things had improved somewhat between me and my father. And now, at this show, he cried when he heard my music," says Formell. "Afterward, he asked if he could record two of my songs with Los Van Van."

"But we said, 'No.' Juan-Carlos didn't escape Cuba and suffer all that pain only to have his music recorded by a Cuban band," says Sullivan. "He needed a chance to record those songs himself."

Between 1996 and 1998, Sullivan tried to interest record companies in Juan-Carlos's music, but to no avail. A friend finally lent them money so that Formell could record a demo. But the couple barely scraped by.

"We lived at a level below welfare," says Sullivan. "It was a horrible, humiliating time."

Then came a turning point. With the release of *Buena Vista Social Club*, a market for a song-based Afro-Cuban music suddenly exploded. Juan de Marcos González, the musical director of the project, was up for a Grammy and arrived triumphantly in New York City in 1998. By chance he happened to call the Formells.

"Juan de Marcos was looking for a videotape or a book he thought we had," says Sullivan. "It was a total fluke, an accident he called. But I happened to tell him Juan-Carlos was playing at the Zinc Bar the following night. I never seriously thought he would come. But sure enough, he showed up the next night with a few friends."

"Talking to him afterward, I knew he understood what I was trying to do with my music," says Formell. "He asked me if I had a record deal, and when I said no, he promised to help me."

González was good to his word. Influential people at Nonesuch Records showed up to see Formell play some time later. That helped create the buzz that eventually led to his being signed by BMG Classics.

"He opened the door for me," says Formell. "And I'm forever grateful."

To those who grew up in Cuba and managed to escape, the music on *Songs From a Little Blue House* comprises a meditation on all that was lost. Not surprisingly, the CD touched off a storm of controversy in the media. Formell was ridiculed not only for daring to be different from his father, but for challenging the widely held notion that Cuba was a place that supported and encouraged musical creativity.

"I can't separate my music from my politics. So I expected to be attacked," says Formell. "But I didn't expect to be incessantly compared to my father, whose music is so different."

If *Songs From a Little Blue House* was based on rural life in Cuba, as filtered down through his grandmother's memories, Formell's second CD, *Las Calles del Paraiso* (The Streets of Paradise), is a decidedly urban recording. At the record release concert, held at downtown Manhattan's Jazz Standard one weekend in early June, the crowds were mostly non-Latin. Both shows sold out, with a large overflow crowd turned away. Dedicated to the late Pello el Afrokan, the legendary singer, dancer, *conguero*, and composer of El Mozambique, *Las Calles del Paraiso* evokes Havana as it was in Formell's youth. He uses acoustic guitar and horns to blend with his honeyed voice, which, though not exceptional, is still lovely.

"In my mind I saw a movie about a day and night in Havana," he says. "It began with carnival on the Malecon and continued as I walked through the neighborhoods I used to know. It's an imaginary movie. I brought my friends, Cuban musicians like Jimmy Branly and Carlito Del Puerto and Vicente Sanchez and Yosvany Terry, who, like me, live here now, to capture that movie soundtrack.

"Life is hard for most Cuban musicians living here. But some of us are creating a new sensibility. I feel leaving Cuba was great for me. I found happiness as a person. I found realization as an artist that I never had. I couldn't be Cuban in Cuba. And even though I'm living in a country where I don't speak the language and I'm not part of the culture, I'm able to be myself here. I was raised in the way most Cubans were raised—with no privileges. And this made me part of the people. My music never had to do with the system that Cuba established, but with the spirit and soul of the people."

It's paradoxical that most of Formell's following at the moment is non-Latin. That's probably because those audiences have a stronger concept of the singer-songwriter. Formell's reference points as an artist are José Antonio Méndez, Compay Segundo, and Los Compadres. And all three are widely unknown to Latin audiences in the United States.

I asked Formell how his relationship today is with his father. He leveled a disarming smile on me.

"Much better. My father changed. He helps me more now than he ever did. He's my number one fan. Which is ironic, because the Van Van fans have a problem with my music. But all that matters is my father, the founder of Van Van, feels otherwise."

❧

On a Sunday evening I took a ride out to Union City, New Jersey. Ever since I'd arrived in New York, I'd been told not to miss the weekly *rumba* held at Esquina Habanera, a local bar. Union City used to be predominantly Cuban up to the 1980s, but the community gradually changed. Central Americans, Dominicans, and Puerto Ricans moved in, and the Cubans, most of them poor, began an exodus to Miami. I asked the cabdriver, an old man from the Dominican Republic, if he knew about the Sunday night *rumba*. "No," he said, dropping me off outside the bar. And it was obvious from his expression that he could care less.

Inside, the music had just started. Up on the small stage six percussionists played the rhythms of Elegguá, the great trickster *orisha*, as a wily male dancer moved through the audience, sticking his hands in people's pockets. When the rhythms shifted to *rumba*, couples leaped out onto the small dance floor. At one point, a very large and beautiful woman—in Cuba, I could imagine the men shouting, "Estás gorda (You're fat)" as a compliment—and her lean, muscular partner expertly danced the *guaguancó*, each reveling in the delicious sexuality their movements evoked, a pantomime of intercourse leading, if only the dancers took it to the next step, into a night of pleasures.

The group, Raices Habaneras, boasted some of the New York area's most extraordinary talent. Pedro Martínez, a young and handsome virtuoso percussionist and singer, had arrived from Cuba a few years earlier and was making a name for himself in a variety of musical settings. And Vicente Sánchez, an older *conguero*, made the skins of his drums sing. The rhythms changed. The dance floor cleared and a lone male dancer exploded to the *jiribilla*, engaging in what amounted to an improvised competition between himself and the *quinto*, the highest-pitched conga drum. With each spluttering crack of the drumhead, this dancer shook and shuddered.

I might as well have been in Havana or Matanzas. All around me were Cubans of every age, shape, and skin hue: old men in white, blue, and yellow guayabera shirts, cigars jutting out of their mouths; women in floral print dresses; and children, waiting for a chance to strut out on the dance floor and take a stab at the *rumba*. On a Sunday night in Union City, New Jersey, Cuba's tree of rhythm had sunk its roots and spread its branches.

"The first *rumba* we had here was March 24, 1996. We started at four P.M. that day and we finished at three A.M.," David Oquendo, the leader of Raices Habaneras, told me between sets. "Right away, we knew we had something magical happening."

Oquendo, who conceived the Sunday *rumba* and sings and plays claves with the group, is broad-shouldered and stocky with prematurely white-gray hair. A month before, he'd gone with Raices Habaneras to Seattle for ten days and every show was mobbed.

"Originally our little *rumba* was only supposed to be here once a month. But people complained the very next Sunday, 'What happened to the *rumba*?' And so Tony"—Oquendo motioned to Tony Sequeira, the club's owner, standing next to us—"made the *rumba* every *other* week. But the people came the next Sunday and demanded, 'Where's the *rumba*?' "

"The club was packed, so I had to make it every Sunday," said Sequeira. "We just wanted to create a place of our own, to remember our roots and our homeland."

"People said Tony was crazy to create a *rumba*," Oquendo says. " 'Criminals will come,' they said. Because in Cuba, if you want to find your enemy, go to the *rumba* and you'll find him. Or her. But here there are no enemies. I bring my mother and my daughter here."

"Why Sunday night?" I said. "Don't people have to work?"

"Because in Cuba Sunday was originally the day for *rumba*," said Oquendo. "During the week the poor people worked. But after the

The great Cuban composer and virtuoso, Paquito D'Rivera.

misa—the mass—everybody went to the *solars* in their barrios. The *solars* are poor apartment dwellings with collective bathrooms and no plumbing, located all over Cuba. I grew up across the street from a *solar* in a neighborhood called Cayo Hueso, in Central Havana. And I always would go to the *rumbas* there."

I saw that a group of people was waiting to talk to Oquendo, including a European filmmaker and her assistant who were considering doing a documentary on the club. I talked with Tony Sequeira. Cubans had come from as far away as Philadelphia and Boston in order to participate in the *rumba*. This was the place that all the great Cuban bands came once they hit New York. Oquendo put his arm on my shoulder. "Tomorrow, we'll talk," he said in his raspy voice, and scribbled down his phone number. Which is how we ended up sitting on a bench overlooking the Hudson River the next day.

"How hard was it to put together Raices Habaneras?" I asked.

"Let me tell you, it's not that easy," Oquendo said. "The people who come from the folkloric world in Cuba are not that easy to get along with. To conduct these musicians you have to show them exactly how to play. Even good *rumberos* will play the wrong tempo or style. They may come from different towns, like Matanzas and Havana, and have their own ideas of what is correct."

Paquito D'Rivera had hinted that Oquendo would have something powerful to say about the war in Angola.

"Were you called up to fight in Angola?" I asked. "Did you go there?"

Oquendo looked startled for a moment. He clearly hadn't been expecting the question. "That's something I have talked about with only a handful of friends and never with a writer. But since you ask, I will tell you. In 1975 there was a war in Angola," Oquendo said. "I was in my last level in the high school. And the military called me up for service. I was just fifteen years old and our unit was going to be the first military unit to go to Angola. Well, me and two or three others resisted. I said, 'I'm not going. If I have to fight for my country, I will. But what is the reason I have to fight a war in Africa?'" Oquendo's eyes went heavy at the memory.

"Well, they told me it was mandatory. I had to follow orders. But I refused, and so they sent me to La Cabaña Prison. I spent two weeks there. And then they sent me to El Pitirre. That was a concentration camp, a prison. The capacity was eight hundred, but they shoved three thousand of us into there. I was locked up at El Pitirre for five years and nine months. I was just a child and they threw me in with criminals. This is a part of my life I never talk about. Just my close friends know. But I never forgot what happened to me there. There were fights every day. And the prison guards—they were the worst monsters."

For eighteen months Oquendo had no communication with the outside world. His mother and father weren't told where he was. And when they finally came to see him, they didn't recognize him.

"I was emaciated, like a survivor in a Nazi concentration camp. And my hair"—Oquendo puts his fingers through his hair—"turned gray overnight. Right now I'm forty-three. But my hair was gray at sixteen.

"In prison I saw things I will never forget. There was, for instance, a giant of a man named Amaro, who was from Matanzas. Amaro was a friend and he was always happy, never made trouble with anyone. He always had a smile. But one day a prison guard asked him why he was smiling. 'That's my personality,' Amaro said. All of a sudden, this prison guard took a metal tray and smashed it into Amaro's face. When I saw that, I knew that guard was in trouble. Amaro hit him once and knocked him out cold. And then he said, 'Don't anybody touch me. Just take me to maximum security.'

"So they took him there. But from my cell I could see seven or eight guards with bayonets go in after Amaro. Amaro was so strong he threw each one of the guards to the ground. But then they sent dogs in after him. Amaro killed one of the dogs. But after that I heard Amaro screaming, 'Killers.' Because the dogs were attacking him and the guards were jabbing him with bayonets, until they finally took him to the hospital. And that was just one of the terrible things I witnessed in El Pitirre."

"What helped you survive?" I asked.

"The music kept me alive. I learned more about music in the prison than when I was free. Why? Because the musicians here were playing from their souls. In prison I learned all about the Abakuá, the Congolese, and the Yoruba music and religions. The Abakuá taught me that the most important thing I had was my character and my spirit. And there was so much time to learn. The day has twenty-four hours. But in prison, twenty-four hours is like a year."

When Oquendo was released in June 1980, he tried to make up for his lost youth. The first thing he did when they released him was to go to his house and open the case of his guitar.

"There were four strings broken, I remember, and I tied the strings in knots, because it was difficult to get new strings. But my fingers wouldn't follow the commands of my mind. And I started crying. Because I realized they took the best years of my youth.

"Every day for the next three months, when I wasn't working construction, I spent every available waking hour practicing guitar or *tres*. My family thought I was crazy. But music was my life. And when I got confident I went out looking for a job with a band." Oquendo got a job with Moraima Secada, a famous *son* singer. He played with Compay Segundo. And for a time he played with the great singer Elena Burke. He worked with dozens of bands all over Cuba, and founded his own group, Alafin, a band that merged jazz, rock, and folkloric rhythms. But making a living was not easy given his prison background.

"The officials made it hard for me," Oquendo says. "In Cuba, when you've served time in jail for something political, you're no one. Nobody cared about my musical abilities. I applied to the music schools, but I wasn't allowed in. So I worked odd jobs as a barber, as a construction worker. And finally I got performing jobs under the table, without the government knowing. And little by little I got more work."

From the moment he got out of prison, Oquendo wanted to leave Cuba. But the opportunity never arrived until relatives secured him a visa to travel to Panama.

"Cousins on my mother's side had lived in New Jersey since the 1970s, and they suggested I go there. So in 1989 I took my mother with me and we never looked back. We stayed for almost two years thanks to the help of family members who sent us $500 each month. That's the only way we survived. But eventually I found work. One day as I was walking around, I saw a beat-up guitar lying on the streets. I picked it up and I fixed it. Soon I was playing with very good musicians in Panama, musicians who loved our music."

Oquendo came to the United States in January 1991, staying in Miami for a couple of days before coming to Hoboken. Word soon spread of his talents, and Paquito D'Rivera ended up collaborating with him on three CDs.

"Paquito is one of the most important musicians I met here. We have chemistry, and he gave me so much. Right now we're working on a beautiful *bolero*."

Oquendo produced four CDs for Johnny Ventura, the king of the merengue, and has recorded with Chico O'Farrill, Cacho, and Patato Valdés. He also has his own trio that plays every Thursday at the Clam House, a club in West New York, a town adjacent to Union City. But whereas Esquina Habanera is a dazzling scene, an efflorescence of Afro-Cuban spirit only a stone's throw from New York City, the Clam House is essentially a dive. There, Oquendo's group plays what in Latin America would be known as *sopa*—standards done in a restaurant environment. Even so, if you listen to Oquendo sing *boleros*, which he does splendidly, you can half imagine yourself in Cuba during its golden age.

"For many years Cuban music was a cliché. But with Raices Habaneras we've had a chance to present the true soul of the music, the deep roots. There's so much I want to do. Right now I'm using two guitars, acoustic bass, and percussion to present *filin*. *Filin* is a form of *canción* that began to be popular in the 1940s. It evolved to include *bolero* and jazz. But I'm trying to create a kind of *filin* that people can dance to, because when you dance the music goes inside of you."

Oquendo looked at his watch.

"I have to meet someone," he said. "When are you coming to New York again?"

"Not until the end of the year," I said.

"Well, I will play for you then and you'll know what I'm talking about."

"I was born in Guantánamo, the only girl in a family of two boys. My father was a professional singer. But when he met my mom he quit. He worked construction and never sang again," says Xiomara Laugart. "And he had a beautiful voice. He sang *boleros,* and when I was a child he would sing me and my brothers to sleep. That's where I learned to sing; he was my inspiration. I remember he sang this old song by Vicentico Valdés."

I ask her if she can remember a lyric, and she smiles and nods before breaking into song, her voice tender and melancholy:

Los aretes que la faltan
A la luna
Los tengo guarados
En el fondo del mar
(The moon lost her
earrings deep in the sea)

"I always sang a cappella. I made up songs as a child and would comfort myself that way. I grew up in Altura de la Lisa, a very poor neighborhood. We had a hard life. Sometimes we didn't have anything more than rice or sweet potatoes. And there were times we just had a broth for dinner," she remembered.

"My family had all these big plans for me," Laugart said. "They wanted me to go to the university and study for a career. But all I wanted to be was a singer. So I studied economics and got my degree. And as soon as I did I gave my parents the diploma and said, 'Now I'm going to be a singer.' "

Her talent was soon known. At an open audition, Pablo Milanes and Silvio Rodríguez, the leaders of the *nueva trova* movement, heard the young singer's extravagantly beautiful voice. Milanes took her under his wing, becoming a lifelong mentor, letting Laugart sing with his group. She toured outside of Cuba with Milanes and eventually married Alberto Tosca, a prominent guitarist-composer. For a while the two performed together in a duo, but while they were in Mexico City, Tosca had an affair with another woman. Laugart, six months pregnant with her future son, Axel, left him. Between 1982 and 1995, Laugart was the chanteuse of Cuba, with all the work she wanted. She traveled all over the world, toured Europe and South America, and recorded six CDs. For five years she fronted a band led by Omar Sosa, touring Spain while living in Cuba. But from the beginning, Laugart was controversial. She wasn't afraid to speak her mind and criticize the injustices she saw everywhere around her.

"I talked about the need for freedom, the need for democracy. I sang about the reality of Cuba, not the propaganda," she said. "And the Ministry of Culture made me pay for it. People have to understand, everywhere in Cuba, at radio and TV stations, at recording studios, there are officials who decide what you can and cannot sing. Anything you want to record they can censor. And that made me more and more angry. In Cuba, I was a star. But as an artist I couldn't say what I wanted."

Her destiny was decided on February 13 and 14, 1995, when the singer used Valentine's Day to present two concerts. The shows, held at Plaza de la Revolución, were ostensibly innocent, devoted as they were to love songs. But it was easy to see what Laugart was getting at.

"I told everyone that we all need to love and be loved, to accept our brothers and sisters in and out of Cuba, because Castro had recently made a hateful speech saying that the American Cubans were worthless. But love is our true heritage, not hatred. All I sang those days were love songs. And when I finished the concert, the police arrested me. I told them, 'I won't sing again in this country until it is a free democracy.' And they handcuffed me and took me away."

Laugart was taken to a jail near the American Interests Section while her mother tried to find out where she was. Authorities told her the only way to be released was to renounce all her beliefs to the Cuban press.

"I said no, never, and they told me I'd never work again or be allowed to tour abroad."

It was the beginning of a long descent into darkness. From 1995 to 1997, Laugart could find no work. The Ministry of Culture had essentially blacklisted her.

"I got very fat then, and I had no hair. I looked like a mean bulldog," she says, and it's hard to imagine the lean, beautifully proportioned African woman as she must've been then. "I gained eighty-one pounds and nobody in Havana recognized me. I was in a deep depression, too. But I had to survive, so I sold marijuana and alcohol. I became a drug dealer, working out of my mom's apartment. I would sell drugs to tourists, musicians, anyone who wanted them. Our house was the base of the empire. My two brothers helped me, and we had people working for us all over Havana.

"My mother was terrified of me getting caught. My father didn't know. My mother would become hysterical sometimes, scream that I would get caught and thrown in prison for life. This was during the special period, when Cuba was starving. The only way to survive was to have dollars, and the only person earning dollars was me. Somebody had to support the family. But if I were caught they would've put me in prison. Not long ago, just being caught with dollars would get you five years in prison."

There was a knock at the door and Ileana Padrón, whose SoHo apartment we were sitting in, entered. Tall, delicately featured, and willowy, Padrón had lived with Laugart for a year and had made her part of Yerba Buena, an Afro-Cuban/hip-hop/Afrobeat ensemble that had recently toured with Dave Matthews. But now she was managing Laugart for the company she and her husband, the producer Andres Levin, ran called Funny Garbage.

"I'm telling him about my arrest," said Laugart.

"But you have to say why else you were controversial," said Padrón, and the two exchanged knowing smiles.

"Well, okay. I was bisexual. And the macho men in Cuba couldn't deal with that. In fact, I was living for four years with the sister of one of the most famous singers in Cuba, Amiaury Pérez."

"And don't forget the story about the TV show," said Padrón.

"Oh, yes. How can I forget that? One day I was invited to be interviewed on a live TV show. So the host of the show began questioning my integrity, my skin color, and my sexuality. He was a racist, macho asshole and he treated me like a piece of shit. This was on national television, and I got so enraged that I stood up and broke a microphone on his head. Well, I wasn't on TV for five years after that."

In 1997, things brightened. Laugart was invited to stay in Italy with some friends, and there she started her career again, learning Italian. A year later she left Cuba and lived for two years in Rome.

"I was living in Italy and on vacation in Cuba when Ileana saw me at the Cohiba Hotel," says Laugart.

"I was working for the Massachusetts Arts Council then," says Padrón. "I was asked to bring artists from Cuba, and when I saw Xiomara I asked her if she wanted to perform in a festival in Massachusetts."

"And of course I said yes. I gave Ileana my passport and a few days later," Laugart said, "I was on my way to Massachusetts. Afterward, Ileana invited me to live with her and we got an apartment together. She got me a gig singing at the Zinc Bar, where I had a trio that mixed jazz with *son*. Kip Hanrahan heard me and we made a record together, *Deep Rumba*. Since then I've recorded with Jacky Terrasson and Manny Oquendo. Every year I go to Japan with Deep Rumba. And Yerba Buena did seven shows with Dave Matthews, which has been incredible."

"Dave heard our EP demo and invited us," says Padrón. "That was an amazing experience."

I hadn't yet seen Yerba Buena perform, but I'd heard their EP. Like such groups as L.A.'s Ozomatli and France's Sargent García, Yerba Buena incorporated a grab bag of world music genres, everything from

Afrobeat and *rumba* to *son* and samba, blending it with hip-hop, soul, and jazz. The band had lost its top songwriter, the talented Descemer Bueno, but Yerba Buena still had the gifted Cuban singer-percussionist Pedro "Manotas" Martínez and jazz saxophonist Ron Blake. Laugart's powerful voice gave the band plenty of sizzle.

"We're opening for Celia Cruz in Central Park in two weeks, and we're coming to the Hollywood Bowl in July with Eddie Palmieri. You want to come?" Padrón asked.

"Sure," I said. But Padrón didn't even hear me. She had taken a call on her cell phone and was speaking rapid-fire Cuban Spanish.

"I didn't use my fame in Cuba here," Laugart continued. "I'm not young anymore. But I wanted to start from the beginning and work my way up. As much as I hated the government and what they have done to artists, leaving Cuba was hard. My father told me, 'If you leave, don't come back.' My son was okay with my leaving. He's made his own career as a musician. He didn't have to live in my shadow. But we talk every week on the phone. And we cry."

"We want to get him out of Cuba," Padrón said, reappearing. "That's my next project."

"I have to go somewhere now. But we can talk later," Laugart said.

So we said good-byes and I grabbed some dinner and headed down to the Jazz Gallery, where the Dafnis Prieto Quintet was playing. Ever since he'd arrived in New York, Prieto, a brilliant twenty-seven-year-old trap drummer from Santa Clara, Cuba, had cut a wide swath through the jazz world. He'd played with Henry Threadgill and Eddie Palmieri's Afro-Latin Jazz Orchestra, with pianist Andrew Hill and bassist John Benitez. In each case, he'd taken the music to a higher level.

Located on Hudson Street, the Jazz Gallery was founded by Dale Fitzgerald, a former anthropology professor who was trying to create a space that could function as an international jazz cultural center. Like a lot of hard-core jazz fans, Fitzgerald had fallen under the Cuban spell. He had researched a project on Chano Pozo and had found time to make sure that a surviving heir of Pozo's was paid royalties on dozens of songs that had become hits.

"I got her something like $30,000," Fitzgerald said, "just by making certain phone calls and being very persistent."

As I sat down I noticed Henry Threadgill. A moment later, the young avant-garde Cuban dancer, Judith Sánchez, Prieto's wife, took a seat next to me. With trumpeter Brian Lynch and saxophonist Tim Ries out front and Luis Perdomo playing piano, Prieto had the perfect engine for his piston-driven sound. A *danzón* turned into a ferocious jam, with Lynch spraying burning choruses over popcorn-popping rhythms. Sometimes Prieto held a stick in the middle of one hand, thereby hitting the hi-hat and the snare at the same time. Subtle rhythmic shifts took the music in unexpected directions. And Perdomo added *iyesá* rhythms from the *batá* drums into his playing. Some of the music had an almost mathematical precision. And in one piece, "Masacoteando," the melody itself was a direct outcome of the rhythm.

"A lot of musicians get lost playing with Dafnis," Perdomo said after the set. "I've seen that. If you're not clear with the rhythms you're going to be in trouble, because Dafnis will change things all the time without any warning. But since I play percussion, including a little *batá,* I understand what he's doing and can anticipate the quick changes."

Prieto is short and muscular, with a face that reminded me of a marten.

"I'm always trying to break forms apart—even forms that seem sacred because they might be folkloric," he said. "At some point those forms had to be invented, right? Well, why not make more forms?"

We talked about music for a while, about Prieto growing up in Santa Clara. But it was late and I needed rest, so I headed back to my hotel. The next morning I took a bus out to North Bergen, a leafy New Jersey suburb where the great Cuban saxophonist and composer, Paquito D'Rivera, lived.

"I bought this house from a black Cuban doctor who was married to a Cuban psychiatrist. In Spain, he played congas at night and studied medicine by day. A perfect life, right?" D'Rivera said.

He led me upstairs, where there were big bedrooms with high ceilings and paintings by famous Cuban artists hanging on the walls. One room was painted sky blue, a color echoed out in the garage, where I couldn't help noticing the gleaming tail fin of a Bel Air jutting out. Seeing my eyes fall on it, D'Rivera opened the door for me to experience the car's sleek inner sanctum.

"For forty-three years I dreamed of having a blue 1957 Bel Air. I can still remember the day it rolled out. I was a young boy in Havana, and when I saw that car, man, I fell in love with it. This car used to be red. I got it a year ago from a company that makes classic cars. But I paid too much. The body itself cost $11,000. But the mechanic had to buy all these parts. Oh my God, by the time I was done it was $65,000. By then, I wanted to kill him."

D'Rivera grew up when Havana was a hothouse of jazz and decadence, a destination for American musicians and movie stars. His mother was a dress designer and his father was a classical saxophonist who owned a small store on Virtudes Street. The young Paquito took his father's little store for granted. It sold instruments, music books, and accessories.

"However, that store was a meeting ground for musicians," said Paquito. "Cachao would come to buy strings for his bass, Chico O'Farrill came to buy trumpets. Bebo Valdés and Chocolate Armenteros and Ernesto Lecuona—they would all drop by. My father was a representative for Selmer, the famous maker of saxophones. He gave me a saxophone when I was five. I made my public debut when I was six years old. I played a *habanera* and 'La Comparsa de Cubana,' by Lecuona. Already I knew I wanted to be a musician. There wasn't really a doubt."

Sitting near the pool behind his house, D'Rivera doesn't look like someone who suffered a heart attack a month earlier. He's dropped some weight and seems completely relaxed. He peppers the conversation with jokes and puns as his wife, Brenda, a soprano singer, brings us drinks.

When I mention the heart attack, D'Rivera rolls his eyes. "The stress of delivering commissions and doing so many concerts must've gotten to me. I had to finish Stravinsky's *The Soldier's Tale* and perform it in Spain, and that was a huge, huge pressure. I have to do all these commissions. Plus the situation in Cuba continually upsets me. It weighs on my soul."

He deals with the pressures and conflicts, the anger and the frustration of living in exile in *My Sax Life,* a rambling, chaotic pastiche of anecdotes that he wants to have published in America. But on this day he seems glad to be a storyteller.

"My father had one of those big RCA phonographs, and that's where I got exposed to classical music by composers like Paul Bonneau. Later we got a record player and my father would play big band music: Artie Shaw, Count Basie, Harry James. One day he played me Benny Goodman, from a 1938 recording at Carnegie Hall, featuring Lionel Hampton and Gene Krupa. And when I heard that, my imagination was on fire."

Seeing their precociously gifted son, his parents deftly orchestrated a stage career. His mother made him suits to wear for performances that his father arranged—on radio and TV shows, at cabarets and nightclubs, in concert halls and wherever else music was heard. The young prodigy performed on the same bill with clowns and cabaret singers, with bikinied *rumba* dancers and comedians.

Soon, he could play Mozart or swing, bebop or chamber music. On clarinet he developed an expressive chalumeau register. He could play with luminous delicacy or else make the instrument growl and groan. As word spread of his virtuosity, the world seemed limitless, but then came the hammer blow, a lunatic 1956 law that suddenly forbade musicians under eighteen to work on TV and radio. It was no use to ask why. And three years later, the revolution shook the country, changing everything, initiating a million descents into darkness and ruptured dreams.

For D'Rivera, as for many artists, the revolution was the beginning of what amounted to an evil spell put upon the country. But even so, there were moments of brightness. Willis Conover, who had a jazz show on

Voice of America, was one. "People in America don't even know who Willis is. But Willis was a hero," D'Rivera said. "He had a show called *The Jazz Hour.* It originated from Washington, D.C., and aired twice a day. And through him I discovered Miles Davis and Tony Williams and Ron Carter and Ornette Coleman. This was post-bop, no tempo, free jazz, and, man, it blew our minds. Listening to it, we could feel connected to the latest developments in jazz."

In the early 1960s, D'Rivera studied music at a conservatory in Marianao and joined Havana's Musical Theater, where Leo Brower was the musical director. There, a fourteen-year-old Paquito played alto saxophone in a group that included pianist Chucho Valdés and Carlos Emilio, the fabulous guitarist and future member of Irakere. But a summons to do three years of compulsory military service woke him up to alternate realities.

"It was there, among the young soldiers, that I first heard of the political prisons in Cuba. Some of the recruits told tales of bayoneting and torture and of prisoners forced to sleep on their shit," D'Rivera says.

"This is what so many Americans don't know. Cuba trained terrorists. Later, when I was in Angola playing for the Cuban troops, I listened as Fidel denied we were in Angola. I was taken to terrorist camps in Cuba where I would see guys looking like Osama Bin Laden."

After the army, he toured with Orquesta Cubana de Música Moderna. But the group he put his mark on was Irakere. It's instructive to hear how different his take on the group is from Chucho Valdés's.

"Irakere was formed because we wanted to see the world. For the Cuban musician, travel—escape from Cuba—is like a psychosis, an obsession," says D'Rivera. "But we also had to hide American jazz behind our music, because jazz was a dirty word. It was considered a form of American imperialism. Now Chucho would tell you a different story, that the group was specifically founded to explore different Cuban traditions. Because he has to say certain things. And that was an achievement, no doubt. But that's not the reason Irakere was formed. We had to disguise jazz, because it was the product of 'a decadent Western society.'

"In the 1970s, the Cuban government destroyed the bohemian spirit of Cuba. They crushed the nightlife. When Chucho called me to be in Irakere, I was sitting around doing nothing. I'd been removed from the group I was in, Orquesta Cubana de Música Moderna, because of the crime of playing jazz. They didn't exactly throw me out. They just said, 'Paquito, you need to rest. Go home. Write music if you want. We'll pay you, but not to play your music.' So I spent two years doing nothing at home. *Nothing*. And how could I complain? I was getting my salary, right?"

Irakere was formed with the cream of the crop in Cuba. The group regularly left the country, and each time he left D'Rivera saw that he was living in a floating prison.

"I loved playing with Chucho and all the great musicians in Irakere. But deep in my heart I knew I would have to leave. Because I had seen New York in 1960. I had performed there, with my father. And I knew what freedom was like."

He has powerful memories of Cuba. He remembers jamming with the legendary Chico O'Farrill at Maxim's, participating in *descargas* with Cachao, and playing with Dizzy Gillespie in 1977, when the trumpeter visited Havana.

He was twice married in Cuba. The first marriage was short-lived. The second marriage brought a son, Franco. But in 1980, after witnessing the horrors of the Mariel Boatlift, D'Rivera was ready to leave.

"Irakere had a European tour which offered a chance to defect. And I knew I had to take it. I came here when I was thirty-two. I was eleven when Castro came to power. Leaving Franco was agonizing. I had to abandon my son and my wife. I wouldn't see them for eight years. *Eight years*."

The ready smile D'Rivera has momentarily disappears. There's sorrow in his voice now.

"I lost the opportunity to see my son grow up. What's more, I had to leave my country as a criminal. But that's what Cuba does to you."

The early years of exile were the hardest. Lonely and broken in New

York, cut off from his family, D'Rivera had no power over events. As soon as he defected, his wife had problems with the Cuban authorities.

"They took our car away from my wife, Eneida, and harassed her. But eventually I got them out. I paid the government something like $22,000 and I brought them to America. But our marriage didn't survive. The Cuban government made sure to destroy that."

We drank some coffee. Then D'Rivera handed me an excerpt of a novel he'd written called *In Your Dark Arms,* based on a lyric from "Noche Cubana," by César Portillo. It's written from the perspective of a musician—or musicians. Cachao, the great trumpeter Alfredo "Chocolate" Armenteros, and Chico O'Farrill appear as characters.

"The novel is about Havana in the forties and fifties. The city is the hero. The story is that a Cuban trombonist disappears on the Nile River. His name is Pucho and he is kidnapped by a tribe of women in the desert in Africa. A strange illness has left the men dead and so the women kidnap Pucho, who just happens to be a good lover."

When he talks of Cuba his voice is both wistful and sad. I ask him why some musicians chose to stay while others left.

"Everyone has their own reasons. But those who stayed had to live with a lie. They had to deny their inner life. Someone like Chucho Valdés—you never know when he is telling you the truth or lying. After forty-three years of living in that regime, you lose your identity. I have seen Chucho saying certain things in public and in front of me, which I can't believe. I was with him a few years ago when a TV journalist asked him, 'How is Havana these days?' And Chucho answered, 'It's beautiful.' And afterward, I said, 'Chucho, how can you say that? They have let the city fall to ruins.' And Chucho just smiled and said, 'No, no. They are fixing it up.' Later Bebo, his father, told me, 'Paquito, what do you expect him to say? He could not survive without saying what the government wants to hear.' "

Few Cuban musicians who've come to America have done as well. Many have seen their careers plummet. But his success is not a matter of luck. Fluent in both the classical and jazz idioms, D'Rivera flourishes in both worlds. He's offered commissions all the time and has trouble turning them down.

"I just premiered a flute concerto with the National Symphony. It's called *Grand Danzón*."

He loves Brazilian music, Portuguese *fado*, Argentinian *tango*, and the folkloric music of Puerto Rico, Venezuela, Argentina, and Colombia. He loves to fuse jazz and classical motifs with Latin American forms.

"I love the music of Astor Piazzolla and *joropo*, a 6/8 Venezuelan rhythm, and their waltzes. For a long time, the world trivialized Latin American music, equated it with Carmen Miranda. It didn't matter where you were from, if you told someone you were from south of the border, they thought of 'La Cucaracha.' But I've composed classical pieces using Latin American forms. And those forms are beautiful."

As a bandleader and soloist, he's on the road most of the year, his itinerary jammed. He reels off a list of upcoming shows: the Library of Congress; a tour with Calle 54, assembled from the Latin jazz documentary of the same name; a clarinet clinic at the New England Conservatory of Music; an appearance at the Double Reed convention in Canada; a Brazilian recording project with the cello virtuoso Yo-Yo Ma.

"And I want to write a contrabass concerto dedicated to Cachao. And to have Edgar Meyer, a bassist from Nashville who's recorded with Yo-Yo Ma, play it. Edgar is a genius."

He would never go back to Cuba as it is because he would have to ask for a visa to visit his own country, an "insanity" he's not willing to participate in.

"The best way for a terrorist nation to bridge any sanctions is through the arts. I remember when Paul Simon went to South Africa to record *Graceland,* in violation of the sanctions against that racist regime. That was wrong. Fortunately, Nelson Mandela triumphed. But Paul Simon didn't help. And think of how many bands are lending credibility to Castro by performing in Cuba."

Cuba, he says, is an absurdity. The country should have toppled. The people should be in open revolt.

"But that's hard to do because everyone is afraid of everyone else. Ninety percent of Cubans worldwide support the embargo. As Cubans we send $1 billion a year to Cuba, to help our families," D'Rivera says. He looks at me hard now. "I send money and instruments. I have to. And isn't that a contradiction?"

"Of course," I said, and saying good-bye, I caught a bus back to Manhattan to meet with Oriente López.

Just as genius is no guarantee of success, musical greatness in Cuba was not necessarily predictive of success in America. Many musicians who'd left Cuba found that life under capitalism was no piece of cake. The paradigm shift from a country where individualism is suppressed to a country where individualism is worshiped is a leap of imagination not easily made.

In Cuba, Oriente López had been a star. A conservatory-trained flutist, pianist, and arranger, he had been part of the seminal group Grupo AfroCuba, which, together with Irakere, had produced a visionary melding of African and Cuban folkloric music and jazz. In addition, he'd worked as the musical director and arranger for Silvio Rodríguez. But in New York, his career had faltered.

For a time he worked with Regina Carter. He played piano with Marc Anthony and was associate conductor for *Capeman,* the failed Paul Simon musical. He'd arranged some compositions for Paquito D'Rivera, with whom he'd just finished doing a soundtrack for an independent Spanish film, *Rosa la China.* He'd written music for various Latin jazz artists ranging from Ralph Irizarry and Timbalaye to the Nuyorican *charanga* band Jovenes del Barrio, but he had yet to form his own band and had unaccountably given up the instrument he'd devoted half his life to—the flute.

"The biggest problem I've had in New York is meeting people interested in my musical ideas," López said sheepishly. "Mostly I write for jazz artists, Latin bands, and eventually I might play with them—but not in a steady way. I haven't achieved the success I expected. I need to network more."

López is lean and handsome, his balding head shaved close. He was dressed elegantly, wearing dark slacks and a blazer. That afternoon, he'd been scheduled to play piano for a brunch concert with a Latin band. At the last minute the show was canceled, and he apologized for having no other gigs for the next week where I might see him live.

His mother was a classical pianist who taught music at different schools. She told her son as a child that music was spiritual. "She always wanted me to approach music that way. And one day, when I was six years old, she took me and my brother and sister and told us we were going to the beach. But in reality, she was taking us to an audition that attracted kids from all over Cuba." López passed the audition easily and was accepted to the first of many elite schools. He started out playing classical violin but switched to flute—an instrument he would study devotedly until age twenty-three—two years later.

"What about your father?" I asked.

"My father?"

"Yes. What role did he play in your life?" The question seemed to flummox him.

"My father worked odd jobs. He was not a musician. He drove a taxi. He was a dreamer," López said, his eyes downcast, his voice trailing off. His sentences seemed disconnected, as if the childhood he was recalling was another's. He seemed lost in some way, and his mournful eyes seemed to hide some secret wound. But there was a reason, as I soon found out.

"Okay, so I will tell you. My father was Ricardo López. When I was six, the authorities came for him. Detectives arrived in the middle of the night and they took my father away."

"What had he done?"

"My father was very high up in the Communist Party. He was a bodyguard for Che Guevara. But there was a power struggle. And Fidel had my father and others arrested. My mother tried to remain optimistic. She tried to keep things together. We would go to the prison and visit my father once a week for two hours. But we could never show our feelings. Because Cuba is like that. Nobody shows their feelings. Then, one day when I was eight years old, my father was brought to the conservatory where I was studying. A teacher brought me to see him. There were police surrounding him and they had allowed him to see all his kids because they were moving him to another prison. But when I saw him I was ashamed and I was scared, because I thought something terrible was going to happen. My mother told me to be careful, that the authorities would look for any excuse to throw me out of the school. And from that time on I hid myself away."

To escape the pain, López threw himself into music and excelled. He went to Havana's elite National School of the Arts and later to the Fine Arts Institute. He loved jazz, a music that was forbidden to be taught.

"But then I heard Irakere," he said. "I knew I wanted to play music like that. And I got a chance when I was at the Fine Arts Institute, because there I began collaborating with Grupo AfroCuba as a composer and performer."

Between 1984 and 1990, López toured the world with AfroCuba. The group had been founded in 1977 by saxophonist Nicolás Reinoso and included some of Cuba's most daring musicians. It drew heavily on African sources and brought new, complex melodies and harmonies to Afro-Cuban forms.

"Nobody in America really knew about Grupo AfroCuba, which is a shame. But it was one of the greatest bands in Cuba. We went to Europe and Latin America. We played long pieces with powerful polyrhythms. There were five horns and three percussionists. It was the best experimental laboratory I could've asked for."

At the same time, López was working for Silvio Rodríguez as a musi-

Dafnis Prieto in New York.

cal director and arranger. It seemed, in retrospect, a world of limitless possibilities.

"I had the chance to create the music I wanted. I loved the folkloric music of Cuba and the rest of the world, and I loved jazz and classical music. And my dream was to mix those with Afro-Cuban elements. But whenever I traveled out of the country I never wanted to come back to Cuba, because Cuba was like a prison."

In the fall of 1990, while touring Mexico with AfroCuba, López decided to defect, but told no one that he was leaving for fear they might betray him. He lived in Mexico City for two years and played with many bands. When he went to Venezuela, where he had family, he stumbled into political chaos.

"That was when Hugo Chávez had been put in jail and suddenly Venezuela was sealed off, and I had to stay eight months instead of two weeks."

In 1993, he went to Miami and stayed a few months before coming to New York. Like many musicians, he couldn't afford the city and found himself living in Union City, New Jersey, part of a large émigré community.

"In Europe, groups like Charanga Habanera and NG La Banda were the favorites. The people like the new music. But here in New York, people like nostalgia music of the fifties, like the Buena Vista Social Club. I would like to compose for films and the stage. And I'm getting a little work. But it's hard."

It was getting late and López seemed edgy. He said he had to return home. But when he noticed a photograph of my five-year-old daughter lying on a table, I saw the eyes of a soul deeply wounded.

"The biggest pain I carry is having missed watching my daughter grow up."

"You didn't mention you had a daughter."

"She was nine when I left, and now she's eighteen. Her name is Greta Liz López. I saw her last Christmas." He looked away and fell into silence.

We walked outside where twilight was settling over the city.

"I'd like to hear some of your recent music," I said. "Could you send me some?"

"Yes. Sure. I'll send it to you," López agreed. But as I watched him walk away, into the crepuscular night, I knew he never would.

6. ACROSS THE WATERS

I think I was playing *rumba* in my mother's womb," Long John Oliva tells me one early spring afternoon. "I nursed with *rumba,* ate with *rumba,* slept with *rumba.* And even when I played shortstop in the minor leagues, I brought the clave sticks with me." Oliva has a sculpted face, with skin the color of butterscotch. His body is coiled with a restless energy, and his eyes—fierce one moment, tender the next—hold the memory of wounds given and received.

"I remember being eight or nine years old and seeing my daddy play at Callejon in the *solar,* in La Habana. Many famous drummers were there: Santa Cruz, Papaito, Puntilla. From the time I was five years old, I knew I wanted to be a *rumbero.* But often I didn't have access to the drums because my daddy had big problems with drinking and was always selling his *tumbadoras.* So I learned to play on boxes and on doors. When I played I was in another world, because the drums have a spirit inside them: Aña. Even today, when I play the *batá* at a *toque fundamento,* I feel the power of Aña. I feel lifted up like I'm flying in the air."

I first got to know Long John Oliva at a benefit concert where we both performed. A friend recommended him as an accompanist for a theater piece I was presenting, an adaptation of an ancient myth from Nigeria set to Afro-Cuban rhythms. After the performance—to which Oliva added a haunting mix of Abakuá, *batá,* and *rumba* rhythms—I mentioned I was headed to Cuba in a couple of days. Oliva grinned and hugged me like a brother, planting a kiss on my cheek.

"Listen, if you get a chance, look up my father, Pancho Quinto," he said, writing down the number he had. "He can tell you the history of Cuban music."

Pancho Quinto was a legend, one of the most famous *rumberos* in all of Cuba. I never could find him in Havana. However, when I returned to Los Angeles I learned that the arts collective I had formed had been awarded a grant to teach music, storytelling, dance, drumming, and theater to an impoverished community of Latin American schoolchildren. As a musician and storyteller, I had studied Afro-Cuban percussion and used it in performances at colleges, prisons, schools, and community centers. I had seen how myths and powerful rhythms combined to draw listeners into the deepest parts of themselves, the places where change and healing can emerge. And who better to teach Latin American kids the rudiments of rhythm than a master drummer from Cuba?

"You just tell me when. Because I want to pass on my knowledge, my legacy, to the children," Oliva said when I asked him if he would teach with me. For the next three months Oliva taught forty-five boys and girls, ages six through ten, how to play and dance *rumba,* and he accompanied me on stories that I told to the children. Some of the kids we taught came from damaged homes and suffered physical abuse; many were full of rage. Most could not listen to anything for more than a minute without an outburst. But as Oliva and I played the rhythms of Cuba on our drums and told them stories, the children began to calm down and listen.

"If you learn these rhythms, in your hands and in your body," Oliva told the students one day, after we had played a long *rumba,* "you can always find the place inside yourself where there is balance. You can make yourself whole even if somebody tells you you're not."

After the class, we went back to my house and Oliva talked about his life.

"I was born a little after the revolution, in 1962, and I grew up surrounded by music. You know about my daddy, a very famous *rumbero*. But my mother was a musician, too, a singer, and she worked every day and sometimes went on the road. We had a house in Old Havana and Niño Rivera might come jam on a Sunday, and the musicians from Los Van Van might show up the next day.

"We had religious rituals at the house all the time," he told me. "But my father had a rough life. He didn't have a childhood. He had to work from the time he was seven years old, because his family had no money. He would clean cars, shine shoes, unload shipments at the dock. And later, he drank."

At age twelve, Oliva got accepted to one of Havana's music schools. He studied music theory and classical timpani. But he quickly became frustrated. The school's approach to music was rigid and the curriculum didn't allow students to listen to, much less learn, the popular idioms of Cuba.

"You couldn't listen to *rumba*. You couldn't listen to jazz or *son*. And I asked myself, 'Why?' I didn't like that. I wanted to hear and learn all kinds of music. Friends would come back with tapes of Charlie Parker, Chick Corea, Dizzy Gillespie, and Thelonious Monk. In Cuba, we loved jazz. But we couldn't call the music 'jazz' because jazz was an 'imperialist' creation. Well, one day when I was supposed to be studying classical timpani, I sat in the practice room and listened to a Charlie Parker recording. I was trying to play the lines he was playing on the saxophone on my drums. Suddenly, the door opened and the teacher came in. That day, I was reported to the administration and they threw me out of the music school."

Oliva gave up his dream of studying music. He played baseball but felt trapped. Then, in May 1980, he heard the announcement all of Cuba heard.

"Castro said he was sending all the criminals and outcasts to the United States," Oliva said, his eyes darkening at the memory. "But a lot of people who weren't criminals made up their minds. The truth is, only a small percentage of the people who set out during the Mariel Boatlift were criminals. The rest were professionals who could no longer stand living without hope. I left Cuba because I wanted to see what life was really like in America. I heard all the propaganda. But I couldn't believe what I didn't see. And I knew I couldn't be free in Cuba."

On Mother's Day, 1980, at sundown, Oliva fled Cuba on a run-down fishing boat that was overloaded with passengers. It was a voyage he would never forget.

"We listened to the loudspeakers that were set up along the beach. Angry voices told us we were trash, that we would be thrown into prison in the United States as soon as we arrived. As soon as I got on the boat I threw my clothes in the water—everything except my shorts—and I strapped myself into a lifeboat. The moment we took off I started singing Yoruba chants, the songs I grew up with. I was scared I was going to die so I called on Yemayá, the mother of the sea, not to take me.

"I never slept. If the boat sank I had to be ready to jump. I saw grown men mess their pants from pure terror. And all around me was chaos. Out on the rolling sea, I saw a boat spin out of control. A woman fell into the sea and disappeared before my eyes. I saw another boat sink, and I saw a father and his little son swimming in the water. The father somehow passed his boy up into the arms of someone on another boat. But then he just sank into the water and drowned because he had no more strength left. It was then that I realized what a monster the Cuban government was to send thousands of people to die in the ocean just to retain power."

Oliva's boat was picked up off the coast of Florida and he was sent to a fort in Pennsylvania where he stayed for three months. There, he played baseball, a sport he had excelled at in Cuba. American scouts heard about the camp and came away impressed with his fielding and batting. Later that year, Oliva signed on with the Texas Rangers and had dreams of being a major-league player. But then came an encounter that changed his life.

"I was never submissive, and when I saw something unfair, I would confront it. One day, at practice, a white player insulted me. He said he didn't want some Cuban stealing his job. 'Go back to your fuckin' country!' he screamed at me. And I just went crazy. I punched him. All the rage that was inside of me came out."

Oliva left the Rangers the next day and moved to Puerto Rico. He played Cuban music in Puerto Rican bands. But a Cuban friend told him that Los Angeles was a good place for musicians. Oliva was ready for a change. He didn't feel he could make an impact in Puerto Rico, so he moved to Los Angeles in 1986.

At first it was exciting. He got an opportunity to play in Willie Bobo's band for a couple of years. Following that, he toured with Strunz and Farah, a group led by two guitarists. With Oliva's subtle Afro-Cuban rhythms, the duo's CD, *Primal Magic,* snagged a Grammy nomination.

Oliva toured with Jackson Browne, Kenny Loggins, and Arturo Sandoval. He played with jazz bands, Brazilian samba ensembles, and hip-hop groups. He made enough money at one point to buy a house. But he never stopped thinking of Cuba and was always comparing it with the United States.

"Cuba made us leave in disgrace. There, I had to live in denial of everything. And the fear was constant, a psychological fear on you all the time. But here in the United States, the control is sophisticated. The government can allow protests, because they don't really threaten the way things are done. This country is all about money. If you don't have it, you're nothing. In Los Angeles or New York, people will spend

$5,000 on their dog, but they wouldn't give healthcare to a homeless person."

In 1991, Oliva married a Puerto Rican journalist with whom he had three kids. But the honeymoon didn't last long. When Oliva's mother, Ana Esther, who had breast cancer, came to live with them, a pattern of anger erupted in their marriage. Oliva watched his mother die in 1992 and saw his marriage fall apart, with his wife getting custody of the children.

For a time he lived in Miami. He played with the great Cuban jazz trumpeter, Arturo Sandoval. But Oliva came to loathe the city for its overt racism against black Cubans and soon returned to Los Angeles. In the late 1980s, Afro-Cuban music had none of the popularity it enjoys now.

"There was no real Afro-Cuban music scene," Oliva said. "I would play a *rumba* in a club in L.A. and no one would show up. Most of the Latin Americans here are from South or Latin America. They're used to cumbia, merengue, and ranchera music. They didn't grow up with clave. And the white Cubans in L.A. didn't know *rumba*. But slowly, over time, the scene changed. We kept playing and pushing and talking about the music. I would send my best students down to Cuba to study with the masters. And when they came back they had new knowledge. I could use a beer," Oliva said.

I came back with a beer that Oliva drained in a few gulps. Ideas were bubbling in his mind now, and the conversation grew more intimate.

"For the last three years I've been alone and that's changed me. My wife and I fought all the time and we had to split up. I was full of rage because I never got the love I needed as a child," Oliva said, his eyes like two open wounds. "When my mother died, I felt empty, like I had nothing left. But alone in my little apartment, I saw that you need to deal with the positive and the negative. I don't get angry anymore. I have the tools to stop myself and give myself a time-out. And when I feel stressed out I play the drums. Inside those rhythms I feel relaxed. Inside those rhythms I can breathe.

"I love myself because I know that deep inside I'm a good person. My dream is to open a school where people could study the music of one country from the ground up. Because when you know the foundations of a culture, you know the people. And I want to pass on my knowledge. Cuba is a complicated, mystic country. It's a place of deep knowledge and great suffering, and I'm always missing it. I grew up in the religion; my father is Changó, my mother is Yemayá. The religion shaped my soul and nourished me."

The afternoon light was fading and I had to pick up one of my sons from a gymnastics class.

"What does the music of Cuba mean to you?" I asked.

"The popular music, the *son* and *changüí* and *guaracha,* are full of life. They come from a marriage between the father, who is Spain, and the mother, who is Cuba. But our sacred music holds the deep memories of the ancestors. The sacred songs and chants hold the anguish of all we suffered as slaves. For me, the music is more important than food or drink, more important than love or money. We hide our pain behind the music, and our impotence as well."

Los Angeles didn't have the concentrated community of Cuban superstars that New York had—everyone from Paquito D'Rivera to Celia Cruz. But it was filled with unsung heroes and little-known geniuses who lived in the shadows of the vast pop star machinery. In 1997, when I started listening more closely to the local bands, I met Alan Geik, who had a Latin show called *Alma del Barrio* on public radio. Geik was then in the midst of recording a tribute CD to the late Cuban DJ, Emilio Vandenedes, a key figure in popularizing Cuban music in Los Angeles and Miami during the 1980s and 1990s. One day he invited me to the studio in Hollywood where it was being recorded, and it was there that I met José Caridad "Perico" Hernández, the musical director and composer for the project.

Hernández's wife had recently died and he was still mourning her. I listened as he sang a sad *bolero*, "Solo y Triste," dedicated to her memory and oversaw the rhythm tracks on a number of other songs. I told him I wanted to interview him, and the next day I drove to his house in Eagle Rock.

"I can't forgive what the government did to me. After the revolution, I went from musician to prisoner," Hernández said when I asked him about his life in Cuba. His eyes, which normally sparkled like a child's, were as heavy as bullets. "They sent me to Camagüey, far, far away from my wife and six children, to cut sugarcane. For six years—I will never forget that. The pain is in my heart still. That's why I have never returned. But Cuba lives inside of me. It runs through my blood. I never forgot the music. When the rhythm is inside your body, you never lose it."

He looks younger than his sixty-three years. His smooth, pecan-toned skin and large, square, majestic head give away his Indian ancestry. He grew up in a small town called La Palma in Piñar Del Río, Cuba's westernmost province. His calling was clear at age eight when he tested out as the most musically gifted student in his class. By the time he was twelve, he was playing congas in a band that imitated the then-popular Conjunto Casino. Two years later, he says laughingly, he was *playing* with Conjunto Casino.

"We would finish up at four A.M. every night. Then we would have parties and continue drinking until the morning," Perico says, shaking his head and rolling his eyes in wonder at the memories those days still summon. "*Everyone* was playing Havana then: Benny Moré, Celia Cruz, Félix Chapotín, Sonora Matancera."

In 1958, Hernández was asked to play with an assortment of the city's top musicians to open the Hotel Capri. It was the gig of a lifetime and a memory he savors.

"We practiced for *three* months—I'll never forget that. We opened on November 28, 1958, and we were sold out every night. I was making $160 a week in Cuba, which would be like—I would say, like $3,000 a week today."

Then came the revolution, the closing of cabarets and casinos and exile to Camagüey. By then, Perico, as everyone called him, and his wife, Esperanza, already had six children. It wasn't until 1964 that they escaped Cuba. Thereafter, he came to California and raised a family.

These days, he sings with Son de la Tierra, a band he put together that plays the full range of Afro-Cuban music. But for years he's been a musician's musician, performing on records and film soundtracks and playing gigs with other better-known Latin bands. Before Son de la Tierra, he led a charanga-style band called Charangoa, where he played congas and sang at El Floridita's, a Hollywood nightspot known for its music and fine Cuban food. There, on Friday nights, many a great musician would stop by to see the master at work. Poncho Sánchez, who recorded a couple of albums using Perico some years ago, including a Grammy-nominated song Perico cowrote, "Guajira Para La Jeva," calls Perico "a great, great" musician.

"Perico plays with his own original style. He knows *all* the early Cuban rhythms and how the music fits together. But he's also a terrific singer and writer, not to mention a beautiful, humble person. The only reason he's not more visible is because it takes so much else, besides musical ability, to make it in this business."

"He's a *sonero,* a composer and a complete musician," Long John Oliva said of Perico. "When we play together, like with Caravana Cubana, magic happens, because together we have so much knowledge."

Caravana Cubana, the all-star group that Geik put together for the first of two CDs, released *Late Night Sessions* in 1999. The CD showcased everyone from Jesús Chucho Valdés and the singers in Bamboleo to salsa trombonist Jimmy Bosch and such L.A.-based Cuban musicians as Carlitos Del Puerto and Lázaro Galarraga. Many of the songs were written and arranged by Perico. And it's his soulful *criollo* voice that caught my attention when I first heard it. The CD came out of nowhere to be nominated for two Grammys, which prompted Geik to produce a follow-up, *Del Alma*.

Geik is tall and lanky, with dark hair, a mustache, and Mediterranean features that could pass for Gypsy, Greek, Jewish, Italian, or Spanish. He grew up in the Bronx in a Jewish family. In the late 1950s and early 1960s, New York City was a musical paradise, and pop music hadn't been segregated into rigid categories.

"Tito Puente would play with Thelonious Monk at the Apollo," he recalls. "Or I'd go to Birdland on a Thursday night and see a double bill of Machito and Duke Ellington's orchestras."

Geik studied at the London School of Economics as the Vietnam War raged—an experience that led him to become a fierce antiwar agitator. He gave up a career in economics and worked in TV in New York before moving to California, where he ended up working as a film editor. He loved Latin music but never gave a moment's thought to being a DJ until he phoned Eddie López, a local DJ for a show called *Latin Dimensions* then broadcast on KCRW (89.9 FM).

"I knew Eddie and he happened to be looking for someone to take over the show. I said, 'What about me?' And he said, 'You'd be fine,' " Geik recalls. "And that was a turning point. I really blundered into this."

That was 1979, when almost no DJs were seriously playing Latin music. *Latin Dimensions* eventually gave way to *Alma Del Barrio*. And the knowledge of Latin American music he amassed down the years, plus his background as a film editor, prepared him well for making *Late Night Sessions* and *Del Alma*.

"I had to use nearly two decades of friendships I developed in the music business just to make people confident I could pull this off," Geik says. He gave me a broad grin. "And amazingly, they trusted me."

One blistering early August morning in the summer of 2001, I got a call from a friend who told me that Los Muñequitos de Matanzas were living in Los Angeles.

"For how long?" I asked.

"Two months."

The legendary folkloric group had come to Los Angeles before, usually for a few days, performing at colleges and conducting workshops and master classes for students and professional dancers and musicians. Inevitably, they squeezed in a few concerts that quickly sold out. But two months was an eternity that offered endless possibilities for the diffusion of their knowledge. I logged onto www.Afrocuba.org, a Website that I visited from time to time, and quickly found where the group was giving its next workshop. The next afternoon, I drove downtown and parked in a no-man's-land of bodegas and businesses. I walked along the tracks next to the Metro. The sun was going down over a smoke-blue sky and the Staples Center, directly across the highway, looked like a massive piece of purple costume jewelry. The class was in a faceless building located a few feet away from the Metro stop. The door was open and there, sitting down watching a Spanish sci-fi video, was the group's leader, Diosdado Ramos.

I saw a few familiar faces. But the two-story loft soon filled up with more than 150 people, an ethnic mélange of Latin and Anglo, Asian and African-American. Other members of Los Muñequitos drifted in: Ricardo Cané, Israel "Toto" Berriel, Freddy Alfonso, Ana Pérez. Finally, Jesús Alfonso, the group's musical director, appeared and half of the Muñequitos, including the dancers, went upstairs for the dance portion of the workshop.

I followed them and watched two lines, with thirty students each, move to the bubbling sound of *rumba*. One student, an old woman with reddish-gray hair and wattles under her chin, had a serene look of bliss upon her face as she moved to the insistent pull of the *tumbadoras,* clave, and voices, her body looking already younger. On a muggy Saturday night in August, a tree of rhythm, planted four centuries ago in the sacred ground of Cuba, had spread its roots and branches into Los Angeles.

I ran into Jorge Luis Rodríguez, the founder of Stage of the Arts, a nonprofit group that had set up the residency.

"How did you get them to come here for so long?" I asked. "And are they doing this in other cities?"

"No, never," Rodríguez said, his eyes twinkling merrily. "I grew up in Matanzas and heard Los Muñequitos playing on the streets in my neighborhood. I lived in Matanzas until 1980, when I came to the United States. In Cuba, I worked in the Ministry of Culture. And when I founded Stage of the Arts twenty years ago, I couldn't bring Cuban artists here because of the embargo. But when the walls between the two countries began coming down, I brought a few of the musicians for extended stays, to teach. This is the first time I brought the whole ensemble."

Over the next five weeks the Muñequitos spread their knowledge all over Southern California. There were dozens of workshops at colleges and community centers. The group, composed of some twenty musicians and dancers, appeared twice at African Marketplace, performed a sold-out show at Santa Monica's Temple Bar, and jammed with Son Mayor, a local Latin funk band, at L.A.'s slick Conga Room. At the historic Wilshire Ebell Theater, the troupe included a stunning Abakuá ritual. Watching Bárbaro Ramos and the other dancers portray the hooded *diablitos,* ancestral spirits, I was reminded of Día de Reyes, Day of the Kings, when the same rituals, performed on the streets of Havana or Matanzas, might result in an unpredictable act of compassion like the freeing of a slave.

One day, the drummers in Los Muñequitos went to Leimert Park, a black community near USC noted for its progressive art scene, and jammed with some of L.A.'s leading young hip-hop artists. The fusion of *rumba,* Cuba's protoplasmic street funk, and the homegrown words and beats of local DJs and break dancers inspired spectacular bursts of rhythm and rhyme. With each foray into the black and Latin American ghettos and enclaves of Los Angeles, Los Muñequitos couldn't help seeing their own destiny but for a twist of fate.

"Here in the United States, the youth are forsaken," Jesús Alfonso told me a few days later, when I caught up with him for breakfast. "There are no elders, no initiations. The people don't know who they are."

"There are initiations, but mostly into gangs," I said. "Few are thinking of the generations to come and the fear we're passing on to them."

"So what do we do?" A sadness fell across Alfonso's face. I could see he desperately wanted an answer to that burning question.

"Elders need to come forward with their knowledge. And the youth here need initiations. Maybe not Abakuá or Santería, exactly, but something with that power, something arising out of our imagination. It would be great to see you and your group working in the poorest barrios in ghettos in Los Angeles or New York, teaching drumming and dance, exposing kids to Afro-Cuban ritual."

"We have to rescue knowledge that's been lost. When are you coming to Matanzas?"

"Soon, I hope."

"We can talk more about this," Alfonso said, giving me a warm embrace.

But a few days later the terror attacks changed everyone's plans. Los Muñequitos were set to perform on TV at the Latin Grammys *on* September 11. But of course that never materialized. With the world turned upside-down, many of the group's members returned to Cuba early. A month later, I caught up with Jorge Rodríguez.

"What did you think of the Muñequitos' residency?" I asked.

"Well, I did some calculations. I figured that over the seven weeks they were here, Los Muñequitos reached over 20,000 people," he said. "Cuba has so much to give to America. Blacks in this country don't have a direct link to the ancestors. But the blacks in Cuba have that connection. The British took away the drums from the slaves here. But in Cuba the slaves kept the drums and the dances. And those rhythms continue to revolutionize our music."

Whenever I returned from Cuba, I always had to readjust my psyche. The moment I stepped off the plane I felt the rhythms change. In Cuba, children would dance to two coins clicking. In Los Angeles, I taught the children of poor Mexican immigrants who, by age eight, were ashamed of anything resembling dance. But when I returned to the United States on New Year's Eve, 2001, I wasn't prepared for the sadness that seemed to drive what passed for life.

I returned to a country trying desperately to forget what had happened on September 11, trying to return to normal, as if normal were anything other than a state of anxiety. Every month or so, a Cuban band would come through town and I would go, hoping to find a connection back to the musical freedom I had experienced in Santiago, Matanzas, and Havana, but invariably I came away alienated.

One night I ended up at El Floridita, one of L.A.'s "hot" clubs. A Cuban-style band, led by Johnny Polanco, was playing straight-ahead salsa. A suave dance teacher was showing off, doing dips and spins and other stylized moves of salsa. No one was actually dancing in time to clave. Instead, the people looked like robots who'd been programmed for Latin-style disco. Out of some masochistic streak, I asked a woman to dance. But when our hands met, her body stiffened. Like people in Cuba, I danced on the two, hooked into clave. But my partner shook her head. She took, she told me, lessons from a different teacher, so dancing together would be "impossible."

The next night, at a gallery opening of Cuban artists, I ran into Alina Mesa, a thirty-year-old dancer from Havana. She danced a *rumba* with a fellow Cuban, Pedro "Muñeco" Aguilar.

"I have the same pleasure from dancing that I have when making love," Mesa said, when I asked her how she felt. "So why should I lie. Dancing is like an orgasm that satisfies my whole body."

We arranged to talk about music and dance and I drove out to Fontana a few days later, past tawdry houses and gang graffiti, where Mesa lived with her mother. She's thin and has a ballerina's taut, muscled body. Her thick black hair hung around her neck like strands of rope.

"I grew up in Havana," Alina said. "My mother was a dancer, too, and she performed with the great Cuban singer-composer Carlos Embale. And she would take me as a small child to see her uncles and aunts, who all danced in the Conjunto Folklórico Nacional de Cuba.

She took ballet classes and her path seemed predestined when she was accepted to the prestigious Gran Teatro de la Habana García Lorca, a feeder school to Cuba's elite classical dance world. But Mesa was different. Whereas her classmates all had light skin, Mesa was the lone dark-skinned descendant of Yoruba slaves.

"When I was studying ballet, the parents and the children would give me weird looks. The parents would say things like, 'What is this black girl doing here?' This was the 1970s, but racism was still a reality. So I made a vow to be better than all of them."

While the other kids were out playing in the streets, Mesa practiced relentlessly, forcing her body into the stiff, formal positions required of the exacting European art form. She learned to dance on pointed toes and execute perfect pliés. And always she held her body rigid.

Then one day, about four years into her ballet studies, Alicia Alonso, the first ballerina of the National Ballet of Cuba and one of the country's most famous dancers, paid the school a visit. A mix of excitement and anxiety descended on everyone.

"Our teacher told us to be in the first position. She told us to stand as rigid as an iron bar. Then Alonso came into class and started sizing us up. She adjusted our bodies, crying, 'Stiffer!' And when she came to me she whacked my butt, pushing it in. And I hated that. It hit me that everything about ballet was rigid. I realized that the folkloric dances of Cuba were so much more beautiful than ballet. Dancing with my family or at *toques* I felt loose and free."

Around her neck she wears a gold chain pendant depicting Ochosi, the *orisha* overseeing the hunt and justice. And encircling one wrist is a bracelet of green and yellow beads that signify Orunla, the holy diviner and patron of all *babalawos,* the high priests of Santería.

"Orunla is the one who gives the final word on which *orisha* is your guardian."

"And mine is Obatalá."

Mesa soon quit the ballet school. At age eleven she enrolled in the training academy for the Conjunto Folklórico Nacional. Two years later, she became part of Cabildo de la Habana, where she had opportunities to perform regularly. When she was sixteen, Mesa went to live in Varadero, the gorgeous beach resort town east of Havana. She taught dance lessons at one of Varadero's big international hotels. And it was here that she met a wealthy young Spanish businessman.

"He owned a construction company and kept badgering me to marry him. And finally my resistance wore down."

A coldness came into her voice. The man she would soon marry had a huge apartment and four servants; she wanted for no luxury. But as soon as she landed a job in television her new husband became insanely jealous.

"Whenever people would call he would grill them with questions like, 'How do you know her? Why are you calling her?' And I began to hate him. Then one day, he fired the servants and told me that from now on I was cooking and cleaning. I told him, 'I'm black but I'm not your slave.' He tried to hit me and that was the beginning of many terrible fights until I called the police and left."

These were her darkest days, living alone in a strange country, far away from her family and caught up in an abusive marriage that ultimately ended in a divorce. Luckily, Mesa had a job on a TV show called *Entre Amigos.* But the stress had taken its toll. She chain-smoked cigarettes and put on twenty-two pounds. The show's producer approached her one afternoon.

" 'You're too fat,' " the producer told me. "And they started recording my weight every day so that I was humiliated."

A friend who lived in Andalucía invited Mesa to stay on a nearby island.

"I jumped at the chance," she said, smiling at the memory. "I was so depressed, so humiliated. But I started exercising every day, until the pounds melted off." Like all Cubans, she regularly sent money home to her mother. But one day in 1994, she got a call from her mother saying she needed a few hundred dollars more.

"I asked my mother why she needed more. But she said, 'Don't ask.' That was weird, so I called a few days later. But no one answered. A neighbor said no one was living there."

While Mesa was living in Spain, life had become a horror in Cuba. At the age of forty-six, her mother, Sonia González, had reached the end of her tether. Secretly, González launched out on a raft with, among others, her husband, Diogenes Quintan and Alina's older sister, Lidia Belkis.

"I found out later, when I got a call from the United States. When I think of what they risked to come here. The food got wet and the oars they had snapped. No one knew how to read the compass they brought. For four days they floated at sea, until a rescue boat miraculously picked them up."

She and her mother are close, and Mesa still dances. She appeared in the film *Dance With Me*. But her career has languished. She wants to go back to Cuba, but not until it's free. She takes me into her bedroom and shows me its altars to Oya, the *orisha* of storms and cemeteries, and Obatalá.

"My mother is a *santera*, a priestess of the Santería religion. I practice but I'm not a fanatic. I go to celebrations when I'm invited because I adore the saints and believe in them. I am a daughter of Obatalá, the father of the *orishas* and the creator of mankind. He asks that I remember that he's there and never forget that he's part of my life."

On a windblown Saturday night in April I showed up for the first of four Afro-Cuban concerts at San Francisco's SomArts Cultural Center. There I saw a performance that took in everything from Spanish *jota* music and Andalusian *punto guajiro* to *rumba* and *songo*. Some twenty-seven musicians and dancers, six of them specially flown in from Havana, were on hand. They played *punto fijo* and *punto libre* from the Cuban countryside and sang *trovas*, *boleros*, *sones*, and *guarachas*. Cuban and non-Cuban percussionists, including a talented Jewish drummer, Michael Spiro, anchored a rhythm section that created everything from Abakuá to *rumba*. Along the way, an orchestra played marvelous *danzones* as couples danced to riffing violins and flutes.

The concert, called *Roots to Timba*, was the ambitious brainchild of Roberto Borrell, the fifty-four-year-old artistic director of Orquesta la Moderna Tradición, a San Francisco–based *danzón* band that had received grant money to stage it. Its goal was to span 150 years of musical history, and to some extent it succeeded. A carnival *comparsa* snaked through the audience at the end, and the three-hour performance did give a sense of the history of the music that I'd never seen before, in or out of Cuba. But that said, the performance had many glitches—the dance of the *nanigo* from Abakuá folklore was weak, and more than a few of the collaborations between the Cuban artists and the homegrown musicians seemed stiff or ragged. But there was a reason for that.

"The American government didn't approve the visas for the musicians until Friday—a week before the concerts. And the musicians didn't come until the day *before* yesterday—*two* days before the shows," an exhausted Borrell told me after the concert. "So there was no time for rehearsal. I was completely out of my *mind*. Alexander Borrell, my cousin, isn't even here, and he was supposed to perform the *nanigo* dance from the Abakuá. I almost canceled the show. And what's worse, it turned out to cost three times as much as we had budgeted."

"Even so," I said, "everyone gave their best. Can we talk tomorrow?"

"Yes. After twelve, please. I have to get some sleep," Borrell said, and he wrote down his Oakland address.

When I'd gone to college in the Bay Area in the 1970s, and even into the 1980s, there was no real Cuban presence. When the Cubans did come, they had to plant the seeds of a musical community.

"When we started playing here in the Bay Area, nobody understood Cuban music," the Cuban guitarist, *sonero*, and bandleader Fito Reinoso, who had come in the early 1980s, told me when I stopped off to see him. "The people didn't know how to dance. They didn't know clave and they didn't comprehend the rhythms. There were not that many Cubans living here, and our music wasn't popular. I remember shows where people would call out for ranchera music. And if we played *rumba*, well, they would stand like statues."

But gradually the Cuban musicians kept coming, their numbers swelled by the Mariel Boatlift. They formed *timba* bands and folkloric groups; they taught *batá* and *tres*. Eventually a *rumba* took hold on alternate Sundays at La Peña, a Berkeley cultural center, where master percussionists like Jesús Díaz would perform. La Peña regularly brought in Afro-Cuban groups. But just as important, various cultural organizations sprang up to create opportunities for American musicians to study in Cuba and for Cuban musicians to teach in America. In Oakland, a nonprofit organization called Plaza Cuba became one of the country's leading groups to sponsor music and dance programs in Cuba. And Global Exchange, also based in the Bay Area, organized trips to Cuba.

"The Bay Area doesn't have the large numbers of Cuban musicians that New York has, but we have a strong community of people who are dedicated to learning about each other's cultures," Ariana Hall told me one afternoon. Hall lives part of the year in the Bay Area and works with Cubanola Collective, a New Orleans–based nonprofit group whose mission is to explore the relationship between Cuba and New Orleans.

"We're bringing the Rebirth Brass Band down for carnival in Santiago in July, and that's really exciting. The goal is to exchange carnival traditions and rituals with *comparsas* and congas in Santiago. A filmmaker is doing a documentary on the whole project. Have you heard of Rebirth?"

"I marched in a second-line parade right behind them ten years ago in New Orleans," I said. "And I'll be in Santiago for carnival, too."

"Well, you're going to have to come and dance with us," Hall said.

When I knocked on the door of Roberto Borrell's apartment, the door was answered by a stick-thin, middle-aged Cuban woman, one of the dancers from the night before. Her name was Marta Mesa.

"Roberto is not here. He went to pick someone up at the airport," Mesa said. "But sit down. He's expecting you."

Borrell returned ten minutes later, looking harried.

"Ah, you're here," he said. "I'm sorry. I've been running around like crazy making sure the Cuban musicians are taken care of. You met Marta?"

"Yes."

"Well, she was my second wife in Cuba."

Borrell is tall and lean and has a bushy head of salt-and-pepper hair. Even when he smiles, a gold tooth glinting, his eyes seem remote. Like a lot of Cubans, he came across the waters in 1980, at age thirty-two, the year of the great Mariel exodus. But the story he tells, of betrayals and anger, of what he had to leave behind, is uniquely his. In the neighborhood where Borrell grew up, Jesús María, there was a famous *comparsa* called Las Jardineras. When he was five years old, Borrell saw them play in front of his house, an explosion of rhythm that made him want to dance.

"There were maybe a hundred musicians and dancers," Borrell remembered. "But my grandmother wouldn't let me dance. And I had to stand still like a soldier. I never forgot this. It was like being hit with a blow. I didn't even know then that I wanted to be a musician and dancer.

But I loved music. I listened to *son* and *rumba*. I heard Félix Chapotín and Arsenio Rodríguez. I listened to Los Muñequitos. I was hungry for music."

Borrell's father had just the opposite view. He didn't want his son to be a musician and even prohibited him from watching *rumba*.

"My parents didn't want their son to be a musician because the whites discriminated against us. Cuba's whites believed all blacks were good for was playing drums and drinking rum," Borrell told me. "But when I was eleven, a social club was built in my neighborhood. There was no money to hire a band so they played albums. And because of that my parents let me go. There, I could dance *danzón, cha-cha-cha, son montuno, guaracha*. Every Saturday I danced, and when I danced, life was wonderful." Borrell went to other social clubs when he was thirteen and fourteen, and there they had great bands. He saw Chapotín when his band had Miguelito Cuní and Lilí Martínez, who was the greatest *son* pianist in Cuba. He saw Orquesta Sublime and Orquesta Sensación, with Abelardo Barroso singing. And during carnival one year he saw Benny Moré and Orquesta Aragón.

When he was fifteen, Borrell was studying accounting, a career his father approved of. But as carnival approached, his feet grew itchy. Borrell knew he had to dance, even if he went against his parents' ultimatum. So he went to a rehearsal for Alimentacion, a food worker's *comparsa* that marched during carnival.

"I hated accounting. But when I rehearsed with Alimentacion's *comparsa* and we moved out on the streets and I was dancing, I felt like I was flying on top of the world. It was paradise. But someone from my neighborhood saw me and told my father. And when my father found out, he got so mad he threatened to throw me out of the house. I remember he said, 'I can't believe you're studying accounting and dancing that shit.' He considered all the folkloric music to be garbage because that was the propaganda he listened to from high society. He said I had to make a choice. But I said I wasn't going to give up dancing. I danced during carnival that year, and though I didn't know it at the time, my father was there watching."

When he was eighteen, Borrell auditioned for Conjunto Folklórico Nacional. The audition was difficult.

"They would show me a complex dance and I would have to execute it. It might be a Congolese dance or a *rumba*. And I had to know how to dance *son, danzón,* and cha-cha. Luckily I was accepted and I performed with the *conjunto* for three years. But when it got political, as everything was in Cuba, I left." Borrell didn't know what he wanted to do. He was totally lost. But one day, he happened to meet a trumpeter who asked him if he wanted to perform in a circus. Soon he was wandering across Cuba for six months, playing music for a circus."

On and off for ten years, beginning in 1970, Borrell taught dance at various cultural centers. Music and dance were his abiding passion, but he saw no future for himself.

"I was apolitical and wanted nothing to do with the revolution. I saw that the revolution was destroying the culture of Cuba. From 1968 to 1974, the regime banned the *batá* and Abakuá. You couldn't play *rumba* in your own house. For that you could go to jail."

When Borrell quit a construction job and took a low-paying position as a professional dancer, he experienced the repression firsthand. Because he quit, Borrell was called to court and given a trial.

"They sentenced me to jail for eight months, but my father appealed the decision and I only spent twenty-four days behind bars," Borrell said. His eyes darkened and his face hardened.

"I didn't want my father to interfere. I wanted to spend those eight months and come out a monster. Because I was full of rage and hate. That's what Cuba had done to me."

The hatred and rage he felt for his homeland only deepened when Borrell turned down an offer to perform at an important political function and faced reprisals.

"I was making money at the beaches, where I was performing for tourists. That's how I was keeping myself from starving. And I would lose that precious money if I played for the politicians. Well, the party officials didn't like my decision. And afterward, they banned me from being a choreographer."

One day, in the spring of 1980, Borrell heard rumors about an opportunity to leave Cuba. News of the boatlift spread like wildfire through Cuba. The only requirement was that you had to be a delinquent. Borrell had a daughter, Marlene, with a woman he'd since broken up with. He knew if he left he might never see her again. But he never thought twice about fleeing.

"I had a criminal record," Borrell said. "So I showed my letter of liberty from when I was in jail for twenty-four days. Two days later, I was on a boat leaving Cuba." At Fort Chaffey in Arkansas, Borrell formed a group called Kubatá that played folkloric music. An aunt in Maryland agreed to sponsor him and introduced her nephew to Luis Salomé, who had a septet called Estrellas de Son. The group's first show happened to be at the Library of Congress.

"I convinced Luis during the break to let me present Kubatá, my *rumba* group. And Dan Sheehy, then a director at the department of folklore at NEA, happened to hear us," Borrell says. "Well, that led to our getting a grant."

Kubatá played in Washington and all over the East Coast. But seeking out a bigger constituency of Cubans, Borrell moved to New York, where he stayed for ten years. There, he played with all kinds of Afro-Cuban groups, including Machito's band. He traveled to Brazil and performed with Latin superstars like Celia Cruz and Sonora Matancera at Carnegie Hall. Then in 1991, a friend sent Borrell a ticket to visit San Francisco.

"The moment I arrived, I knew I didn't want to leave. And when my flight back came up, I didn't get on the plane."

Borrell taught dance and percussion. And though there wasn't a large Cuban community, word of his abilities spread. He played with an early Bay Area Cuban band called Conjunto Céspedes and a group led by Fito Reinoso. There, Borrell met up with Tregar Otton, a violinist and arranger with the Berkeley Symphony Orchestra. Otton set about convincing Borrell that they should found a *danzón* band, but making that happen was anything but simple.

"I had to work with Tregar for five years—*five* years—before we got the clave right. You see, Cuban music has to be accented just right or the rhythms don't work. But Tregar listened to many, many *danzones* and eventually he mastered the style so that he could arrange the music.

"Many white people in Cuba love the *danzón* and think it's purely European and has no roots from Africa. But the truth is, the *danzón* is Afro-Cuban. The percussion is black. And the *paillas*—the early *timbales*—and the *güiro*, the notched scraper, are instruments Africans pioneered."

In fact, the roots of *danzón* were deeply embedded in the history of slavery and revolution. After blacks revolted in Haiti, slaves and French colonists fled to Cuba where the latter established their plantations and highbrow culture. They brought the *contradanza*, a European-based popular dance music that eventually evolved into *danza*, out of which the *danzón* was born. You can hear the French-black influence in Failde's *danzones*, where the *cinquillo* rhythm gives its distinctive sound.

"The original *danzón* was created in 1879 by Miguel Failde. Miguel Failde was black and so was his orchestra," says Borrell. "If you listen to the *danzón*, you see it begins with a four-bar introduction and *paseo*, which are repeated and followed by another melody. The dancers do not dance during these sections; they choose partners, stroll onto the dance floor, and begin to dance at precisely the same moment—the fourth beat of the *paseo*, which has a distinctive percussion pattern. When the introduction is repeated, the dancers stop, flirt, greet their friends, and start again, right on time as the *paseo* finishes."

By the 1920s, *danzón* gave way in popularity to *son*, which, according to the musicologist Alejo Carpentier, became the preeminent expression of Afro-Cuban culture. But the beauty of the music is timeless.

"The *danzón* we play is true to the spirit of the 1950s, the last period of innovation," says Borrell. "We're not out to violate the integrity of the genre. Everyone loves this music. Old people and young people come to our concerts. Once a month, on a Sunday, we play *danzón* at a party. And the children love to dance. I want people to understand that Cuba's music is much more than the Buena Vista Social Club and goes much deeper than Van Van and Bamboleo."

Borrell was in Cuba the previous November for the sole purpose of making the arrangements for *Roots to Timba,* and he was astonished at how the country had deteriorated.

"I was in a state of shock. The people have nothing. Like all Cubans, I send my parents money. But I tell them the truth about America. The music is strong within me. When I came to the United States the only thing I knew how to do was play and dance the music I grew up with and drive. For me, music is food, medicine, and life, whereas this culture is all about materialism. My daughter wants to come here now, but I warn her that community does not exist here, that she will lose things by coming here. To feel yourself, you have to look inside; if you open your heart it comes out. But people in the United States have to look outside to feel themselves. Do you have a copy of our CD?"

"No," I said.

Borrell excused himself and came back with a copy of *Goza Conmigo.* My eyes happened to fall on an old recording of Los Muñequitos that was sitting out on a table. I had recently spent a few hours with Jesús Alfonso, the group's legendary percussionist, and mentioned it.

"Ah, Jesús is a close friend of mine," Borrell said. "But I only came to know him because Marta, my second wife, is the daughter of Juan Mesa, the founder of Los Muñequitos. And there's a story I have to tell you now. When Juan Mesa died in 1976, as you can imagine, there was an extraordinary funeral for him in Matanzas. Juan was the greatest folkloric singer Cuba ever had. When he sang *rumba,* you would cry to hear him; when he sang to the *orishas,* he would take possession of your soul. Well, at his funeral, the *nanigos* came first and did a ritual to honor him because he was an initiate of the Abakuá. Then, Los Muñequitos played for him. And after that, the *bataleros* played for him, because Juan was a *santero*. But as the *bataleros* played, a woman was possessed by Oyá. She moved so violently that she fell headfirst against the coffin's glass window. Her face smashed into the glass and pieces of glass and blood spurted all over. Of course, no one was expecting this."

I looked at Marta Mesa, who had been listening silently to our interview, and saw her shake her head. Tears began to form in her eyes, and Borrell put his arm around her.

"When Marta saw this, she knew she had to see her father one more time. But when she looked into the coffin and saw the blood and the glass on her father's face, she became so wild that she lost control. Four men couldn't hold her, until I finally stepped in and calmed her down. One of the men asked me who I was, and when I told him that I was her husband, he understood. Well, in 1992, when the Muñequitos were on their first American tour, I spent some time with them. And Jesús Alfonso and I got to talking about Juan Mesa's funeral. And when I told him about my memory of the woman crashing into the coffin, Jesús looked at me. You see, he was the one who had grabbed hold of me at the funeral. I didn't remember him. But Jesús remembered me."

Omar Sosa spends most of the year in Barcelona and the rest of the time in the Bay Area, where his producer, Scott Price, lives. But even though I'd seen the thirty-three-year-old Cuban pianist in Havana at two Santería celebrations in his honor, I scarcely got to talk to him. Now that we were in the same city, I made it a point to see him.

Sosa had made seven CDs since moving to San Francisco in 1995 and had forged a reputation as one of the brightest figures in Afro-Cuban music. His roots were in jazz—Thelonious Monk was his most obvious influence—but his vision extended to Brazil and Ecuador and took in hip-hop, funk, and other world music. The latest incarnation of the band merged Afro-Cuban jazz, *orisha* incantations, and funk with rap, *montunos,* and the music of North Africa. *Sentir,* his newest recording, was nourished with the rhythmic richness of Morocco and full of Islamic melodies and singing that made overt what was always present in Cuban music. When I went to see the band that night, the CD was just a point of departure for a deeper exploration of a mystic triangle between Cuba, the Americas, and Morocco. The *montunos,* pared back to evince their raw power, gave way to short, jabbing explosions of jazz that reminded me of Herbie Hancock and Wayne Shorter. A Venezuelan percussionist, Gustavo Ovalles, pounded out sheets of rhythm on *batá* and congas. The Moroccan vocalist and *guembri* virtuoso, El Houssaine Kili, made the connection between Cuba and Morocco explicit.

"My music has always been going along the path of spirit. I call on the ancestral spirits, the *egun,* and ask them to come when I play," Sosa said after the show. "I feel Afro-Cuban music is a great eruption of spirit from Africa. It feeds my soul. But in Brazil I explored *orixá* music, because it's the sister of our Yoruba music. And in Morocco I was drawn to the *gnawa* music, which is all about spirit-possession. The *gnawa* musicians are descendants of slaves who were held in captivity in Africa, so that spirit of freedom is in their music.

"Jazz *is* freedom. The first time I heard Thelonious Monk was when a German musician I knew played him for me. Then I saw this documentary on Monk and I started to cry. I saw the beauty and the soul of his music. I saw the deep history of jazz. Monk taught me about what it is to be free. The most important things in this world are freedom and peace. Without freedom, we're slaves, and without peace, we kill each other," he concluded.

Since I'd last seen him, Sosa had toured all over the United States. Soon, he would move on to France, Germany, Austria, Turkey, and

Reunion Island. His band—bassist Geoff Brennan, drummers Elliot Kavee and Ovalles, saxophonist Eric Crystal, vocalist Martha Galarraga, rapper Sub-Z, and the Moroccan singer-instrumentalist El Houssaine Kili—was playing jazz festivals all over the world. With the help of a Rockefeller grant, Sosa had written a three-movement orchestral work that would be performed with the Oakland Symphony in 2003.

"The symphony is based on the musical traditions of Cuba, Brazil, Morocco, Ecuador, Venezuela, and Colombia," Sosa said.

I remembered that I had some photos to give him from the time we spent together in Havana. But when Sosa flipped to a shot of him and his wife, the Ecuadorian artist Shirma Guayasamin, I only had to take one look at his eyes—which suddenly went dead—to know that something terrible had happened.

"My marriage fell apart in Cuba," Sosa said, handing me back the photo. For a moment I thought he would cry, but instead he looked away, broken and lonely. "I'm not feeling so great. We were married ten years and I think I will love her all my life. But she wasn't part of the religion, and that came between us. That was one of the revelations of the *orishas* I received in Cuba. Because a husband and wife are supposed to be in this together."

"Most people, even the critics, believe that there were no significant Cuban percussionists in New York before Chano Pozo arrived. But that's not true," Cuban *timbales* master Orestes Vilato told me.

"Before Chano came, Cuban musicians were in New York jamming with great American jazz musicians," said Walfredo de los Reyes, the acclaimed Cuban percussionist. "Armando Orefiche's band came through. And during the early 1940s, Ernesto Lecuona's Cuban Boys traveled the world. You would call them a big band. They went to New York and Europe, and when they got to New York, they would go crazy

Long John Oliva in Los Angeles.

looking for jazz clubs and late-night jam sessions. I know this because they would come to our house. My dad was a musician in Cuba, and when we moved to New York in 1940, we lived on Forty-ninth Street in Hell's Kitchen and all the great Cuban musicians would come by our place."

"Guillermo Álvarez was in New York then," said Vilato.

"Guillermo Álvarez was a terrific Cuban drummer who," said Reyes, "was in New York in those days. Unfortunately, he killed himself in Miami. But Diego 'Morfeta' Iborra played *bongó* and *tumbadora*. He played with Charlie Barnet and Artie Shaw. This is the mid-1940s, before Chano Pozo arrives. And already Cuban musicians are jamming. They're jamming with Miles Davis, Dizzy Gillespie, Charlie Parker, and Bud Powell. So there was a great dialogue between the two countries."

It was a gorgeous, sunny day in Walnut Creek, and Reyes's studio was jammed with every conceivable Afro-Latin percussion instrument: *timbales,* congas, trap sets, *cajones, bongó,* cowbells, and *chekeres.* In a lifetime of music, Reyes, now sixty-eight, has played *descargas* with Cachao and held down the rhythm section for the likes of Frank Sinatra and Wayne Newton. He can swing a whole orchestra or power an avant-garde jazz quartet. I glanced at old black-and-white photos of him down through the decades, in Cuba and in New York, and Reyes gave me captions and contexts for each shot.

Reyes and Vilato could not be more physically different. Whereas Vilato is pudgy, moon-faced, and short, Reyes is tall, lean, and angular. Vilato is openly bitter about being neglected by Latin jazz historians, while Reyes has an optimistic outlook on life and is confident of his place in the Afro-Cuban firmament. But there's a musical bond between them: Both left Cuba at an early age, have played and recorded together, and both helped shape the history of Latin jazz and Afro-Cuban music in their adopted country.

Vilato lived in New York for twenty-five years and was renowned as one of the great stylists on *timbales.* He played with everyone from

Johnny Pacheco and Rubén Blades to Celia Cruz and the Fania All-Stars. You can hear his *timbales* on 300 recordings, but for all his brilliance, he cannot get enough work.

"I came to New York as a twelve-year-old," said Vilato, "and I saw these drummers with incredible technique. And I said to myself, 'I can't imitate them.' So I tried to create my own style. And the foundation of my style was *rumba*. But I added other sounds, too, rhythms that I heard on the tabla."

"Orestes was one of the players who kept the Cuban sensibility alive," said Reyes. "He didn't get into jazzy, flashy styles of playing. He had a clean, crisp sound and a perfectly tuned instrument. He knew when and where to play the right notes."

From 1980 to 1989, Vilato helped power the rhythm section of Carlos Santana's band. And along the way, he played or recorded with a who's who of pop and jazz stars, everyone from Herbie Hancock and McCoy Tyner to Wynton Marsalis and Linda Ronstadt.

"I can play in any style," said Vilato. "But it always retains the flavor of Cuba." Reyes arrived in New York as a child in 1940. His father, Walfredo de los Reyes II, was a trumpeter and singer in Casino de la Playa, a band that, in the 1930s, boasted the great singer Miguelito Valdés. But when Walfredo's father got a contract to play at the Sans Souci nightclub, the whole family decided to move back to Cuba.

"In the 1950s, the great Cuban drummer Guillermo Barreto and I were playing set drums bebop style in Cuba. We had a *bongó* and conga and a big band. We played jazz tunes," said Reyes. "Because while American jazz bands were incorporating the conga drums into jazz and bebop, things were changing in Cuba, too. When bebop hit Cuba, bands led by Armando Romeo, Jr., and Bebo Valdés were mixing the drum set with Cuban folkloric instruments and forging their own sound."

"See, there's a secret history to the evolution of Afro-Cuban rhythms in American and Cuban music that nobody knows about," said Vilato.

"And we know it because we helped create it. The Cubans were not teaching *timbales* in 1979, and the tradition was in danger of dying out. Changuito told me that when I met him then. But the Cuban musicians in New York helped bring it back. Walfredo was born in Cuba, came here as a child, and then went back to Cuba to teach the musicians there"

"The great Cuban trap drummers in Cuba were listening to me and Guillermo Barreto and Danny Pérez," said Reyes. "I know this may sound like bragging, but it's not meant to be. We were *pioneers* of rhythm. So, for instance, Changuito used to watch me all the time. And in Cuba, when I was on vacation with my family, I would go check out Candito Segarra at CMQ Studios and be blown away with how he played multiple percussion instruments at the same time. Later, I integrated the drum set, the *timbales,* the congas, and the *bongó* and played them all at once.

"Man, I could tell you stories. My band was playing at the Hotel Nacional in 1954. We were hired by Meyer and Jake Lansky. They paid us very well. I would eat filet mignon with Jake and know he was the Mob. But after the revolution, the Castro regime was throwing musicians in jail. You had to have a permit from the government to have a set of *batá* drums or hold any religious ritual. And American music—forget it. They put the great young Cuban drummer Horacio "El Negro" Hernández in jail for playing rock and roll."

"Meanwhile, in the United States, the music was undergoing huge changes, especially with rhythms," Vilato said.

"Where did the *timbales* come from?" I asked.

"They were derived from the timpani and became popular about a hundred years ago in Cuba. They were mainly used in *charanga* and *danzón* bands," said Vilato. "But you could hear them in the early *son* groups that played in rural areas outside of Havana. They represent African-based rhythmic concepts blended with the tradition of symphonic music. Plus there's elements that came from other countries besides Cuba, like Puerto Rico.

"In 1924, Sonora Matancera created a style of playing *timbales* like the *bongó*. Sonora Matancera used to travel all over the world. But the people in Cuba don't know that. It was Sonora Matancera that added two trumpets into *son*. And they traveled to Mexico and that's where the trumpets entered mariachi. The small *timbales* were called *timbalitos* and were played with small mallets. Most of the playing was on the head, which you could tune to the tonic and the dominant. In New York City, where I'd been since 1956, most of the bands had a set drummer with a *timbale* added. That's where the technique of the *timbales* was started. And it came from trap drummers like Walfredo, Umberto Morales, and Monchito Muñoz."

"That's because I was one of the Cuban musicians in New York in the early 1950s who was playing trap drums and *timbales*," said Reyes.

"And we have to give credit to the Puerto Rican musicians. If Cuba is a bird, then one wing was Cuba and the other was Puerto Rico, whose musicians kept the music alive in this country," said Vilato.

"There's so much to tell you, you would have to spend weeks with us," Reyes said. "When Cole Porter wanted to write a *bolero,* he went to Cuba. That was the inspiration for *Begin the Beguine*. And when Leonard Bernstein composed the music for *West Side Story,* he also went to Cuba. Rock and roll got its early riffs from Cuban *rumba*."

"And all the rhythms of funk came from the *batá*," said Vilato. "Listen." Vilato pulled two conga drums toward him and tapped out one of the basic *batá* rhythms. What I heard was the root rhythm of 1970s funk, of James Brown and a thousand hip-hop bands.

"That's the root of funk right there," Vilato said.

"I love bebop. But bebop died because no one could dance to it," Reyes cut in. "So they went looking for a rhythm to replace it. And that's where rock and roll came in. Here. Listen."

Reyes picked up his drumsticks and played the basic, syncopated Afro rhythm from Cuba, then followed it with rock and roll's foundation groove.

"You hear the similarity between the Afro-Cuban groove and rock?

Now, most American jazz musicians couldn't play Afro-Cuban rhythms. They couldn't play in 2/4, which is what most Afro-Cuban music is written in. And they couldn't pick up on the bass."

"So they changed it to 4/4 time," said Vilato, "so Americans could dance to it."

"And the person most responsible for that was Pérez Prado," Reyes says, referring to the Matanzas-born bandleader who simplified Cuban mambo recordings and gained pop chart success.

It was getting late and Vilato had to leave. His face seemed sad, his eyes rueful.

"Do you get much work with Latin bands here?" I asked. And as soon as the question came out I could see it touched a raw nerve.

"The Bay Area has a reputation of being a brotherhood," said Vilato. "But that's all bullshit. I don't get telephone calls. Cuban drummers come over and call up musicians I've played with and offer to undercut me. They'll play for next to nothing, just to steal a job. I perform in Colombia and Panama. But when I come back here, I'm nobody. The Bay Area ignores the great Cuban musicians that are here. I recorded on three hundred albums. I played with Carlos Santana for almost a decade. But I don't know how I'm going to pay my rent this month."

When Vilato left, Reyes showed me some more photos from his heyday in Cuba and New York. But Vilato's bitter words weighed on his mind.

"Cuban musicians have to scuffle," Reyes said. "But Orestes's view is only his view. There is a community of Cuban musicians here, especially in Oakland."

I asked Reyes where he saw Afro-Cuban music going?

"It's going in amazing new directions, but *without* losing its Cuban heritage and feel. Take a group like Columna B, with Dafnis Prieto and Yosvany Terry."

"I'm going to see them in New York," I said.

"Well, you're in for a treat. That group is playing an abstract fusion of

Cuban funk and jazz. They're playing rhythms in multiple time signatures. Not everyone can play this; it's very difficult. The older musicians of Cuba sometimes criticize the younger musicians. But me, I love what the young ones are doing. Cuba has an inexhaustible supply of genius. You could spend a lifetime traveling in Cuba and you wouldn't find all the secrets of the music. And the music just keeps coming."

7. CARNIVAL IN SANTIAGO

In the weeks just before carnival, a kind of fevered delirium seizes the city of Santiago. Massive papier-mâché figures known as *muñecones* must be readied, masks made, costumes and capes created with feathers, rabbit skins, beads, and glass. Songs have to be rehearsed, dances perfected, complex choreography synchronized. For carnival, an explosion of rhythm, song, and spirit meant to lure every sentient being into its swirling vortex is a fierce competition as well as an unfolding of sensual dementia. I came to Santiago during a sweltering July to experience the city's historic bacchanalia. A few weeks earlier, Festival del Caribe, a weeklong orgy of music and dance that honors a different Caribbean region each year, served as a warm-up. By the time I arrived, on carnival's opening weekend, the air hummed with electricity as I walked through the streets of Sueño and Trocha, famous carnival neighborhoods, and then down Garzón, where the jury stands were set up for the spectacular processions that would pass by each night.

The heat was merciless, my shirt drenched minutes after I hit the streets. I walked to the headquarters of Conga de Los Hoyos, Santiago's legendary carnival group, where I found an unusual scene taking shape. Here, in a room drenched in carnival history, the Rebirth Brass Band, which had come all the way from New Orleans with a contingent of some fifty Americans, was preparing for its first of many performances in Santiago.

Rebirth's cofounders, Philip and Keith Frazier, were talking to a San Francisco–based film crew that had come to Santiago to make a documentary about the musical exchange between their band and Conga de Los Hoyos. Both groups were legends in their hometowns. Rebirth was one of New Orleans's seminal brass street bands that had reinvigorated a musical tradition more than a century old—a tradition that was one of the deep roots of jazz. And Conga de Los Hoyos, celebrating its hundredth anniversary, was the most famous of Santiago's six congas, winner for ten years running of carnival's first prize. Beholding this scene, I couldn't help smiling at the serendipity of it all. Twelve years ago, I had marched with Rebirth through the backstreets of New Orleans in a second-line parade that had first awakened me to the rich history of early jazz and black carnival. And now, thanks to Cubanola Collective, a nonprofit group dedicated to exploring the cultural connections between New Orleans and Cuba, Rebirth would share its artistry with a group that was, in many ways, its Spanish-speaking counterpart.

"We were supposed to do this last September, at Festival Benny Moré," Ariana Hall, Cubanola's director, said as Rebirth's musicians tuned up. "But that got canceled because of the terror attacks. We lost most of the grant money, but then amazingly, we were able to put this trip together. The idea is to exchange street performance traditions in New Orleans and Cuba. Street performance is about the interaction between musicians and the community, and the use of public space. And Conga de Los Hoyos and Rebirth both have a similar conception of public space and their unique role in their neighborhoods. They're both dedicated to building community."

By now the room, whose walls were adorned with old carnival banners and ancient photos, was jammed. Scores of Santiagans poked their heads in through the open windows to get a better look as Rebirth suddenly launched into some second-line funk, a performance carefully watched by the musicians in Conga de Los Hoyos. Félix Bandera, the wiry director of the group, listened to Rebirth's funky music with undisguised joy.

"To me, this is a once-in-a-lifetime wonder," Bandera said as Rebirth's horns riffed wildly. "The music they play is the real jazz, which was born long ago in New Orleans."

Knowing it was the hundred-year anniversary of Conga de Los Hoyos, I asked Bandera what his conga's theme would be this year. He raised his eyebrows and flashed a mischievous smile.

"That," he said, "is a secret. You will have to wait until Thursday, when we march in costume and perform in the streets and before the jury."

Soon it was the Cubans' turn to perform. Conga de Los Hoyos played a *rumba* first, then a medley of carnival songs on more than a dozen drums, including a majestic, melancholy "La Comparsa," a super-funky version of "Manisero," and a wild song called "A Gozar en el Platanal" about a whorehouse, all of it highlighted by the piercing solos of the *corneta china,* a horn that became synonymous with carnival in Santiago back in 1916. I noticed Philip Frazier shaking his head, grooving on the beat.

"Whoa, man, the people here are just like us," he told me. "They hang out in neighborhoods that remind me of New Orleans, of *our* 'hoods," Frazier said. "And the music is *deep.* It reminds me of the carnival music of the Mardi Gras Indians. But it's different because of the clave beat. So I'm trying to soak it up so we can find some common ground to jam later."

Moments later, after Conga de Los Hoyos finished up, Frazier took his tuba and, with the rest of Rebirth, headed outside. A small army of onlookers, including the New Orleans contingent, now fell in with Rebirth as it marched down Martí Avenue. With each passing block, more people swarmed around the group. Parents held tiny children on their shoulders and danced wildly. Young girls and boys shook as if with palsy to Rebirth songs like "Tornado" and "Always There." The red-hot music, a mix of jazz, funk, soul, and pop, triggered spontaneous songs from the Cubans, who had no trouble coming up with improvised lyrics. Then, thirty or so minutes later, it was over.

"What you have seen is nothing," a Cuban woman told me. "Wait until Conga de Los Hoyos take to the streets."

Since that would be in two days, I had time to wander through Santiago and take in the sights and smells of carnival. That night, I let myself get lost in Sueño, a middle-class neighborhood by Santiago standards. I passed endless kiosks with vendors hawking pork sandwiches carved from the greasy carcasses of whole pigs set out on rough wooden tables all up and down Céspedes Street. At the intersection of Calle K, I heard the wild squeals of children and beheld Santiago's version of Disneyland. For here the streets were filled with amusement park rides that defied the embargo: coasters and teacups and Ferris wheels and merry-go-rounds, all of them hand-soldered and ingeniously constructed from salvaged metal piping and old motors. The base of one ride was clearly constructed from the differential of an abandoned truck. The ride had carnival's wild colors and designs painted on it.

"Where did you get the motor?" I asked the operator, handsome and shirtless.

"We found it in a dump and repaired it," the man said, scratching his stomach and smiling. "If I had the resources I would make it more beautiful."

"My family designed this machine," another operator proudly said of his whirligig teacup ride that spun at a forty-five-degree tilt and was doing steady business at two pesos a pop.

There were cotton candy and paper cones of popcorn and *ayaca,* Cuba's equivalent of a tamale, for sale. I turned down another street and saw an astonishing carousel with carved horses that spun me back to my own childhood in Coney Island. At the corner of Céspedes and G Streets, a crowd congregated around a most unusual grouping of musicians. Out front, a tall, young black percussionist played *pailas*, a kind of *timbales*, a tom-tom, and a hi-hat, alongside another musician who played the *güiro*. But it was the boxy instrument behind them that caught my attention: an apparently ancient player organ that utilized a hand crank with notched paper rolls that fed through it. The sound of this trio was something altogether wondrous, like hurdy-gurdy mixed with *son* mixed with modern lounge music. Inside the circle was something just as strange: a trio of transvestites lost in their own magical dance. When the song ended I made my way behind the organ.

"Where did you find this instrument?" I asked the man behind it. "I didn't find it—I made it myself," said Roberto Ramos. "I grew up in Bayamo and my family built and repaired these organs. It's a family tradition handed down to me."

"There are only two real carnivals—the one here and the one in Bahia," Julian Mateo, a Santiago-based folklorist and former art history professor, said the following afternoon when I stopped by his house. "When I was a young boy, carnival in Santiago would last a month. Can you imagine that? And I would go to Guantánamo in August, right after ours ended, and experience their carnival."

"Enrique Bonne has a song called 'If I Didn't Have the Carnival, I Couldn't Live,' " the Santiagan artist Antonio Ferrer Cabello recalled when I came to his studio to talk about carnival. "And that's how I feel about it. I have danced in the streets. I have followed the conga lines and shaken my body to those rhythms.

"I've always been interested in the rituals of carnival. I've made *muñicones*, designed floats, and created masks. There have been many governments who've tried to repress carnival. But the people have always defended it. At the beginning of the revolution, carnival was strong, but later on it lost some of its power because civilian leaders, most of them from Havana, tried to impose their vision on it. Carnival here was unique, unlike in any other part of Cuba. It's always been a spontaneous eruption. It's part of the celebration of Santiago de Campostela. And since the majority of the people are black and mestizo, it was their music and rituals that colored everything. Even in my lifetime, the government depicted carnival as the creation of savages. In the mid-1920s, I remember clearly, the local government here established another carnival in February. And for two years they staged it—without congas and without *comparsas*—at a theater in Vista Alegre. That was an elite area, for the wealthy whites, and they paid to have their seats decorated. My father, who was also an artist, helped design the theater's decorations. But the carnival was not successful; it fizzled out. Because carnival comes from the streets, from the people."

In Europe and other parts of the world, including Brazil, carnival takes place in February, part of the pre-Lenten festivities that have roots that go back to pre-Christian times. But in various Caribbean countries carnival occurs in the summer. How Santiago's carnival came to be in July reveals the city's unique colonial history. For once upon a time, Santiago did have a winter carnival. Accounts tell of women dressed in linen gowns, their powdered faces dripping with disdain for anyone below their stature. The philharmonic societies held masked balls—but only for whites. But sometime in the eighteenth century an alternate celebration, known as *fiesta de mamarrachos,* evolved for the black slaves and freed people of color.

The word *mamarrachos,* which literally means "masquerading" figures, was itself disparaging when applied to black carnival, according to the sociologist Nancy Pérez, who wrote a groundbreaking book on the origins of carnival in Santiago. The word could be African or have come from a corruption of Momus, the name for the ancient Greek god of blame and ridicule. But whatever its origin, the celebration gained momentum with each passing year. Whereas winter carnival was celebrated indoors by a privileged class that danced dainty mazurkas, rigadoons, and minuets, *mamarrachos* took place in the open streets in the blazing heat of deep summer and unfolded to fantastic drumming and dancing.

"The blacks hardly wore any clothing and they put on masks and painted their faces," Pérez told me one afternoon when I came to visit her. "In the nineteenth century, the newspapers started calling the black celebration Carnavales de Verano. But eventually this carnival became a huge spectacle because Cuban Creoles liked the music, dancing, and percussion of the blacks. *Mamarrachos* had spirit and passion, whereas the white winter carnival was boring."

Pérez is thin and spindly, with a birdlike face, a sloping nose, and deep-set eyes. These days she lives on a minuscule pension in a sprawling, run-down high-rise development in El Salado, a twelve-minute drive east of Santiago. The walls of her apartment are painted graffiti style with snatches of poetry, and the rooms are jammed with books on Afro-Cuban history, literature, religion, and folklore.

"I once had thousands of books, but I had to sell them during the Special Period in the 1990s," she said apologetically, remembering the time when Russia pulled out of the Cuban economy and the country spun into economic chaos.

No one knows precisely when *fiesta de mamarrachos* began. But as early as 1795, the king of Spain was issuing edicts forbidding it because of the "moral and physical damage" it produced. And from this time on, its history is that of the Spanish authorities trying to suppress it. In 1815, Santiago records show, *mamarrachos* was forbidden because it encouraged race and class mixing and sexual lewdness. And in 1823, all masking and *mamarrachos* were outlawed due, according to newspaper reports, to "the escape of slaves into the mountains."

In 1869, in the first year of a ten-year-long insurrection against Spain that would lay the foundation for a national identity not based on racial divisions, the governor of Santiago prohibited *comparsas* from parading in the streets because of the potential to "foment revolution." Two years later, members of various black carnival *comparsas* were caught and jailed, according to city records.

The black *cabildos*, religious brotherhoods, and mutual aid societies formed by the Spanish Catholic Church are a foundation of carnival culture. From the very beginning, slaves participated in the *cabildos*. In the eighteenth century, the *cabildos* were actually seen as a tool for controlling racial unrest. By giving the slaves some social cohesion and encouraging them to believe in Christianity, slaveowners envisioned, like the ruthless capitalists they were, a better return on investment.

Of course, just the opposite occurred. The black *cabildos*, in fact, contained the seeds of Spain's undoing. By allowing slaves to reunite along tribal lines, to sing, dance, drum, and conduct ancestral rituals, the *cabildos* were the perfect incubators for nurturing resistance and promoting revolution. Though authorities tried to suppress carnival during the 1895 Cuban War for Independence, Santiago's black congas and *comparsas* served as covers for life-and-death political struggles. For it was the chaos and boisterous distractions the groups created during carnival that allowed *mambises*, or freedom fighters, to engage in their clandestine operations.

"Carnival musicians had to rehearse and move all around the city. And secretly they would remove the skins of their drums—the *requintos*, the *bocús*, and the *tumbas*—and put guns and machetes inside them," Pérez said. "In this way, they were able to take weapons from the city to the countryside. Of course, they were risking their lives."

Some of the fiercest freedom fighters who took on the Spaniards were ex-slaves who came from Baracoa—Cuba's oldest city—to live in the countryside and figured prominently in carnival. The Carabalí, who came from a region of Africa called Calabar, were especially known for their bravery, recalled in their carnival songs. But many *mambises* came from the barrio of Los Hoyos, including the black generals Antonio and José Maceo and Guillermo Moncada. Indeed Moncada, who rose from the rank of private to become a legendary leader in both of Cuba's wars for independence, had his own *comparsa* group, Los Negros de Limón.

As far as I knew, Los Negros de Limón no longer existed. But on an insufferably humid Tuesday night I decided that I would march with Carabalí Isuama and Conga de Los Hoyos. I showed up at Isuama's headquarters first and there witnessed a sight that reminded me of the pleasure clubs of New Orleans. Out on the streets, Isuama's king, queen, prince, and princess and other assorted royalty had gathered wearing their crowns and splendid dresses and suits. The queen—beautiful, silver-haired Angela Lubo—was seventy-eight and had had a thirty-year reign. But the king had recently died, so a temporary carnival king—Javier Sagarra, all of thirty-five—accompanied her on the carnival route. Many of Isuama's members are old, and their music—slow, stately conga rhythms set off by the pealing of the *campana,* a brake drum hit with an iron clapper—was powerful to hear.

Isuama's *cabildo* can trace its history back at least 200 years and is the repository of a tradition unparalleled in Santiago.

"Isuama has preserved the chants, songs, and dances of the original Carabalí slaves," Gladys María González, a researcher at Casa del Caribe, told me as we marched east on Carnicería. González, who goes by the name La India, has studied Isuama's traditions for years. She would never miss an opportunity to march with them during carnival or sing their praises to a foreign visitor.

"Isuama has a school in this neighborhood, too, that teaches all the rituals to the youth," she said. "It's the same way the slaves taught their children the songs, dances, and rituals. Slavery is the root of carnival. In all the congas and *comparsas,* you can hear the sorrow and anger and violence and sexuality in the songs. There's a carnival song lyric that goes: '*Con el cuero hinchao le dio un bocabajo.*'

"Well, of course, there's a double meaning. The phrase could mean 'with a swollen penis he fucked her.' But this idiom comes from the days of slavery and also translates to 'with a swollen whip he beat her.' "

We were just then turning north on Maceo, and Isuama was chanting songs in Carabalí.

"During one carnival I saw a man cut his girlfriend's face with a knife after discovering she had betrayed him," La India said. "And sometimes a man will discover his wife is cheating on him and kill her. I saw that happen a few times in past carnivals. Last year was the worst. During carnival a woman was killed by her husband. And this year, the woman's son killed the stepfather in revenge."

Changó and Ochún at a celebration in Vedado.

"How is it he was not in prison?" I asked.

"Ah, he was. But he escaped to his fate."

"Where did it happen?"

"Right here in Los Hoyos," La India said, lighting a cigarette and inhaling deeply.

I wanted to move out with Conga de Los Hoyos and so said good-bye and took off for their rendezvous point, near the house of Chan, the fabled director of the group who had died three years before. A sizeable crowd had already assembled there. The conga's twenty-five drummers were all wearing T-shirts emblazoned with Rebirth Brass Band, and most of the New Orleans contingent were scattered about.

"I'm a gardener for the city of Santiago, but tonight my heart is focused on this drum," Ángel Marcial, thirty-five, told me. Strapped around his chest he carried one of Hoyos's dozen cylindrical *bocús*. "If I make it speak, I'll feel free and happy all night."

"Carnival is when I feel free to be crazy," said Rey Salazar, who plays *bocú* and *campana* with Hoyos. "When I march I'll put the *campana* on my head like a hat and play it. It's something I saw an old man do a long time ago."

Bottles of rum and pitchers of beer were passed around. The film crew arrived and positioned itself out front. Then, at a signal from Félix Bandera, the musicians fell in formation. Suddenly, the keening cry of the *corneta china* pierced the night air and Conga de Los Hoyos, 250 members strong, rolled out, to the thunder of drums, followed by a crowd of revelers that increased exponentially with each passing block.

Like New Orleans, Santiago has a second line—only it's wilder and more dangerous. As Conga de Los Hoyos threaded its way up Martí, a mob began closing in on all sides, drawn by the music. Smiling thieves surrounded me and stuck their hands in my pockets but came up empty, for I'd been warned of them and carried nothing but my camera held tightly around me. Nevertheless, Marcial grabbed my arm and yanked me up front, in tight between him and another member of Hoyos.

"Be careful," he said. "They'll steal whatever you have."

By now, there was no escape. A crush of humanity pressed in on me from all sides. Out of nowhere, a woman materialized directly in front of me. She had black eyes, flat nostrils, and full lips that looked almost carved. Thick black hair fell to the nape of her neck, and as she smiled at me over her shoulder she took both my hands and placed them on her gyrating hips. The look she gave me was unambiguous: I would be a prisoner of her desire. And for the next few blocks she bent forward and ground herself forcefully against me. When I responded in turn, the men all around me cheered approvingly.

It took a few hours to get to Plaza de Martes where all the carnival groups stopped to await their turn before heading out to the bleachers and the jury. I spotted Philip Frazier, his face and shirt drenched with sweat.

"So what do you think of this second line?" I asked.

"Oh, man, *too* intense. Women done things to me here that'd never happen in New Orleans. They're all just free spirits. They shake with every part of their body, and don't ever stop."

In Cuba, carnival is nourished by a powerful slave celebration that was outlawed in the 1880s by colonial authorities. The celebration, known as Día de Reyes (Day of the Kings), was held on January 6 of each year and occasioned an eruption of passion that was unparalleled. Historical accounts of the day, openly racist, depict "savage" blacks running wild in the streets, creating an uproar, asking for gifts. But for blacks, January 6 was a moment when the horrors of slavery were stopped in an illusion of freedom brought on by what the Cuban folklorist Fernando Ortiz termed "an orgy of ritual, dance, music, song, and cane spirit."

History tells of slaves being freed on Día de Reyes, their masters moved by a sudden spirit of compassion or, more likely, guilt. We can only imagine the confluence of emotions that must've overcome Cuba's slaves on such a day: the fervent hope for freedom, the collective memory of so much suffering and sorrow, the need to lose oneself in ritual. (Soon after Día de Reyes was banned, in 1888, the *cabildos,* too, were outlawed because they had functioned as centers for revolution.) Ortiz devoted a whole essay to Día de Reyes. In it, he said that no one knows, and possibly no one ever will know, the origin of the Day of Kings celebration because it did not "come about by ordinance but through the collective spontaneity" of the blacks. But if the celebration was banned, its essence was resurrected in carnival. For it is the congas and *comparsas,* singing, drumming, and dancing during Day of the Kings, that became the spine of carnival.

Why did Santiago's carnival unfold during the third week in July? The answer was traceable to the city's beginnings and very name. In Spain, the road to Santiago de Compostela in the city of Santiago was firmly established as a sacred pilgrimage back in medieval times. An astonishing cathedral that was more pagan than Christian, Santiago de Compostela drew the faithful from all corners of Europe in the belief that here lay the grave of the apostle James. The Santiago pilgrimage was "a gigantic migratory flow, a movement of millions of extras, an unceasing stream of . . . pilgrims from all corners of Christendom, who found shelter and sustenance . . . on their way to the Pyrenees and beyond, until they reached the camino to Santiago," the Dutch writer Cees Nooteboom writes in *Roads to Santiago: A Modern-Day Pilgrimage Through Spain.*

The cathedral in Santiago de Cuba is nothing like the original in Spain, and of course there is no pilgrimage like the one Nooteboom writes about. But from the beginning, St. James, the patron saint of Cuba's easternmost city, occasioned a celebration that took place in the latter part of July.

"Carnival's occurrence in Santiago has to do with the celebration surrounding the cult of St. James, who is the patron saint of Santiago," notes Raúl Fernández, a musicologist who grew up in Oriente and consults for the Smithsonian Institution. "And those festivities took place on his days, around July 25. As far back as the sixteenth century you would have seen large numbers of people out on the streets then."

"The slaves and free mulattos could play drums and sing and chant at the end of the saint's procession," Julian Mateo said when I asked him about the cult of Santiago de Compostela.

I'd talked to Cubans who swore that Castro hijacked carnival and moved it to July in order to commemorate the attack in 1953 on the Moncada barracks. Raúl Fernández laughed when I mentioned it.

"They have it exactly backward. Fidel picked that day in July to attack *because* of the diversion carnival offered him. He used all the noise—all the drumming and celebrating—to give him cover."

On the surface, Santiago's carnival seems all jubilance. But underneath the eruption of joy there is a lament. For carnival was born of the streets and came from the sorrows of this world, the tragedy of slavery and its aftermath, a long legacy of racism. In the days of slavery, carnival, whether it was *mamarrachos* or Día de Reyes, was one of the moments when Africans in Cuba could escape the injustice of their lives and remember their ancestral heritage.

I'd heard the lament of carnival in various contexts. It was in the words of certain songs that the *comparsa* groups sang as they twisted down the streets of Santiago. But mostly it lay submerged in the songs the *cabildo* members sang, songs that spoke to the heroism and the suffering of thousands who died fighting for freedom.

"You can find traces of the sorrow in some of our carnival songs," Pérez said. "But there's more humor than sorrow. And the humor of Cuba is black humor. Wait"—she lights a cigarette, inhales deeply, and blows out a stream of smoke. "I have a story.

"In 1997, during the Special Period when we were all starving, there was a fish sold here that had a million bones. You could hardly eat it; it would take you a year. Well, people dubbed the fish with a new name: *marabú*, which is the name of a bush in Cuba that's full of thorns. During carnival that year, I was on the streets and I fell in behind a *comparsa* and they were singing a song:

Marabú, Marabú, que se
Lo coma el barbú

(Marabú, Marabú,
let the bearded one eat it)"

Pérez chanted. "You understand?" she said, arching her eyebrows. "The Cubans don't take their sadness to the streets. They take their irony and sarcasm and leave the sadness at home."

When I asked Pérez if she'd ever been to carnival in Havana, she shook her head and threw her bony hands out, fingers splayed, in a dismissive movement of disgust.

"Havana? In Havana, there was no second line, no *piquete,* no theater. It was—and is—all about watching floats pass by in the street. In fact, only relatively recently have the people of Havana begun having fun during carnival, by imitating *us,*" Pérez said, smiling with satisfaction. "I remember a group of Santiagans I was with once in Havana during carnival. This would have been 1961 or 1962. Carnival was already under way. So we went to see it. Soon, we started our own *piquetes.* But the police stopped us. 'You can't do that here,' a policeman yelled. 'Go back to Santiago with that.' You see, in Havana you watch; here you are part of it all."

(Pérez was partly right. Throughout Cuba, the ruling class of whites saw carnival as an eruption of a "degenerate" African spirit, and consequently sought to repress it. But the animus toward black *comparsas* was particularly strong in Havana. During carnival in 1913, Havana's black *comparsas* were accompanied by police and vigilantes who forbade them from dancing or using their African instruments. And while blacks in other cities, including Santiago, experienced racist assaults on their carnival culture, there's evidence to show that Havana's edicts were more consistently enforced.)

There is a carnival museum in Santiago that holds artifacts from a bygone era. One day I wandered around the exhibits and got a glimmer of what carnival was like a century or more ago. I saw nineteenth-century *farolas* (illuminated lanterns), brilliantly designed *muñicones,* and fabulous masks. One display had a dazzling cape, its colors muted but still vibrant. Other walls held faded black-and-white photographs of celebrants wearing rough, straw *campesino* hats. The faces that looked out from those photographs bore the marks of hard physical labor.

In the nineteenth century and through most of the twentieth century, Santiago's carnival lasted a month. Work barely went on. Certain crossroads, like La Trocha, known for their wild partying, entered legend. Wandering through the museum, I half imagined the *piquetes,* the spontaneous groups of celebrants akin to the fabled second line of New Orleans parades, marching on their own, banging brake drums and pots and pans, singing songs of jubilation. For the sons and daughters of slavery, carnival had to be a shout of defiance, of freedom.

Carnival was suspended many times for political reasons. In 1958, during the civil war, there was an order from the revolution not to celebrate carnival in Santiago. Yet Batista tried to use carnival for his own ends.

"A handful of blacks and mulattos showed up in the streets," Nancy Pérez said. "And this was the song they sang:

Los blancos pa' la loma
Los negros pa' la conga
(Let the whites go to the mountains
Let the blacks go to the conga)

It was Batista's vain attempt to quell the rebellion by using race. But it didn't work. That year, there was no carnival. Blacks and whites were being killed fighting for their freedom.

"I think Santiago's carnival is historically the most important in the world," says Pérez, who did research for Santiago's carnival museum. "And there's a reason for that. Here we evolved a theater tradition called *teatro de relaciones,* in which a group of friends or families would take a

A master of the corneta china *at carnival in Santiago.*

curtain and go to some areas of the city at carnival time and stage a play they had rehearsed. It might've been something that happened to the family or in the neighborhood; something funny or tragic or satirical. Sometimes the theater criticized the government; other groups staged plays by Calderón de la Barca, one of our great Spanish playwrights. And of course, the actors would make their own masks and costumes. At first it was only blacks doing the theater. But soon the mulattos and whites began participating. And this tradition continued into the twentieth century, right up until the socialist revolution."

I saw some evidence that the *teatro* tradition was reviving one morning when I spotted a costumed carnival theater group performing on

Martí Avenue. The group put on a funny skit about the perils of ignoring the precautions that have led to the control of dengue fever, caused by mosquitoes. But the piece, which included actors dressed as the fever-bearing, striped-legged mosquitoes, had the feel of a public-service announcement.

"Our carnival was among the most important in the world, but economic factors have sent it into decline. *Teatro de relaciones* disappeared long ago, and the actors who knew that form found work in regular theater," Rodulfo Vaillant, the president of UNEAC in Santiago and an accomplished composer, said when I met him at his office. "UNEAC has been working hard to rescue the tradition, and in the last four or five years we're finding it coming back. But it's difficult. The trick is not to impose something that has to have a life of its own and grow spontaneously. We're trying to improve the *comparsa* music and bring in artists who can once again create the fabulous masks that you would have seen in the old days. I was for years part of the carnival committee, and I worked with the *piquetes*. They used to be rich with music and spontaneous. But now they don't play the role they once had. When the state organized them they became stiff and lifeless. So we have a challenge. Recovering traditions is the theme of this year's carnival."

The next morning, Raúlito Campos, an accomplished guitarist, accompanist, and arranger who regularly appears at Casa de la Trova, took me to visit Enrique Bonne, the legendary Cuban composer and creator of the *pilon* rhythm that is a mainstay of Afro-Cuban *son* and jazz. Less than a year ago, his son had died in a tragic accident in Argentina.

"Bonne is still in mourning, and he can be moody," Campos warned me. "But he has a deep knowledge of carnival."

The man who met us at the door was nobly proportioned. Tall, with long arms and broad shoulders, Enrique Bonne could've been a former athlete. He looked fifteen years younger than his actual age, seventy-five, and stood ramrod straight, his handsome face topped off with a thick head of graying hair.

On this particular day, he was getting over the flu. But he greeted us

Carabalí Isuama's royalty outside their cabildo *during carnival.*

warmly. In his heyday he wrote beautiful *boleros* and *danzones,* classics of
Cuban music. But for twenty-nine years he was president of Santiago's
Carnival Committee. When I asked him to talk about that part of his life,
his eyes, which had been melancholy before, lit up.

"Carnival's rhythms have been nourished by the music of the
Dominican Republic and Puerto Rico, and of course our own rich
rhythms and melodies of Oriente. I created a carnival group from many
members of different groups. It had fifty-two percussionists and a *corneta china* player, though now it just has twenty-one drummers. But in
1967, I led one hundred and fifty carnival drummers in performance. We

played every night at the intersection of Trocha and Corona. This is the heart of carnival culture in Santiago, and unlike other places where people just look, here everyone dances. Well, I wrote some of the *comparsas* that we sang, and we made a great noise.

"Up until 1967, Santiago's carnival lasted an entire month. The musical groups would jam on a makeshift stage. And my group would close the night. Santiago had the greatest carnival in the world. Brazil's carnival is based on one or two rhythms, principally samba. But in Santiago, the *comparsas* offer many, many kinds of music. For instance, the Comparsa La Placita will play music from countries all over the world. But we could do better if we had more resources. During carnival, all of us come together, without religious, racial, or class distinctions. We are all one family."

I asked Bonne about *teatro de relaciones*. Had he seen it?

"It had declined already before I was born," he said wistfully. "But in the 1970s and 1980s, it was being revived somewhat. One of the plays I saw was *Santiago Apóstol,* and I remember that it satirized the Catholic religion."

Carnival culture started into decline when the revolution came. People enjoyed wearing masks and doing tricks, but after the revolution, masking wasn't permitted. The regime charged that people were using that as an excuse to commit crimes. I told Nancy Pérez about what Vaillant said about the signs of a reemerging *teatro* tradition, urging her to consider helping to resurrect the culture. But she shook her head. I told her she had more power than she thought, that the passion of one person, armed with knowledge, could reawaken the old rituals. She gave me a doubtful look.

"I have no power," she said. "The Ministry of Culture is in control of that."

Midweek during carnival I paid a visit to Julian Mateo and found him in the company of one of Santiago's poets, Jesús Cos Causse, a slender man in his early fifties, with deep-set eyes. Both of them seemed well lit up with rum, though it was only 10:30 A.M.

"Here, take a look at this tape," Mateo said, seating me in his living room, full of African masks and art, and jamming a tape into the VCR. "It's a film I shot of the funeral of a famous carnival director, the leader of Conga de Los Hoyos—Sebastián Herrer Zapata, otherwise known as Chan."

Mateo, Cos Causse, and I watched a trio of drummers playing as friends came to the casket and put flowers on Chan's corpse, taking a last look at the open coffin.

"What you're seeing is people honoring a last promise they made in Chan's life: to put a bottle of rum in his right hand or some flowers near his face."

Musicians surrounded the dead carnival leader and sang in a combination of Yoruba and Spanish. "Chan was a great musician and choreographer, a great leader of the *comparsas,* and a great friend of mine," Mateo said. "And so when he died, I owed him a visit."

I'd witnessed a jazz funeral in New Orleans once. In front of the casket, a horn section broke into wailing lament. But later the horns shouted with joy, to celebrate the release of the soul to the next world. The similarities were strong. As Chan's funeral progressed, the music was continuous, a constant wave of chattering rhythms and chants. Watching the film, I was reminded that a Cuban government edict in 1792 sought to suppress black funeral celebrations by making it illegal for blacks "to conduct, to the *cabildos,* the cadavers of blacks, in order to sing or cry as is customary in their native land." Certainly, it wasn't hard to imagine Cuba's black funerals in the days of slavery as potentially dangerous gatherings, able to foment rebellion.

At one point the drummers began to play a *rumba* and people lined up to speak to Chan's corpse. A woman came carrying a huge bundle of leaves.

"She's a spiritist," said Mateo. "And she's trying to speak to the spirit of the corpse. But the truth is, she was faking it."

Cos Causse lit a cigarette and poured a large glass of *aguardiente*.

"This film is very important," Cos Causse said, "because it shows the powerful rituals surrounding the death of a very important figure in Santiago's musical community."

"Yet nothing is typical," Mateo added. "The funeral for a musician in another *cabildo* would be different. At this funeral there were thousands of people because Chan was such an important figure in Santiago. Now, would you like some special rum?" Mateo asked, a twinkle in his eye. And without waiting for my reply, he began pouring me a glass of 40-proof La Occidental.

"This rum is very difficult to get. It just disappeared for twenty years at one point. It's got *guayabitas* at the bottom, see? And look. Now you're going to see the carnival procession move out. This funeral started in the morning and went on into the night. Even the governor of the province wouldn't get this kind of funeral."

"For a long time, the tradition of musical funerals fell into obscurity," Cos Causse said. "But in the last five years, I would say, it's begun to reemerge. Musicians now come and perform when important artists or musical figures die."

"If the Haitians have a funeral, it's altogether different," Mateo said. "Certain family members *must* come, often from far away, to make the proper burial. And in that case you have to wait for them, even if it's days. If officials or police try to force the burial rites, the Haitians would come at them with sharpened machetes and there might be full-scale riots. I've seen fights because of that."

The film was coming to an end. A funeral *comparsa* wound its way down to the cemetery. The music was carnival music. People hit *companas* and drummers pounded out the conga rhythms. A man sang a final song while the casket was lowered into the ground.

"Look, if you watch carefully," Mateo said, "you can see that while some people are smiling, some are crying, too. Because there's sorrow and joy in life."

But the image I couldn't get out of my mind, as the film ended, was that of a young boy dancing on Chan's grave. He danced wildly, with all of his young, focused energy.

"No one was expecting him to die and it was a great shock," Juan Palacios, a young musician with Conga de Los Hoyos, said when I asked him about Chan's death later that afternoon. It was dusk, but the heat was still fierce at the headquarters of Conga de Los Hoyos. "Chan was trying to pull out a small ceiba tree in his yard. The ceiba is a sacred tree; you're not supposed to hurt it. Well, Chan fell backward and smashed his head. He was in the hospital five days and then he was gone."

"Chan was like a father to me," said Félix Bandera. "He was a great leader who dedicated his life to music and culture. He studied the traditions and history of carnival. When the *espiritistas* met at a *toque* nine days after Chan died, his spirit came down and possessed one of the people, who pointed to me as the successor. That's how I was chosen.

"All the musicians in our group will get a big funeral procession when they die," he said. "It's part of our tradition. The funeral and carnival traditions come from the same source. When people die we sing:

Se va un amigo, se va un hermano
(A friend is leaving, a brother is dying.)"

EPILOGUE

People come to Cuba for many reasons. Divers travel there for pristine coral reefs, spelunkers seek out massive caves with underground rivers, mystics come looking for magic, and leftists come to reconnect with some imagined revolutionary epicenter in the hemisphere.

Why had I come? For rhythm, I told myself. For the music and the folklore. But there was more to it than that. Like all travelers, I was seeking out my own numinous spirit and answering some as-yet obscure call of destiny. For music in Cuba, I soon discovered, is not merely art. Fire and water, blood and seed, poetry and mystery, music is the high road to initiation, a shaking and breaking of the soul, which mythologist Michael Meade wrote requires death and rebirth as well as "a return to the roots of knowledge, the roots of consciousness and the seeds of meaning hidden in each person."

In Cuba, the roots of knowledge are everywhere. I was not a devotee of Santería when I first arrived in Cuba, but I respected the *orishas* and instinctively knew that the land I tread upon was sacred ground. A *santera* told me I was a son of Yemayá, the mother of the ocean; another told me that Changó, the lord of thunder, was protecting me. Beyond that, the spirit of my paternal grandfather, long dead, was apparently watching out as well. And this was true whether I believed it or not, because every soul in the world is born under an *orisha*. I could dismiss such pronouncements as mystical hocus-pocus. But unusual things were happening since I began visiting the island.

In the summer before my third trip to Cuba, I spent a weekend with my family up at Big Bear Lake. I had wanted to take my son out on a kayak, but as there were none available, I foolishly let myself be talked into renting an outboard motorboat that I had no experience operating. With my wife and three children aboard, I pulled on the throttle and the boat suddenly took off like a rocket. I tried to slow it down, to control it. Then, when nothing happened, when the metallic taste of fear was in my mouth, I went into a panic. As we headed straight for the pylons of the opposite pier, suddenly, mysteriously, without me doing any steering, the boat did a looping 180-degree turn until it pulled alongside the original pier and came to rest.

What had happened was a miracle; my wife and I knew that. The next night, in a dream I would never forget—a dream that I knew was connected with what happened on the lake and the territory of the *orishas*— a creature flew into my room, its wings beating too rapidly for me to determine what it was. Eventually it flew under my bed. When I bent down to look I beheld a glorious vision: a miniature Pegasus looked back at me, its milky white wings fluttering as fast as a hummingbird's.

A close encounter with death brings you further into life. And Pegasus is a horse of power, a mythic visitation from the other world. Mythologically speaking, such horses augur change and carry you into the unknown. Which fit with my experiences. For Cuba, I soon realized, was a place for discovering forgotten knowledge. Here, I heard forgotten rhythms and forgotten songs, witnessed lost dances and lost rituals that never made it to the United States, where slave owners banned the drum and systematically shattered African families. Beyond that, there were lost ideas that had fallen into the cracks. One of those forgotten ideas was that when you were falling apart and abandoned, into your addiction or into your madness, when the sweetness of life was gone and perhaps the purpose, too, a teacher might appear, as if directed to you by an invisible shaft of light. As I traveled through Cuba, I met such people. They fed me with knowledge. They recognized my passion.

In Cuba, nothing happens as you plan it. A Cuban once told me that in his country "the possible is often impossible, while the impossible is often possible." This is borne out every day. Communications, primitive at best, break down unexpectedly and the gods of chance take over. No matter how meticulously I had planned something, it inevitably went awry. But once I admitted to myself that I didn't know where I was going and that anything could happen, I was fine.

When I first left for Cuba, I was married, a father of two children. But six years (and one daughter) later, my marriage collapsed and took me on a journey through the darkness that eventually allowed me to change. I found rhythm. But the rhythm I discovered had preexisted inside me. Ultimately, it was about restoring balance: a way of breaking across the threshold of fear that keeps us from seeing and feeling beauty. Deep within our souls, there is the certainty of change, the anticipation that our old life will open up to new paths. I don't know where those paths will lead, but I'm confident that they will take me where I need to go and back to Cuba sometime in the not-too-distant future.

APPENDIX A:

SELECTED DISCOGRAPHY

ADALBERTO ALVAREZ
La Salsa Caliente
(Sonido/Vogue)
Adalberto Alvarez is one of Cuba's great bandleaders. The founder of the seminal group, Son 14, he has released several wonderful recordings with his current group, Adalberto Alvarez y Su Son. This outing captures the group's explosive *timba*.

MARIO BAUZÁ
My Time Is Now
(Messidor)
A fabulous trumpeter and bandleader, Bauzá was the key figure in the development of Cu-bop, or Afro-Cuban jazz. From playing with Dizzy Gillespie in the Chick Webb and Cab Calloway Orchestras of the 1930s, Bauzá went on to collaborate with the likes of Miguelito Machito, and the legendary drummer Chano Pozo. This whole recording shines with Bauzá's brilliant arrangements and dazzling ensemble work. But Chico O'Farrill's "Tanga Suite," in particular, is sumptuous.

BUENA VISTA SOCIAL CLUB
Buena Vista Social Club
(World Circuit)
Ry Cooder went to Cuba and gathered together some forgotten masters, musicians whose careers had been eclipsed by the new bands and music styles of contemporary Cuba. Of course, everyone knows the results: a multiplatinum Afro-Cuban franchise that's still going strong.

Cynics might claim that it's only non-Latinos who are impressed with this "retro" music, but no one can deny the soulful beauty and intelligence of the playing.

CELIA CRUZ
The Best of Celia Cruz con La Sonora Matancera
(Rhino)
The universally accepted "Queen of Cuban Music," Celia has recorded dozens of memorable songs both in Cuba with the great Sonora Matancera and in New York with Tito Puente and Willie Colon. This recording showcases some of her best work in Cuba.

ARMANDO GARZON WITH HIS QUINTETO ORIENTE
Boleros
(Corason)
Based in Santiago de Cuba, Garzon is a classically trained singer with an operatic voice. Here, he turns *boleros* into glorious anthems of passion.

CUARTETO PATRIA
A Una Coqueta
(Corason)
Gorgeous music from the best *son* group in Oriente, led by the guitar playing and voice of Eliades Ochoa.

¡CUBANISMO!
Malembe
(Hannibal)
Expatriate Cuban trumpeter Jesús Alemany rounded up some of the hottest players for this disc, which features the remarkable singer Rolo Martínez. His flexible, rich voice, developed in Havana's nightclubs during the 1950s, is stunning to hear.

BALLET FOLKLÓRICO DE CUTUMBA
Ballet Folklórico
(Egrem)
Cutumba is one of the two best folkloric groups in Santiago, and this recording, mostly tributes to the *orishas,* is stellar.

PAQUITO D'RIVERA
Paquito D'Rivera Presents 40 Years of Cuban Jam Session
(Messidor)
To hear him at his peak, you should seek out the albums he made with Irakere. But this outing, drawn from shimmering *descargas,* is one of his best.

CARLOS EMBALE
Rumbero Mayor
(Egrem)
For many years Embale was the lead voice with the Septeto Nacional de Ignacio Piñiero. But it's a pity we don't have many sessions like this one, where the greatest *rumbero* of them all unleashes a voice for the ages.

Que Buena Canta Embale
(Egrem)
Another Embale recording that features him also as a *sonero* (a singer of the most common and flexible genre of Cuban music, the *son*). Once listened to it is easy to pick his voice out in the many recordings he has participated on.

ROBERTO FONSECA
No Limit
(JVC World Sounds/Victor Entertainment, Japan VICG)
The young pianist on fire, doing everything from *descargas* and *boleros* to *son montunos* and *rumba.*

JULIO GUTIERREZ Y SU ORQUESTA
Cuban Jam Session Vol. II (With Cachao)
(Panart)
All the roots of salsa are here. A turning point in music. In the late 1950s, one of the vibrant styles of music in Cuba was the *descarga* (jam session), which gives the players a lot of room to improvise around a common theme. Some of the musicians later remarked that they thought it was a party in a recording studio and were surprised to see it in record stores in Paris ten years later.

IRAKERE
Misa Negra
(Messidor)
This is the seminal Latin jazz orchestra. Under the direction of its founder, Jesús Chucho Valdés, this group was the greenhouse for many of Cuba's, and now America's, premier players, including Arturo Sandoval and Paquito D'Rivera.

The Best of Irakere
(Columbia/Sony)
A reissue of the group's live 1978 record with a few mediocre tracks added, this CD captures Irakere at its best, with Paquito D'Rivera and Arturo Sandoval. *Misa Negra,* the Black Mass, is the masterpiece, unfathomably mysterious and exciting to this day.

From Havana with Love: Live From Belgrade
(Westwind)

Homenaje a Benny Moré
(Messidor)

LAS ESTRELLAS AREITO
Los Héroes

(Nonesuch 79551)

Culled from five albums of legendary *descargas,* this two-CD set captures the glorious sound of Cuba as it once was.

ISRAEL "CACHAO" LOPEZ
Master Sessions, Volume 1
(Crescent Moon/Epic)

Master Sessions, Volume 2
(Crescent Moon/Epic)

Cachao's career began in the very early thirties when he played bass at the age of twelve with the Havana Symphony. His path defines the growth of Cuban music to this day. As one of the seminal figures in the development of the mambo, *danzón,* and *descarga,* Cachao makes music that is timeless. Taken together, these two works are a distillation of Cachao's genius.

LOS MUÑEQUITOS DE MATANZAS
Rumba Caliente
(Qbadisc)

Pure *rumba* played by the masters and showing the subtle beauty, the roaring fire, and the aching sadness of the *rumba* as it evolved in Matanzas.

LOS VAN VAN
Dancing Wet—Bailando Mojao
(World Pacific)

A group that redefined Cuban music after the revolution, Van Van has been Cuba's premier dance band since the late 1960s. Under the musical direction of bassist Juan Formell, powered by the great percussionist José "Changuito" Quintana, and fronted by vocalist Pedro Calvo, this group has recorded hit after hit and has toured the world many times. Van Van's recordings are incredibly uneven and rarely capture the band's inspired playing when live. But this one manages to capture the gritty excitement of the band that created *songo*.

MACHITO AND HIS AFRO-CUBAN ORCHESTRA
Tremendo Cubano and Cuarteto Caney featuring Machito: 1939–40
(Tumbao)
A fine sample of the band that created Latin jazz.

MARACA
¡Descarga Total!
(Ahi-Namá Music)
Orlando "Maraca" Valle is one of the world's most accomplished flautists. A product of a generation of music virtuosos, his band demonstrates a rocking blast of Cuba's new dance music.

MONGO SANTAMARÍA
Skin on Skin, The Mongo Santamaría Anthology (1958–1995)
(Rhino)
The great conga master and stylist influenced two generations of musicians. Mongo has been the template of conga playing since he emerged in the early 1950s as a member of Tito Puente's big band. He soon joined Cal Tjader's Latin jazz quintet and then formed his own bands that were incubators for many young, now established players.

BENNY MORÉ
The Most From Benny Moré
(BMG)
The peerless singer, Cuba's greatest, singing some of the songs that made him a national treasure.

LONG JOHN OLIVA AND HIS AC TIMBA JAZZ PROJECT
Lucumi

(Orishas Records)

An explosive blend of *rumba, timba, son,* and jazz.

ORQUESTA ORIGINAL DE MANZANILLO

Puros

(Qbadisc)

Charanga music that blends the modern and keeps the traditional in balance. Many of their numbers were written by singer Candido Fabre, who was with the violin-based band for many of their most memorable songs.

ISAAC OVIEDO

Isaac Oviedo—Routes of Rhythm Vol. 3

(Rounder)

If it only boasted "Coballende," which epitomizes the lyrical genius of the old-school *son Afro,* this would be a treasure. But recorded just before Oviedo died as part of a documentary, this disc has other wonders—*guaracha sones, bolero,* and even a Mexican *huapango.* And then there's Papi Oviedo, heir to his father's genius.

PÉREZ PRADO

Havana 3 a.m./Mambomania

(Bear Family Records)

Gorgeous mambo from a master of the form. Prado developed the mambo in Mexico and on the West Coast of the United States, while his contemporaries, Puente, Tito Rodríguez, and Machito, were bringing this genre to a larger audience in New York.

PELLO EL AFROKAN

Un Sabor Que Canta

(Vitral)

His real name was Pedro Izquierdo, and his fame rests largely on the fabulous mozambique rhythm, drawn from carnival music, that became the foundation of his sound.

PERUCHIN
Piano Con Moña
(Egrem)
Known as Peruchin, Pedro Justiz became the father of Latin jazz piano. If you have to have one CD by him, this is it, with most of the material on the groundbreaking *The Incendiary Piano of Peruchin*. Plus the peerless percussion of Tata Güines and Guillermo Barreto.

CHANO POZO
El Tambor de Cuba
(Tumbao)
As a featured player with Dizzy Gillespie, Chano Pozo brought Afro-Cuban rhythms into jazz. Who knows what he might have accomplished if he hadn't been murdered. But as it is, many of his original compositions have become standards in Latin jazz. And his place in the history of jazz, as this boxed set shows, is formidable.

GUILLERMO PORTABLES
Lo Mejor de 16 Exitoso
(DHCD)
Portables is known as the musician who brought the *guajira* (a country, guitar-centered genre) into the salons of Havana in the 1940s. But as this CD shows, he was a singer of great intensity, a master of the melancholy and an exponent of what the Spanish would call *duende*.

RAICES HABANERAS
Raices Habaneras
(Havana Corner Records)
Though it's recorded in the United States, this *rumba* recording is a

gem and a fine example of the group that plays each Sunday at New Jersey's Esquina Habanera. The sound is open and rich, the drums perfectly balanced, the singing exquisite.

ARSENIO RODRÍGUEZ Y SU CONJUNTO,
Dundunbanza: 1946–1951
(Tumbao)
Rodríguez is a towering giant of Cuban music, a creator of new rhythms and sounds, a master on the *tres* and a musical revolutionary. He led a cutting-edge band from the late 1930s until his death in Los Angeles in the early 1970s. This is my favorite single work of his, but the CDs below hold other aspects of his genius.

Legendary Sessions 1947–53
(Tumbao)

Leyendas/Legends
(Sony Tropical)

LÁZARO ROS
Olorún
Ros is the greatest *akpwón*—spiritual singer—of his generation. Here, he is caught calling to eleven *orishas,* beckoning them down to earth.

GONZALO RUBALCABA
Supernova
(Blue Note Records)
The Cuban jazz pianist at his most explosive.

EMILIANO SALVADOR
Nueva Vision
(Qbadisc)
Salvador died tragically young, recorded few CDs, and lacked the

recognition that should've been accorded him. But here is some of his towering genius.

Ayer Y Hoy
(Qbadisc)
Originally released in 1979, this is Salvador's last recording, a work of poetic intensity from start to finish.

Ñico Saquito
Goodbye Mr. Cat
(World Circuit, UK)
Saquito was one of the legendary *trovadores,* and it's only a pity there aren't more recordings of him.

Septeto Nacional de Ignacio Pineiro
Sones de Mi Habana
(WS Latino)
Piñeiro was one of Cuba's legendary composers and bandleaders. "Echale Salsita," one of the earliest *sones,* was recorded by Septeto in the 1920s. Pineiro's work inspired both George Gershwin and Aaron Copeland. This band, which carries his name, continued long after his passing. For many years it featured the wonderful vocalist Carlos Embale.

Sexteto Habanero
Las Raices del Son
(Tumbao)
One of the first recorded groups featuring the *son cubano,* Sexteto Habanero has had a presence in Cuban music from 1920 until the present. It also spawned one of Cuba's greatest *soneros,* Abelardo Barroso, who began singing with this group as a very young man.

Sierra Maestra
Tíbiri Tábara

(World Circuit/Nonesuch)
A modern reworking of many traditional songs, this is a splendid example of Cuba's great musicianship.

¡Dundunbanza!
(World Circuit)
If anyone doubts that Cuba's classic *son* band has mastered all the genres of Afro-Cuban music, let them hear this disc, whose title song by Arsenio Rodríguez is so memorable.

OMAR SOSA
Sentir
(Otá Records)
Sosa is fast becoming the most innovative voice in Afro-Cuban music, fusing his own explosive jazz with everything from Ecuadorian folk music to Moroccan *gnawa* music. This disc, an homage to Sosa's love of Moroccan music, is a gem: lustrous, deep, and funky.

TRIO MATAMOROS
La Cina en la Rumba
(Tumbao)
Miguel Matamoros and his trio began in Santiago de Cuba in the mid-1920s. By the time they passed from the music scene, they had left dozens of memorable songs.

CARLOS 'PATATO' VALDÉS
Patato y Totico
(Mediterraneo)
This features one of the great *rumba* singers, Eugenio Arango, known as Totico, and the great melodic *conguero* Carlos Valdés, Patato. This is a must-have recording that includes two music legends, both Arsenio Rodríguez and Israel Lopez, "Cachao."

Jesús "Chucho" Valdés
Lucumí Piano Solo
(Messidor)

Bele Bele en La Habana
(Blue Note Records)
Valdés can sometimes be too flashy for his own good. But these two recordings—one for solo piano and the other a recent group recording—show the master at the top of his form.

Various Artists
Cuban Counterpoint: History of the Son Montuno
(Rounder)
A brilliant, indispensable anthology, with great notes by ethnomusicologist Morton Marks, that takes you into the soul of *son*.

Various Artists
Ahora Sí! Here Comes Changüí
(Corason)
A spellbinding collection of *changüí*, a root of *son*, from Guantánamo.

Various Artists
Afro-Cuba: A Musical Anthology
(Rounder)
These songs, chants, and dances, drawn from the four divisions of Afro-Cuban culture—Arará, Lucumí, Abakuá, and Congo—represent the radical roots of the tree of rhythm.

Various Artists
Rapsodia Rumbera
(Egrem)
Another spellbinding set of *rumba* by some of the *baddest congueros* in Havana.

APPENDIX B:

TRIPS AND FESTIVALS

A number of organizations run trips to Cuba that fulfill all the legal requirements for travel to the country.

PlazaCuba, an organization out of the San Francisco Bay Area, has programs each year, including the following:

Popular Music and Dance Program (annually in February). Classes are at Havana's National School of Art and focus on salsa, *son*, and Latin jazz. The program is aimed at salsa dancers and musicians on all instruments.

Afro-Cuban Folkloric Percussion and Dance Program (annually in July). Classes and accommodations are in Old Havana, the exciting center of the city, and are geared to dancers and percussionists of all levels.

SalsaMania (yearly in July) runs concurrent with the above program in mid-July at the same location. This program focuses on salsa, *son*, and other popular music and dance forms. For dancers and percussionists of all levels.

An excursion to the Havana International Jazz Festival, held every even-numbered year in mid-December. A behind-the-scenes look at Cuban music and culture, the trip includes passes to all the events of the Jazz Festival, accommodations at the Hotel Riviera, excursions, workshops, and more.

To find out about these trips or customized ones for groups of fifteen or more, visit www.plazacuba.com. E-mail them at plazacuba@yahoo.com or call them at (510) 872-9590. Their address is P.O. Box 3083, Berkeley, CA 94703.

The Center for Cuban Studies takes a group to the Havana International Jazz Festival every year it's held, around mid-December, and will customize trips as well. In addition, the group's Website has the clearest explanation of travel restrictions regarding Cuba. You can visit the group on the Web at www.cubaupdate.org or call them at (212) 242-0559. Their address is 124 West 23 Street, New York, NY 10011.

Cubanola Collective, a nonprofit group dedicated to exploring the connection between New Orleans and Cuba, has a trip in July that goes to carnival in Santiago de Cuba. For more information call (504) 948-7788 or e-mail them at info@cubanola.org.

Finally, Global Exchange organizes a trip called Cuban Rhythms: Dance Percussion. You can visit them on the Web at www.globalexchange.org or call them at (415) 255-7296. Their address is 2017 Mission Street, Room 303, San Francisco, CA 94110.

MUSIC AND DANCE FESTIVALS

There are many opportunities to travel to Cuba and experience the varieties of music, dance, and folklore. Of the following festivals and workshops, some recur yearly, others every other year, and others twice yearly. Here are some of the important ones. Note: The dates are all approximate and change from year to year. In addition, festivals may be canceled.

JANUARY

Longina Canta a Corona
Dates: Early January, yearly
Villa Clara
Ph: (537) 570210
E-mail: ahs@ujc.org.cu
A festival in honor of one of the great *trovadores* of Cuba, Manuel Corona.

FolkCuba
Dates: Mid- to late January and early to mid-July
Havana
Ph: (537) 303939
Fax: (537) 34395
E-mail: cnae@min.cult.cu
A workshop with Conjunto Folklórico Nacional, dedicated to the dance and choreography based on Cuban folklore.

APRIL

International Festival of Percussion
Dates: Mid-April, yearly
Havana
Ph: (537) 238808
Fax: (537)336633
E-mail: percuba@mail.com
Folkloric and popular symphonic music from Cuba and the world, including percussion competition and theater and dance.

MAY

Cubadisco
Dates: Mid-May, yearly
Havana
Ph: (537) 311234
Fax: (537) 333716
E-mail: icm@cubarte.cult.cu
A convention that features popular performances by groups from Cuba and other parts of the world.

JUNE

Golden Boleros Festival
Dates: Mid-June, yearly
Santiago de Cuba and Havana
Ph: (537) 320395
Fax: (537) 333158
E-mail: uneac@cubarte.cult.cu
A festival dedicated to *boleros* from Cuba and the world.

JULY

Fiesta Del Fuego
Dates: A week in early July (usually around the fourth), yearly
Santiago de Cuba
Ph: (53226) 23569
E-mail: caribe@cubarte.cult.cu
A celebration of Cuban and Caribbean culture, focusing on a different region of the Caribbean each year.

AUGUST

An Encounter of Political Songs
Dates: Early August, annually
Guantánamo
Ph: (537) 570210 and 570181
E-mail: ahs@ujc.org.cu
A festival featuring performances by young *trovadores*.

SEPTEMBER

International Festival of Popular Music Benny Moré
Dates: Second half of September, every two years
Santa Isabel de la Lajas, Cienfuegos, and Havana
Ph: (537) 311234 and 323503
Fax: (537) 333716
E-mail: icm@cubarte.cult.cu
A festival of music inspired by the work of Cuba's greatest popular singer, Benny Moré.

NOVEMBER

African Roots Festival "Wemilere"
Dates: Late November, yearly
Havana and Guanabacoa
Ph: (537) 970202
Fax: (537) 979187
E-mail: paradis@turcult.get.cma.net
A festival dedicated to Cuba's dance, music, and art inspired by its African roots.

Festival Cuba Danzón
Dates: Late November, every two years
Matanzas
Ph: (5352) 243512
Fax: (5352) 614736
E-mail: coral@coral.atenas.cult.cu
Dedicated to Cuban dancers of *danzón*.

Festival of Rock
Dates: Late November, yearly
Villa Clara
Ph: (537) 570210 and 570181
e-mail: ahs@ujc.org.cu
A gathering of the best Cuban rock bands.

DECEMBER

International Jazz Festival
Dates: Mid-December in even-numbered years
Havana
Ph: (537) 311234 or 662286
Fax: (537) 333716
E-mail: cnmc@cubarte.cult.cu
Organized by Chucho Valdés, this is the island's big jazz festival, which
invariably attracts some American jazz stars.

Fiesta a la Guantanamera
Dates: Early December
Guantánamo
Ph: (5321) 322296
Fax: (5321) 324676
E-mail: chacon@gtmo.cult.cu

A celebration of *changüí*, La Tumba Francesa, and Franco-Haitian folk-lore.

Carnival
Carnival in Santiago is held the third week in July each year.
Carnival in Havana is held in mid-February every year.
Carnival in Matanzas is held the third week of August.

Abakuá Secret society of men that originated in Africa and reestablished itself in Cuba.

Aché Spiritual force.

Akpwón A singer who calls down the *orishas* of Santería.

Arará An African tribe that settled in parts of Cuba.

Babalawo High priests of Santería and experts in divination.

Batá Three sacred hour glass drums employed to summon the *orishas*. In order of size, from largest to smallest, the *batá* are: the *iyá, itótele,* and *okónkolo*.

Bongó A Cuban percussion instrument, played between the knees, with two drumheads.

Botija An instrument made from a ceramic jug.

Cabildos Mutual aid societies that allowed Cuba's slaves to reunite along tribal lines and transmit their African culture and religion.

Cajón A box or crate that was originally played as a drum by slaves.

Catá A log drum used in La Tumba Francesa.

Cencerro A cowbell used in Afro-Cuban music.

Chekere An instrument made from a large gourd, around which nets of beads are strung.

Changó The *orisha* of thunder and founder of the drums.

Changüí A root music of *son* that was developed in the east and is played with *tres, maracas,* a *guiro, bongó,* and a *marímbula*.

Cinquillo A rhythmic pattern of five beats that is part of the *danzón* and *contradanza* and came to Cuba via the French in Haiti.

Clave The fundamental pulse of Afro-Cuban music; the two wooden sticks used to play the rhythm of clave.

Conjunto Larger musical group that surfaced in about 1940.

Comparsas Afro-Cuban carnival street band organized by barrio or city district.

Conga A musical group with many percussionists that competes during carnival.

Conga drum An African-derived drum created in Cuba and used in all styles of music.

Danzón A nineteenth-century couples' dance developed in Matanzas.

Diablitos Masked male dancers from the Abakuá brotherhoods. They've become a national symbol of Cuba.

Día de Reyes January 6 and coinciding with Epiphany, this holiday allowed blacks to sing, dance, and drum in the streets.

Egun An ancestral spirit.

Eleggua The *orisha* who opens the crossroads and is known for being a trickster.

Espiritismo A mixed religion of eastern Cuba that took elements of Santería, voodoo, and European spiritism. Fundamental to the religion is the belief that the souls of the dead can speak through the living.

Farol A lantern carried aloft during carnival.

Guaguancó One of several forms of rumba.

Güiro A grooved musical instrument made from a gourd; also, a spirit-possession ceremony.

La Tumba Francesa An Afro-Haitian association that performs a music and dance based on the French plantocracy.

Lucumí The name for the Yoruba people and culture in Cuba.

Mambises Cuban rebels who fought the Spaniards during colonial days.

Maracas Two small gourds with seeds inside that, when shaken, produce a fundamental rhythm of *son*.

Marímbula A wooden box with steel keys, used to create bass rhythms.

Montuno The chorus of the *son*.

Nengón Slang for a black; also an early form of *son*.

Ochún The *orisha* of lakes and rivers and love.

Ogún Warrior *orisha* associated with iron.

Olokun An *orisha* who rules the deepest parts of the ocean.

Omiero Herbal liquid used in sacred rites of Santería.

Orishas The ancestral deities that form the pantheon of Santería. They have their Catholic equivalent in various saints.

Palo A religion from the Congo that took root in Cuba. Called Palo Monte in eastern Cuba.

Quinto The highest pitched of the trio of conga drums.

Rumba An African-derived song and dance created in Cuba and played with conga drums and clave sticks. Three principal styles developed in Matanzas and Havana.

Santera(o) Initiated priest of Santería.

Son The national music of Cuba. A fusion of African rhythms and European melodies, Cuban *son* is the root of salsa.

Tambores Drums.

Timbales A special percussion instrument played with sticks, which became popular in the nineteenth century and was developed by Cuba's military bands.

Toques de Santo A sacred spirit-possession ritual with percussion and song.

Tres Cuban guitar with three sets of double strings; the heart of *son*.

Trovadores The singers of *trova,* the traditional music of Cuba.

Vacunao The stabbing thrusts the male dancer makes at the female during *rumba guaguancó*.

Yemayá The *orisha* of the ocean, mother of humanity.

BIBLIOGRAPHY

Bettelheim, Judith, ed. *Cuban Festivals: A Century of Afro-Cuban Culture.* New York: Marcus Wiener, 2001.

Canizares, Raul. *Walking with the Night: The Afro-Cuban World of Santeria* (Destiny Books, 1993).

Carpentier, Alejo. *Music in Cuba.* Edited by Timothy Brennan. Minneapolis: University of Minnesota Press, 2001.

Hagedorn, Katherine. *Divine Utterances: The Performance of Afro-Cuban Santeria.* Washington, D.C.: Smithsonian Institution Press, 2001.

Jahn, Janheinz. *Muntu: An Outline of the New African Culture.* New York: Grove Press, 1961.

Moore, Robin. *Nationalizing Blackness: Afrocubanismo and Artistic Revolution in Havana*, 1920–1940. Pittsburgh: University of Pittsburgh Press, 1997.

Nunez, Luis. *Santeria: A Practical Guide to Afro-Caribbean Magic.* Spring Audio and Journal, 1992.

Orovio, Helio. *Diccionario de la Música Cubana.* Havana: Editorial Letras Cubanas, 1981.

Ortiz, Fernándo. *Los Bailes y El Teatro de los Negros en el Folklore de Cuba.* Havana: Editorial Letras Cubanas, 1951.

Thomas, Hugh. *Cuba: The Pursuit of Freedom.* Cambridge: Da Capo, 1998.

Thompson, Robert Farris. *Face of the Gods: Art and Altars of Africa and the African Americas.* New York: Prestel, 1993.

Thompson, Robert Farris. *Flash of the Spirit: African and Afro-American Art and Philosophy.* New York: Vintage, 1984.

⚜ ACKNOWLEDGMENTS ⚜

To the many people who shared their musical knowledge—Helio Orovio, Alan Geik, Raúl Fernández, Walfredo de Los Reyes, Felix Varela, Orestes Vilato, Long John Oliva, Raúl Campos, Perico Hernández, Katherine Hagedorn—I am grateful.

For his generous time and his deep knowledge of the history of Santiago de Cuba, I thank Hebert Pérez. Salud to Ferrer Cabello for his gorgeous paintings and carnival reminiscing. And a hug to Nancy Mikelsons for her encouragement all along the way, and Felix for his jokes and good company.

To my agent, Sarah Lazin, who believed in the project from the beginning. And to my editor, Lisa Hamilton, who cured me of writing tics. I offer thanks to Michael Meade, who helped me reach an understanding of myth and ritual that forever changed my life.

And finally, I thank the many, many Cuban musicians and dancers who shared their stories with me.

For any mistakes or omissions made—*mea culpa.*